D0200499

THE
COST

Trump, China,
and American Revival

MARIA BARTIROMO

and James Freeman

Threshold Editions

New York   London   Toronto   Sydney   New Delhi

Threshold Editions
An Imprint of Simon & Schuster, Inc.
1230 Avenue of the Americas
New York, NY 10020

Copyright © 2020 by Bartiromo Productions LLC and James Freeman

All rights reserved, including the right to reproduce this book or portions thereof in any form whatsoever. For information, address Threshold Editions Subsidiary Rights Department, 1230 Avenue of the Americas, New York, NY 10020.

First Threshold Editions hardcover edition October 2020

THRESHOLD EDITIONS and colophon are trademarks of Simon & Schuster, Inc.

For information about special discounts for bulk purchases, please contact Simon & Schuster Special Sales at 1-866-506-1949 or business@simonandschuster.com.

The Simon & Schuster Speakers Bureau can bring authors to your live event. For more information or to book an event, contact the Simon & Schuster Speakers Bureau at 1-866-248-3049 or visit our website at www.simonspeakers.com.

Interior design by Jaime Putorti

Manufactured in the United States of America

10 9 8 7 6 5 4 3 2 1

Library of Congress Cataloging-in-Publication Data

Names: Bartiromo, Maria, author. | Freeman, James, 1950– author.
Title: The cost : Trump, China, and American revival / Maria Bartiromo and James Freeman.
Other titles: Trump, China, and American revival
Description: First Threshold Editions. | New York : Threshold Editions, 2020. | Includes bibliographical references.
Identifiers: LCCN 2020033160 (print) | LCCN 2020033161 (ebook) | ISBN 9781982163983 (hardcover) | ISBN 9781982163990 (trade paperback) | ISBN 9781982164003 (ebook)
Subjects: LCSH: United States—Politics and government—2017– | Trump, Donald, 1946– | Economic development—United States. | United States—Foreign relation—China. | China—Foreign relations—United States.
Classification: LCC E912 .B37 2020 (print) | LCC E912 (ebook) | DDC 327.73051—dc23
LC record available at https://lccn.loc.gov/2020033160
LC ebook record available at https://lccn.loc.gov/2020033161

ISBN 978-1-9821-6398-3
ISBN 978-1-9821-6400-3 (ebook)

For Vickie and Jono

Contents

Introduction

At Donald Trump's Mar-a-Lago Club in Palm Beach, it takes a while to make the chocolate cake. In pursuit of flourless chocolate sponge perfection, the pastry chef must first bring egg whites and sugar to medium-peak meringue before slowly adding the egg yolks. The Guayaquil mousse and vanilla punch also demand painstaking attention before they are combined with the chocolate sponge to yield the president's favorite dessert.[1] And no rendering of this sumptuous sweet was more important than the one plated on the evening of April 6, 2017. One slice in particular carried special importance, as it was carried through the grand dining room at the Florida luxury resort. That's because it gently landed in front of Chinese dictator Xi Jinping. Had he ever tasted anything like it in Beijing?

"I was sitting at the table. We had finished dinner. We're now having dessert and we had the most beautiful piece of chocolate cake that you've ever seen. And President Xi was enjoying it," President Trump told Maria a few days later.[2]

Almost anyone would enjoy it, and the Chinese strongman certainly seemed to be enjoying his first visit to the United States since the inauguration of America's new president. But Xi didn't realize that while they were getting acquainted, his American host was planning to respond to a chemical attack by the Syrian government on its own citizens.

President Trump recalls that, during that cordial dinner with his Chinese guest at Mar-a-Lago, "I was given the message from the generals that the ships are locked and loaded. What do you do? And we made a determination to do it. So the missiles were on the way. And I said, 'Mr. President, let me explain something to you.'" Trump then informed Xi that fifty-nine missiles were in the air and headed for Syria.

Xi "paused for ten seconds and then he asked the interpreter to please say it again. I didn't think that was a good sign," says Trump. Given Beijing's friendly relations with the Syrian regime, China's top communist might have been expected to condemn the U.S. action. But then Xi said through the interpreter that it was acceptable to attack anybody who would use poison gas against children.

"Xi had planned a carefully crafted meeting of equals. Instead he was upstaged by a firepower demonstration," observes Australia's former ambassador to China, Geoff Raby.[3] All fifty-nine U.S. missiles hit their intended targets. America's new president had sent the world a message that he wasn't afraid to exercise U.S. military force. The same message was delivered personally to the head of China's Communist Party, but bundled with the additional note that Trump wanted to build a working relationship. Mr. Trump recalls that, after a productive day of meetings at Mar-a-Lago, he didn't want Xi to return home and be told, "You know, the guy you just had dinner with just attacked a country."

President Trump clearly understood the competitor he faced on the other side of the table. This would be the first of many negotiating dances the new American president would have with China's dictator. Trump had been elected on a promise to "make America great again," and a key part of his plan for U.S. economic revival was to change the trade relationship with China. Even if it went unmentioned over chocolate cake on that balmy night in Florida, Xi had plans of his own to make China the greatest of the world's superpowers.

These days the mention of Xi Jinping doesn't inspire thoughts of delicious cake but of a deadly virus which has ravaged the world. Its precise origins are still debated and many can't help but wonder what exactly Xi's government was cooking up inside its Wuhan virology lab in China's Hubei province in 2019. Wuhan's Huanan wet market, with its live exotic animals, was linked to early cases of the novel coronavirus and its deadly Covid-19 disease. But U.S. senator Tom Cotton of the Armed Services Committee says it's important to keep investigating. "The virus went into that food market before it came out of that food market. So we don't know where it originated. But we do know that we have to get to the bottom of that. We also know that just a few miles away from that food market is China's only biosafety-level-four super-laboratory that researches human infectious diseases," says the Arkansas Republican.[4]

Those inclined to believe in coincidences must also reckon

with the fact that Xi's regime hid the truth about the virus from its own people and the world for critical weeks, costing thousands of lives. The communist cover-up included the case of Dr. Li Wenliang, who had warned others of the new health threat before he was taken in by police, interrogated for spreading "rumors," and forced to sign a document criticizing himself. Several weeks later the thirty-three-year-old ophthalmologist was dead from the coronavirus, leaving behind a young child and a pregnant wife.[5]

Almost three years before the world learned about one of China's deadliest exports—and the deception surrounding it—Trump wanted to clarify that the United States had a new agenda and a new kind of leadership. The man sitting across the table from Xi Jinping at Mar-a-Lago and serving dessert was also making a display of American power that put the Chinese dictator on notice. Trump's recounting of the meeting then offered the entire world an early window into this unconventional presidency.

The United States may never have another president as loved and hated as Donald Trump. And it's hard to imagine one being subjected to so many investigations. The Dos Equis beer ads had it wrong: *America's forty-fifth president* is the most interesting man in the world. And his administration deserves a fair accounting, not unqualified condemnation or praise. We intend to make the case that Donald Trump is an underrated chief executive—and that the abuse of federal investigative power *against* him is the greatest scandal of his era.

We also intend to explain how a White House that appears so chaotic and has been so fiercely resisted by the nation's press and political establishment has managed to enact so much of the agenda promised to voters in 2016. Reporters like to present Trump as a catastrophe for the country, but it's time to also consider the cost of not having him as president. Difficult as it may be for many media observers to comprehend—and regardless of the results of the 2020 election—Trump has achieved a successful presidency hidden in plain sight.

It's perhaps all the more surprising given that he came to the job with no experience in elective office. The real estate developer from Queens rode down an escalator in one of his eponymous Manhattan skyscrapers to announce his campaign for president on June 16, 2015. After arriving at the bottom, he unleashed a raw tirade that resonated with blue-collar voters even as it repelled the nation's political and media establishment.

Just before Trump arrived at the podium, his daughter Ivanka promised the enthusiastic gathering that her father would "outwork anyone in any room" and that he was "the opposite of politically correct." Nearly four years into the Trump presidency, it's hard to argue with either claim, especially considering the people who tend to populate Washington meeting rooms. Ms. Trump also lauded her father's "refusal to take no for an answer" in negotiations and said that "he has the discernment to understand what the other party needs and then to get exactly what he wants." She added that he's a "dreamer" but also a "doer."

At the conclusion of her remarks, speakers in the Trump

Tower lobby blared Neil Young's "Rockin' in the Free World," which fired up the crowd and has been annoying Young ever since. Donald Trump then ascended the stage, and after thanking people and commenting on the size of the crowd, said:

"Our country is in serious trouble. We don't have victories anymore. We used to have victories, but we don't have them. When was the last time anybody saw us beating, let's say, China in a trade deal? They kill us. I beat China all the time. All the time."

Not exactly the Gettysburg Address, but he did get right to the point. The new candidate then made a boast that must have seemed preposterous to reporters covering the event: "I will be the greatest jobs president that God ever created."

Two years and seven months later, U.S. job openings hit a record high of 6.3 million. The record would be broken several times in the Trump era. Also remarkable was that, for the first time since the government began tracking such data, there were just as many job openings as unemployed Americans.[6] Newspaper "fact-checkers" are free to opine on whether they think God created Trump, but they can hardly argue with the numbers.

Back in 2015 at Trump Tower, amused reporters may have failed to appreciate, that while Trump had never held political office, he was the most skilled communicator in the presidential race. We're not just talking about his ability to make his case in fewer than 280 characters. Maria went to Trump Tower in 2016 to conduct a television interview with the rookie Republican candidate and former host of NBC's *The*

Apprentice. Before any discussion of economic plans or foreign policy priorities, Trump insisted on rearranging the television lights so that the brightest coverage was on the interview subject rather than the interviewer. Well played. He knew that, for any journalist, getting an exclusive with the country's new preeminent newsmaker would take priority over aesthetics. The meticulous rearrangement of the lighting has continued to be a pre-interview Trump ritual during his presidency.

Trump brought the same attention to detail to the crafting of his campaign message, which was almost entirely focused on winning over swing districts in Middle America with a promise of economic revival. He argued that step one was defeating an entrenched media and political elite.

Upon accepting the 2016 Republican nomination in Cleveland in July, Trump said: "America is a nation of believers, dreamers, and strivers that is being led by a group of censors, critics, and cynics. Remember: all of the people telling you that you can't have the country you want are the same people telling you that I wouldn't be standing here tonight."

He promised that Republicans would "lead our country back to safety, prosperity, and peace" and then described an economy in disrepair:

I will tell you the plain facts that have been edited out of your nightly news and your morning newspaper:

Nearly four in 10 African-American children are living in poverty, while 58 percent of African-American youth are not employed.

Two million more Latinos are in poverty today than when President Obama took his oath of office less than eight years ago.

Another 14 million people have left the workforce entirely. Household incomes are down more than $4,000 since the year 2000—16 years ago.

He then proposed "reforms to add millions of new jobs and trillions in new wealth . . ."[7]

What's perhaps most striking today is that the agenda he promised in Cleveland is precisely the one he has been pursuing ever since. On that summer night in Ohio four years ago he said, "We are going to enforce all trade violations against any country that cheats. This includes stopping China's outrageous theft of intellectual property." Then he elaborated on the heart of his economic program:

We are going to start building and making things again.

Next comes the reform of our tax laws, regulations, and energy rules. While Hillary Clinton plans a massive tax increase, I have proposed the largest tax reduction of any candidate who has run for president this year, Democrat or Republican. . . .

. . . Reducing taxes will cause new companies and new jobs to come roaring back into our country. Then we are going to deal with the issue of regulation, one of the greatest job-killers of them all. Excessive regulation is costing our country as much as $2 trillion a year, and

we will end it. We are going to lift the restrictions on
the production of American energy. . . .

It was a promise of a better life "for the people I have met
all across this nation that have been ignored, neglected, and
abandoned." He described "the forgotten men and women
of our country. People who work hard but no longer have
a voice." He promised to be the voice for industrial workers whose industries had been closing U.S. plants, especially
in the Midwest.[8] And throughout the campaign this message
was remarkably consistent. At times during his debates with
Hillary Clinton, he sounded like he was running for governor
of Michigan. One of the great ironies of 2016 is that the first-
timer understood the rules of the game better than the political
pros. Unlike most candidates, Trump ran a campaign premised
on the fact that the Electoral College really does decide U.S.
presidential elections.

Meanwhile the rugged and rude Trump style inspired—or
at least provided an excuse for—opponents in politics and the
press to discard the normal rules for objectivity, fairness, and
governmental restraint. The campaign to impeach him began
almost the moment he won the election in November of 2016.
On his first full day in office in 2017, hundreds of thousands
gathered in Washington to protest his presidency—an event
organized well before his presidency had even begun.

Trump's critics styled themselves "the Resistance," as if
they were confronting a tyrant at the head of an invading army
rather than their duly elected president. Most disturbing was
the resistance movement inside the federal government, which

in 2016 included at least one FBI attorney falsifying an email and duping the U.S. Foreign Intelligence Surveillance Court into approving a wiretap on a Trump campaign volunteer. Reports from the Obama-appointed inspector general of the Justice Department and others revealed that a cabal at the FBI repeatedly misled the court in its effort to investigate Team Trump and failed to disclose that the bogus "Steele dossier" of accusations against Trump was paid for by the Hillary Clinton campaign or that the government already had reasons to doubt it that were never shared in warrant applications.

In December 2019 the court found that FBI personnel had provided information to the court "which was unsupported or contradicted by information in their possession." The court ordered the FBI "in a sworn written submission" to explain what it was doing to prevent such abuses.[9] In 2020 the Justice Department acknowledged that at least two of its approved warrants were invalid. In March of 2020 the court effectively banned FBI agents involved in the Trump campaign wiretap abuses from appearing before it on any other matters.[10]

The FBI's surveillance of Trump associates is perhaps the worst abuse of federal power in recent history. But fortunately a more encouraging trend was also happening in America at the dawn of the Trump era. A surge of optimism among business owners was translating into plans for new investment that would eventually lead to that record-setting job market. This surge of optimism caught much of the media by surprise— but not the coauthors of this book. While many journalists were reeling from the shock of Trump's victory in November of 2016 and predicting economic doom, Maria told television viewers that she'd be "buying the stock market with both hands."[11] Investors who acted on that sentiment enjoyed significant gains.

Trump's trade policy was an unknown, but a president promising significant tax and regulatory relief was sparking broad enthusiasm among business owners from Wall Street to Main Street. By the time Trump took office on January 20, 2017, that enthusiasm was translating into expanding opportunity for American workers.

The National Federation of Independent Business's chief economist, William C. Dunkelberg, reported that the month Donald Trump took office a rise in the percentage of small business owners planning to create jobs added up to "the strongest reading since November 2006." And, unlike 2006, this burst of hiring wasn't occurring during a housing bubble. Trump's arrival at the White House brought still more good news for workers. Reports of increased worker compensation in the NFIB survey hit a ten-year high.[12]

The good news on U.S. employment would continue for the first three years of the Trump presidency as the promise of a lighter burden on American business was fulfilled. This unconventional political approach of Trump meaning what he said on the campaign trail has marked him as a Beltway oddity even more than his colorful Twitter commentary. And perhaps that is one reason why much of the Washington establishment still cannot forgive him. His presence upended their power structure.

Many of our media brethren have proven unable or unwilling to report on Donald Trump objectively, and a few have even explicitly made the case that he doesn't deserve traditional journalistic standards of fairness. Media criticism of President Trump has been so constant and so intense that most Americans probably don't even remember the moment in 2017 when CNN declared that the restoration of an FCC policy that had been in place for decades meant the "end of the Internet as we know it." [13] Also largely forgotten are the warnings of economic and societal catastrophe as a result of his tax cuts.

In the second month of the Trump presidency, a news report in the *New York Times* essentially predicted that the highest elected official in the United States would ultimately lose a power struggle with Washington's unelected establishment. *Times* reporters faulted Mr. Trump for "believing he can master an entrenched political press corps with far deeper connections to the permanent government of federal law enforcement and executive department officials than he has." The *Times* report added that the president "is being force-fed lessons all presidents eventually learn—that the iron triangle of the Washington press corps, West Wing staff, and federal bureaucracy is simply too powerful to bully." [14] Of course Donald Trump was elected precisely because many voters were searching for someone to protect them from Washington's bureaucratic bullies.

In that mission he has largely succeeded, although it hasn't always been pretty. Most politicians go to great lengths to conceal character flaws. Donald Trump wears them on his sleeve. Most presidents try to appear dignified and restrained in response to criticism. When a former cabinet secretary questioned the president's competence, Trump called him "dumb as a rock."

Speaking of former administration officials, Trump is setting records for acrimonious partings with senior staff. And America's forty-fifth president is often no more diplomatic in the way he conducts foreign relations. He called the leader of one of America's closest allies "very dishonest and weak"[15]— but also managed to strike a new trade deal with him.

Trump's impolite and unconventional style partly explains how he could manage to get impeached without being accused of any crime in either of the two impeachment articles passed in the U.S. House. And even people who find the Biden family's mining of overseas wealth appalling may not like the president's handling of relations with Ukraine.

But Trump's odd manners and methods also obscure the substance of a highly consequential presidency with significant achievements. Much of the press corps may now be dedicated to cataloging the inaccuracies in the president's rhetoric. Yet it's hard to name an elected official who has more faithfully pursued his campaign agenda—or has disclosed more of his thoughts and opinions. And his well-documented faults appear smaller the more we learn about the surveillance abuses conducted by his detractors within the federal government beginning in 2016. If such abuses of power can target even a successful presidential campaign and White House through wiretaps, informants, and a media leak strategy, then there is little hope of fairness for the rest of us.

Three years into his term, Donald Trump is neither the dignified statesman that some Americans hoped he might become nor the abusive authoritarian that media critics claimed he would be. But Trump can—and often does—boast of impressive results when it comes to the central promise of his 2016 campaign: restoring economic opportunity for the average worker. As we'll describe, in the years before Covid the U.S. job market set a series of records.

Trump has accused many members of the media—including Maria and the *Journal* editorial page where James serves as assistant editor —of spreading "fake news." Yet media organizations are thriving in the Trump era. The question is no longer whether they will remain free to criticize him but how they will continue to generate such robust ratings and revenues after he leaves the Oval Office.

Now it's time for Americans to review the record and decide how long he should stay there.

1

Morality and Prosperity

Judging the presidency of Donald Trump naturally involves a question of style versus substance. It's not surprising that the boorish billionaire who crashed the Republican presidential debate party in 2015 is still tweeting disrespectful comments about his political adversaries. Most people don't change all that much after the age of seventy. But what is remarkable is that the political novice is now concluding one of the most consequential first terms in recent history.

After Trump's stunning victory in 2016, one might have expected the former star of reality television to preside over an entertaining but ineffectual administration. One might even have had fun imagining Trump's celebrity pals lining up for nominations to the federal bench. But who would have guessed that, four years later, legal analysts of both parties would be acknowledging the exceptional quality and quantity of Trump judicial appointments?

The cost of supporting Donald Trump is enduring awkward moments when he says things that presidents shouldn't say. The benefit is that he champions American liberty and prosperity, and a free and prosperous America is a benefit to people all over the world.

In 2016, U.S. voters decided to take a chance on Trump because they figured that, for all his rough edges, he seemed willing and able to confront the bullying Washington bureaucracy—and bully it right back. In Trump's favored metaphor, Americans decided he was the guy to wade into a Beltway swamp that needed draining. The voters had no idea how right they were. As we'll discuss in chapter two, the culture of Washington turned out to be much more corrupt and rotten than almost anyone could have imagined.

Since moving into the White House, Trump hasn't become highly popular. He never was. But he has surpassed any reasonable expectation for his performance in office. In important ways Trump has reduced the federal footprint on the daily lives of U.S. citizens. Meanwhile, his adversaries are promising that when he departs the White House that footprint is going to get much larger.

In 2016, many of Trump's adversaries in politics and the press were saying that his various ill-advised comments portended a dark night of authoritarianism in America. They were wrong. Trump's regulatory and tax reforms and his appointment of judges committed to the rule of law have resulted in a federal government that exercises less power than the day he was inaugurated. And, unlike an actual authoritarian, he accepts the decisions of judges even when they rule against him, just as he accepted the decision of voters to hand the U.S. House of Representatives to Democrats in 2018.

A few journalists, like Doyle McManus of the *Los Angeles Times*, have been honest enough to acknowledge that the 2016 hyperventilating over a potential dictatorship was overdone. "Not long ago, the 'Never Trump' half of the nation was gripped by fear of an authoritarian takeover," wrote McManus in 2019. "But the specter of an autocratic president running roughshod over democratic institutions has ebbed," he admitted, as the courts and Congress maintained the usual restraints on the White House.[1] But many of Trump's critics have simply moved on to claiming that he violates vaguely defined constitutional "norms." Such claims often come from people who favor violations of actual constitutional *rights* and spend much of their time pressuring judges to ignore the plain language of the first two amendments.

Trump doesn't trample our rights and he doesn't start wars. He says things that offend people.

Another thing that Trump sometimes says is that Americans "have no choice"[2] but to vote for him given his economic policies. We always have choices, but he has a point for voters who prize limited government. As we write this in the summer of 2020, with virus lockdowns ravaging the economy and triggering the highest unemployment rates in more than seventy years, Trump's presidential election opponent Joe Biden is stubbornly maintaining that what the U.S. economy needs is a $4 trillion tax increase. Biden has also proposed a much larger increase in federal spending, plus a wave of new federal regulation. This fall voters have a clear choice between a candidate who favors economic growth and one who has other priorities.

The massive exception to Trump's limited government agenda is, of course, the rise in federal debt during his presidency; sadly this is the one area in which he has proven to be an utterly conventional politician. But if voters choose to reject him on this basis, they will elect a candidate promising to spend and borrow much more.

The Republican president Trump is the imperfect champion for foundational liberties at a time in our history when socialism is increasingly embraced by Democratic candidates. In this context, it's possible that Trump's controversial tweets will end up as forgotten footnotes.

One can argue with the slogan "Make America Great Again," on the grounds that America never stopped being great. And the United States is not just one of the great countries of the world. It's the greatest. No other country has done nearly as much as the United States to liberate and enrich people all over the world. Trump the salesman actually understated the case.

Still, the important thing about Trump is that he believes in American greatness, wants America to be the most prosperous country in the world, and prioritizes a thriving America above all other considerations. In another time and place, it might be obvious that a president puts the interests of his country first. But Trump came along at a time in America when too many politicians seemed to view America as one of the world's challenges, rather than its greatest asset. Trump's predecessor

President Barack Obama began his tenure by making a series of memorable speeches overseas in which he described American flaws. In France of all places, he castigated America for "arrogance."[3] Critics dubbed it Obama's "apology tour."[4] By Obama's last year in office it had become standard operating procedure, even when visiting Marxist dictatorships, to recall alleged U.S. misdeeds against the host nation. During a visit to Cuba he noted that the United States had once sought to "exert control" over the country and no doubt many suffering Cubans were wishing that we had.[5] Trump doesn't apologize for America. When it comes to foreign relations, he thinks that in many ways we've been too nice. He presented himself to voters in 2016 as an experienced negotiator who could cut better deals on America's behalf.

Trump correctly casts the United States as a model for the world. And regardless of the number of odd messages he may post on Twitter, he's done as much as any recent president to maintain the constitutional governance that made us great and allows us to exercise the global leadership the world needs. In a September 2019 speech to the United Nations General Assembly, President Trump said, "I have the immense privilege of addressing you today as the elected leader of a nation that prizes liberty, independence, and self-government above all. . . . Americans know that in a world where others seek conquest and domination, our nation must be strong in wealth, in might, and in spirit. That is why the United States vigorously defends the traditions and customs that have made us who we are."[6]

Trump then encouraged the leaders of other nations to honor their own cultures as the foundation of a patriotism that inspires people to defend their independence. But he might just as well have been talking to Americans who have lately witnessed a flood of media stories about attempts to destroy U.S. monuments, even ones dedicated to great abolitionists. Trump stands squarely against efforts to trash our history and understands that while America has often fallen short of its founding ideals, the answer is not to reject such ideals but to extend them to people everywhere. He said at the U.N.:

> The core rights and values America defends today were inscribed in America's founding documents. Our nation's Founders understood that there will always be those who believe they are entitled to wield power and control over others. Tyranny advances under many names and many theories, but it always comes down to the desire for domination. It protects not the interests of many, but the privilege of few.
>
> Our Founders gave us a system designed to restrain this dangerous impulse. They chose to entrust American power to those most invested in the fate of our nation: a proud and fiercely independent people.
>
> The true good of a nation can only be pursued by those who love it: by citizens who are rooted in its history, who are nourished by its culture, committed to its values, attached to its people, and who know that its future is theirs to build or theirs to lose. Patriots see a nation and its destiny in ways no one else can.[7]

Of course such soaring rhetoric is often followed by undignified Twitter commentary. For years this has led many observers to cast Donald Trump as the guilty pleasure of American politics. It's been a recurring theme in media circles ever since he began running for president. The argument is often framed as selfish voters accepting an unpresidential occupant of the White House in exchange for economic benefits. As Trump seeks reelection, it's a good time to revisit this popular media morality tale.

Guilty or not, many voters have certainly experienced pleasure watching Trump torment the Washington establishment. In 2015, Christopher Orr argued in the *Atlantic* that the Republican primary race was the political equivalent of the movie *Caddyshack*, with Trump playing Rodney Dangerfield's character Al Czervik and Jeb Bush taking over the role of Judge Elihu Smails from Ted Knight.

"Pretty much everyone in America would like to have more money, obviously," wrote Orr. "What they don't want is to think that wealth would fundamentally change who they are. This is a basic democratic credo. Most Americans don't want to be rich so that they can develop a taste for fancy French cuisine to be enjoyed over polite repartee with their fellow snobs at the country club. They want to be rich so they can do whatever they want and never have to take crap from anyone."

Orr added that Trump was "an aggressive anti-snob who says whatever the hell he pleases and misses no opportunity to stick it to the establishment. The GOP is Bushwood Country Club (*Bush*wood!) and Trump the obnoxious interloper who, owing to his wealth, can't be tastefully ignored."[8]

In 2016, Josh Barro of Business Insider called Trump "the guilty-pleasure candidate" and wrote about the future president's brand identity: "Trump Steaks. Trump Vodka. Trump Wine. These are not luxury items so much as they are indulgence items. His is a brand that says, *screw your cardiologist, have a steak. You earned it.*"

Barro went on to observe: "There is a lot of money to be made selling virtue-signaling goods and services to affluent people, but Donald Trump is not Martha Stewart, and he is not Gwyneth Paltrow. The appeal of Trump is not just that he's rich, but that because he's rich he gets to do whatever he wants—and he does not want to drink kale juice."[9]

In a similar vein, comedian Seth Meyers noted a suspicion among some political analysts that candidate Trump was more popular than reported because voters were reluctant to admit to pollsters that they backed his controversial ideas. Said Meyers: "Guys, that's a red flag. Your president shouldn't be a guilty pleasure." Meyers then pretended to be a voter struggling to make the decision and said, "Uhhh—I know I should be getting a salad, but I'm just going to vote Trump. I am so bad right now!"[10]

Whether Trump's unique style of commentary elicits laughter or outrage—or perhaps a little of both—there is now a presidential record to consider. In this era the stakes are high for America and the world, and who would say that a tasteless tweet should overrule a presidency that supports liberty and the rule of law?

Trump's media detractors have known all along that they weren't going to get anywhere blasting the president's *Caddy-*

shack style if the *substance* of his agenda was yielding positive results for most voters. So reporters at major media outlets spent a few years promoting without evidence a theory that Trump had betrayed his country. Unhinged opinion writers like Paul Krugman at the *New York Times* suggested that tens of millions of American voters were willing to accept a Russian conspiracy to rig U.S. elections as long as they could gain partisan advantage or tax cuts.[11]

If the claims of collusion with Russia had been true, they surely would have proven that voters made a devil's bargain in backing Trump. But the point was always to try to shame his supporters, not to conduct a thorough examination of the available evidence. In March 2018 the House Intelligence Committee released a report on Russian efforts to interfere in American elections, and like every other government report on the subject it found no evidence of Trump's involvement in such efforts. Three days later, Chairman Devin Nunes (R-Calif.) told Maria, "What strikes me most is that we had seventy recommendations and findings, yet I think you might be the first person to actually cover" them.[12]

The collapse of the collusion case makes it hard to claim that Trump voters should feel guilty about anything. On the other side of the ledger, the tragic events of 2020 have only served to underline the moral imperative of electing a U.S. president who prioritizes American prosperity and liberty.

During the first three years of the Trump presidency, while American workers were often enjoying record-setting levels of job openings, perhaps it was easy for media pundits to take such conditions for granted. Wage gains were dismissed as insufficient compensation for Trump's flaws. Such pundits will now have a hard time persuading the former owners and employees of shuttered businesses that, hey, it's only money.

In the spring of 2020, state and local governments responded to the coronavirus by ordering the shutdown of much of American society. Mandated closures of businesses and other organizations inflicted a financial toll that would have been almost unimaginable just a few weeks earlier. Exactly how many trillions of dollars this will cost Americans is still to be determined.

Long lines suddenly appeared at food banks nationwide, even in some of the country's most affluent communities. Aerial views of thousands of cars whose drivers were waiting for emergency food assistance circulated on the internet. Many people had never relied on charity before and were shocked to find themselves needing help. In San Antonio, National Public Radio interviewed a forty-two-year-old bank employee named Erica whose ex-husband had lost his job and could no longer make child support payments.

"I never, ever could have even imagined anything like this," Erica told the public broadcaster. "I was almost ashamed, to be honest, to even pick up food from the food bank because somebody might look at my used Cadillac and be like, 'What is she doing in the food bank line?' But I had to get past those feelings of shame. There's no shame in feeding my children." [13]

In April alone the shutdowns destroyed more than 20 million jobs as the national unemployment rate surged to nearly

15 percent. Unemployment was even worse than it initially appeared because the rate didn't account for the millions of people who had recently been on a payroll and had not even started looking for another job during the lockdown.

But the unemployment rate was still historically awful. "The U.S. jobless rate eclipsed the previous record rate of 10.8% for data tracing back to 1948," reported Sarah Chaney and Eric Morath in the *Wall Street Journal*. Economists estimate that the unemployment rate during the Great Depression was much worse—close to 25 percent. Still, by one measure the U.S. economy really did fall all the way back down to 1930s-style disaster territory: "The job losses due to business closures triggered by the pandemic produced by far the steepest monthly decline on records back to 1939." [14]

It will take a long time to identify and measure all the negative consequences of the enforced isolation of Americans in response to the virus. Right now America needs economic revival. And American economic revival is the cause that has defined Donald Trump's presidency. The Trump agenda to remove the tax and regulatory barriers to growth resonated with U.S. voters in 2016. After taking office, he delivered on his promises to enact historic reductions in business regulation and slash what until 2017 had been the industrialized world's highest tax rate on corporate income. Business investment soared in response and the number of U.S. job openings set a series of new records.

In 2020, after a global economic catastrophe, the growth agenda may now resonate with voters worldwide. When the U.S. economy experiences a sudden contraction, it's not just a catastrophe for Americans. When it comes to the health of the poorest countries on the planet, it's clear they suffer humanitarian disasters when the United States and other advanced economies suddenly demand fewer goods. You won't hear it on many college campuses, but a faltering America is a disaster for the world.

For example, according to *New York Times* East Africa correspondent Abdi Latif Dahir, "Already, 135 million people had been facing acute food shortages, but now with the pandemic, 130 million more could go hungry in 2020, said Arif Husain, chief economist at the World Food Program, a United Nations agency. Altogether, an estimated 265 million people could be pushed to the brink of starvation by year's end."

Reporting in April and May, Mr. Dahir described a deadly stampede in Kenya at a flour and cooking oil giveaway, and red flags hanging from the homes of starving people in Colombia. The *Times* correspondent also told the story of Nihal, a migrant worker at a soup kitchen in New Delhi, India: " 'Instead of coronavirus, the hunger will kill us,' said Nihal, who was hoping to eat his first meal in a day. Migrants waiting in food lines have fought each other over a plate of rice and lentils. Nihal said he was ashamed to beg for food but had no other option. 'The lockdown has trampled on our dignity,' he said." [15]

The people of the world need a prosperous America, and not just because they want to be fed. The worldwide public health crisis of 2020 is a sober reminder of how the world would suffer without a vibrant medical research enterprise in the United States. This jewel of the U.S. economy is also the hope of patients worldwide as they await vaccines and therapies to fight diseases for which there is currently no cure.

BIO (Biotechnology Innovation Organization), a biotechnology trade association, notes that in 2018 emerging medical companies in the United States received a record $12.3 billion in venture capital funding, more than twice the total raised by such companies in the rest of the world combined. That same year emerging U.S. therapeutic companies also raised more than twice as much in initial public offerings as the rest of the world combined.[16] This is the financial fuel for innovation, funding the new discoveries and clinical trials that will yield new medicines and save lives in years to come.

Why does so much of this activity happen in the United States? Because inventors trust that the traditional American rule of law that protects our liberty also protects our property. Creators of new medicines and new technologies are free to grow their businesses and profit from their inventions. Intellectual property is constitutionally protected. In Article 1, Section 8, of the Constitution, America's founders gave Congress the power "to promote the Progress of Science and useful Arts, by securing for limited Times to Authors and Inventors the exclusive Right to their respective Writings and Discoveries." Well beyond the issues of intellectual property and medicine, America's open markets, protected by a reliable and predictable application of the law, give people around the world the confidence to invest in U.S. companies.

No president has done more than Donald Trump to appoint judges who will faithfully interpret the Constitution and protect the American rule of law. Even the president's harshest critics concede the quality of the more than two hundred judges he has appointed and the Senate has confirmed to seats on America's courts. Left-wing legal activist Ian Millhiser probably didn't enjoy writing the following words, but give him credit for acknowledging the truth: "There's no completely objective way to measure legal ability, but a common metric used by legal employers to identify the most gifted lawyers is whether those lawyers secured a federal clerkship, including the most prestigious clerkships at the Supreme Court. Approximately 40 percent of Trump's appellate nominees clerked for a Supreme Court justice, and about 80 percent clerked on a federal court of appeals. That compares to less than a quarter of Obama's nominees who clerked on the Supreme Court, and less than half with a federal appellate clerkship." Adds Millhiser: "In other words, based solely on objective legal credentials, the average Trump appointee has a far more impressive résumé than any past president's nominees."[17]

As a candidate in 2016, Trump made promises about the people he would appoint if elected, even supplying lists of potential Supreme Court justices. But there was little in his background to suggest an abiding commitment to constitutional originalism. Yet, unlike conventional politicians, he has kept his promises and made outstanding appointments.

The benefits of Trump's rock-solid commitment to constitutional liberty are not just economic. Improbable as it may have seemed, the thrice-married star of tabloid gossip pages has become the stalwart champion of Catholic nuns seeking to preserve their core First Amendment right to religious exercise. The Little Sisters of the Poor is a nonprofit religious order that runs homes for the elderly poor across the country. The Obama administration threatened to impose fines of tens of millions of dollars upon the Little Sisters if the nuns would not agree to violate their beliefs and pay for contraceptive services in their health plan. After taking office, President Trump used an executive order and then two federal rules to ensure that the Little Sisters of the Poor could continue their mission without having to sacrifice their faith. It's safe to say the nuns wouldn't approve of a lot of Trump's comments, but many of them no doubt recognize that he has proven to be an important defender of their God-given rights.

Speaking of enjoying the freedom to live according to the dictates of one's own conscience, it is very much related to economics. U.S. prosperity enabled American individuals, foundations, and corporations to give an estimated $449.64 billion to U.S. charities in 2019, according to *Giving USA 2020: The Annual Report on Philanthropy for the Year 2019*. The report is compiled each year by the Indiana University Lilly Family School of Philanthropy.

"The solid growth of giving in 2019 brought total giving close to the record level set in 2017, which means that the past three years are the three highest years on record. Clearly, Americans prioritize generosity as a key part of their lives," said Rick Dunham, Giving USA Foundation chairman, as his organization released the new findings in June of 2020. "Giving increased substantially in 2019, ending the decade on a high note," he added.[18]

Americans' capacity and willingness to help others doesn't end at the water's edge. The simple fact is that a prosperous

United States is one of the best things that's ever happened to the world. Billions of people around the planet are better off today because America defeated the twin terrors of the bloody twentieth century, national socialism and communism. And America has never stopped lending a helping hand to the world. The uniquely American entrepreneurial culture that created places like Silicon Valley has generated unprecedented prosperity, which among many other benefits enables historic levels of charitable activity and foreign aid.

A 2016 report from the Hudson Institute found, not surprisingly, that the U.S. government gives far more to developing countries than any other government in the world. But what may have come as a surprise was that Washington's official development assistance was dwarfed by the amount of money flowing from other sources in the United States to the poor countries of the world. Private philanthropy, private investment, and remittances from relatives and friends in the U.S. to the developing world added up to roughly ten times the amount of U.S. government development assistance.[19]

Our point is to highlight the contributions Americans make as taxpayers as well as donors, and as always they are making a lot of them in the fight against infectious disease. "For more than a half century, the United States has been the largest contributor to global health security and humanitarian assistance, saving lives all over the planet. The United States led the fight against Ebola, HIV/AIDS, tuberculosis, malaria, and other infectious diseases, as well as humanitarian responses around the globe, including the current crises in Venezuela and Syria," said Secretary of State Mike Pompeo in May.

Pompeo was announcing the latest round of U.S. government assistance, but he also recognized the contributions made by U.S. private citizens: "Even while battling the virus on the homefront, the American people remain the world's greatest humanitarians. Together, private American businesses, nonprofits, charities, and individuals have provided nearly $4 billion in donations and assistance, in addition to government aid. All together, Americans have provided nearly $6.5 billion in government and non-government assistance and donations to the global COVID-19 response, accounting for nearly 60% of global totals."[20]

And of course American charity goes far beyond medicine. The Charities Aid Foundation, based in the United Kingdom, creates what it calls a *World Giving Index*. In 2019 the organization reported on ten years of research conducted by the Gallup opinion research firm, which examined the charitable habits of people around the world. The foundation says the results represent the views of more than 1.3 million people in 128 countries and is the largest such survey "ever produced and made freely available."[21]

The foundation explains:

In order to ensure that giving is understood in its various forms, the report looks at three aspects of giving behaviour. The questions that lie at the heart of the report are:

Have you done any of the following in the past month?

- Helped a stranger, or someone you didn't know who needed help?

- Donated money to a charity?
- Volunteered your time to an organisation?[22]

In other words, the index is not a measurement of how much money the citizens of a country donate but rather a reading on how likely its people are to help others in one way or another. "The United States of America occupies first place over the last 10 years," reports the foundation.[23] Yes, Americans are generous with their money, but the U.S. received its highest score in the category of helping strangers, an extremely common American habit.

What about the other end of the scale? Out of the 128 countries surveyed, which one displays the least charitable activity? The foundation reports that "China has the lowest Index score over the 10 years . . . and in fact is the only country that appears in the bottom 10 for all three measures we ask about; helping a stranger, donating money, and volunteering time."[24]

This probably has less to do with China than with the tragedy of its particular form of government. When a country has been run by a communist dictatorship for seventy years, where expressions of faith are routinely and sometimes brutally suppressed and independent thought can result in prison time, it's a culture in deep need of repair. In observing the long struggle of Cubans living under another communist regime, Cuban exiles often express both a passionate love for their homeland as well as an ambivalence about returning to live there, even in the event the dictatorship finally collapses. Many fear that the great Cuban culture has been broken by six decades of Marxist tyranny.

The tragedy of Chinese political oppression, despite the country's phenomenal economic rise in recent decades, is perhaps the greatest reason why a prosperous America is a moral necessity. Whether the American constitutional republic or the communist dictatorship based in Beijing ends up sitting on top of the world's largest economy has profound moral implications for the entire world. "America First" is a controversial slogan in the United States. But what many people around the world truly fear is the prospect of living under the influence of China first. The country is ruled by an unelected regime which denies its people the most basic liberties, including free speech, freedom of the press, and due process of law.

This means Americans have a job to do as we seek to rebuild our economy and ensure the success of open markets and free societies. The ranking Republican on the House Ways and Means Committee, Representative Kevin Brady of Texas, says that as America bounces back from the virus, the playbook for growth hasn't changed: "The key is to make sure temporary job losses don't become permanent ones—that's what Congress ought to be focused on. We ought to follow those same elements that created the Trump economic boom: keeping taxes low, incentivizing businesses, making sure that work pays for our workers."[25]

He's talking about policies that created the rare and wonderful occurrence of many more job openings in the United States than unemployed people.[26] There's nothing immoral about that. And who should feel guilty about ensuring that Americans and people everywhere can enjoy the pleasures of liberty and prosperity?

2

The Coup That Failed

This should never happen to another president," said Donald Trump in 2019, "because most presidents wouldn't be able to take it."[1] He was talking about the Russian collusion fraud that haunted his presidency—the evidence-free claim that he had somehow worked with Russia to rig the 2016 election. Trump has been known to say outlandish things, but in this case voters should take him both seriously and literally. The American republic cannot survive if government officials are routinely able to mislead judges into approving surveillance campaigns against political opponents.

In the old days before media organizations sanctioned just about any effort to take down Donald Trump, the FBI's activities in this era would have been fodder for a dark Hollywood thriller. The federal government used wiretaps, informants, and even doctored evidence against Trump associates—while hiding the real exculpatory evidence for years. If such outrages become a regular part of U.S. politics, the cost to political freedom will be severe. In this case the heavy cost was not just to Trump associates who had their most basic liberties violated; the cost to the people's business was also significant. We'll discuss other challenges of the Trump era in the chapters ahead, but what's clear is that collusion claims dominated public debate for more than two years of his presidency.

The collusion investigation was not an economic event. But America's free economy and world-leading financial markets, which have created wealth and opportunity for people around the world, can exist only under a predictable rule of law. The unprecedented campaign by senior government officials against an opposition candidate and then a duly elected president was a fundamental assault on our rule of law. Destructive claims of Russian collusion poisoned our public discourse for years.

It's impossible to understand the Trump presidency or provide a fair accounting of Trump governance without noting the extraordinary obstacles he faced. Attorney General Bill Barr told Maria in June 2020 that it was "the closest we have come to an organized effort to push a president out of office since Lincoln's assassination."[2]

It's also worth noting the message of the markets in this era. While many of our colleagues in the media industry ran with bogus conspiracy claims and cast Trump as an existential threat to our way of life, investors clearly never bought that story. The era of Russian collusion hysteria in the press was an era of rising wealth in stocks. Investors tuned out the anti-

Trump circus, focused on Trump tax and regulatory reform, and then confidently made bigger and bigger bets on American business. When markets tumbled in recent years, it was usually due to a reaction to Trump trade policy, or, most dramatically, when a virus from China and the overreaction of state and local politicians shut down much of the U.S. economy.

The average investor figured out pretty quickly that Trump was actually *not* a traitorous authoritarian bent on destroying our republic. But all Americans should understand the threat his adversaries posed to the rule of law on which our liberty and prosperity depend.

We can now see that, for many proponents of the collusion theory, the purpose of the investigation wasn't really to search for evidence of Trump conspiring with Russian strongman Vladimir Putin; there wasn't any. The point was to create headlines about the investigation and use this flow of controversy and suspicion to destroy a presidency.

As Trump took office in January of 2017, a historic flood of deceptive leaks by government employees kept the new president on the defensive. Senate Committee on Homeland Security and Governmental Affairs chairman Ron Johnson (R-Wis.) has tabulated "a leak a day, 125 leaks in the first 126 days, and 62 of these leaks threatened national security, by President Obama's own definition of that . . ."[3] Johnson adds that the volume in this most serious category of leaks in the early days of Trump's tenure added up to more than six times the levels of the Obama or George W. Bush administrations.

We call these leaks deceptive because the search for collusion evidence had come up dry despite aggressive and illegal efforts by FBI officials to procure such evidence. Yet the flood of selective leaks, packaged for media consumption, suggested a rising mountain of proof of Trump treachery. Compliant reporters, anchors, and pundits took it from there, citing anonymous sources and weaving dark tales of walls closing in around an embattled president.

We don't think well of people who mislead us, but for some reason many in our industry have decided not to turn on the sources who fed them a massive deception. Johnson correctly notes that even if the leakers remain anonymous to the public, leak recipients in the press corps clearly know who they are. He points out that leaks were routed "to 18 different outlets. And I haven't seen too much investigation, reporting, or investigatory reporting, from the media in terms of how they were either duped or complicit in this corruption of the transition process." [4]

Attorney General William Barr states: "It's been stunning that all we have gotten from the mainstream media is sort of bovine silence in the face of the complete collapse of the so-called Russiagate scandal, which they did all they could to sensationalize and drive.

"And it's like not even a 'whoops,'" he continued. "They are just on to the next false scandal."

Barr adds that it "has been surprising to me that people aren't concerned about civil liberties and the integrity of our governmental process." [5]

What follows is the story of the historic corruption and abuse of federal power, enabled and encouraged by news organizations that abandoned journalistic principle in the pursuit of ideological ends.

In 2016, supporters of Hillary Clinton began circulating a bogus dossier of smears alleging that Trump had been compromised by the Russian government. The creation of the dossier was funded by the Clinton campaign and the Democratic National Committee during a presidential election year. They used a law firm called Perkins Coie, which hired a company called Fusion GPS to build the dossier against their opponent. The author of the dossier, former British spy Christopher Steele, was staunchly opposed to Trump. Steele's information came from a "Primary Sub-source" who by 2017 had told FBI agents that some of the most sensational claims were simply made in "jest."[6]

This effort to brand Clinton's opponent a traitor didn't prevent her defeat in the 2016 presidential race. But it helped inspire Trump's adversaries in Washington to turn the national security machinery of the federal government against American citizens participating in politics. To employ the surveillance tools usually reserved for terrorists and other foreign enemies against an associate of Donald J. Trump, U.S. government officials committed a series of frauds upon a federal court and the American people.

It would take until December 2019—almost three full years into Trump's presidential term—for the Justice Department's inspector general to lay out Steele's connections to Russian oligarchs. This information had been sitting in the FBI's own files but was ignored in the quest to make a collusion case against Trump. Not until April 2020 did the public learn that even *before Trump took office* the FBI began receiving intelligence reports saying not only that key dossier claims were false but that they had been invented by the Russian government.[7] After years of political warfare fueled by accusations against Trump, the U.S. election meddler with Russia ties turned out to be Hillary Clinton.

This doesn't mean that anyone should "lock her up." It may be immoral but it's not illegal to share self-serving unverified rumors with the FBI and urge an investigation to determine if your political rival is conspiring with a foreign government. The greatest fault lies with those in government who accepted this reckless partisan scheme and used it to assault the U.S. political system and individual liberty. It's time for a reckoning to ensure this never happens again.

Director James Comey's Federal Bureau of Investigation said that it officially began targeting Trump campaign associates in July 2016 with the opening of a case called "Crossfire Hurricane." We say "officially" because it is unlikely that that was the true start of the investigation, as we'll discuss later. What's not in dispute is that, almost thirty-two months later, special counsel Robert Mueller reported to the Justice Department that he'd found no evidence of anyone in the Trump campaign colluding with Russians.

The absence of evidence wasn't for lack of trying by the special counsel. Mueller took over the Russia investigation in May 2017 after Comey's firing sparked calls for an independent inquiry. Mueller stacked his team with activist Democrats, including generous donors to Obama and Clinton campaigns and staff who had been promoting the collusion narrative long before they went to work for Mueller. In May 2020 an embarrassed Biden for President campaign would cancel a fundraiser featuring top Mueller prosecutor Andrew Weissmann. But it was too late to hide the fact that Trump had been investigated by ideological opponents.

What's also now clear is that, months before Mueller was hired in 2017 and before Trump was even *inaugurated*, FBI officials already knew they had no collusion case. Richard Grenell, as acting director of national intelligence in 2020, declassified voluminous witness testimony proving the government never had any collusion evidence. Says Grenell: "The Russian investigation had all sorts of red flags from the beginning and when you look at the transcripts, when you look at the declassified footnotes from some of the investigations, it's clear that there were multiple people from multiple agencies that were raising red flags. However . . . those red flags and those voices were pushed aside, classified, and never shown to the public. And so very few people knew the truth . . ."[8]

Justice Department inspector general Michael Horowitz, who was appointed to his post by President Barack Obama, has been documenting the numerous problems with Steele and his dossier, including the many reasons not to believe it. Democrats weren't Steele's only clients.

"Steele had multiple contacts with representatives of Russian oligarchs with connections to Russian Intelligence Services (RIS) and senior Kremlin officials," reports the inspector general.[9]

"Steele's frequent contacts with Russian oligarchs in 2015 had raised concerns in the FBI Transnational Organized Crime Intelligence Unit," adds the IG's report, but this information wasn't even shared with members of the FBI team using Steele's reporting to investigate the Trump campaign.[10]

The December 2019 inspector general's report described questions related to a particular unnamed ally of Russian ruler Vladimir Putin: "We asked Steele about whether he had a relationship with Russian Oligarch 1. Steele stated that he did not have a relationship and indicated that he had met Russian Oligarch 1 one time. He explained that he worked for Russian Oligarch 1's attorney on litigation matters that involved Russian Oligarch 1 but that he could not provide 'specifics' about them for confidentiality reasons."[11] So, according to Steele, he did not have a relationship with someone who was funding his work?

As for his infamous dossier, Steele wasn't actually doing much work at all. "Steele himself was not the originating source of any of the factual information in his reporting," says the inspector general's report.[12] Steele had farmed out the task of reporting to somebody else and Steele never told the FBI who it was.[13]

To summarize, an anti-Trump former foreign spy whose clients included representatives of a Russian oligarch and the Hillary Clinton campaign provided the critical evidence in the collusion investigation from a source he did not disclose.

Believe it or not, this was enough—along with the suppression of exculpatory evidence—to get a wiretap on an associate of the Trump campaign named Carter Page. Some Trump opponents have spent years pretending that Steele's dossier was just one part of a huge mosaic of solid evidence justifying the surveillance and the overall investigation.

But the Obama-appointed inspector general found that without Steele's claims there would have been no Justice Department request for a wiretap under the Foreign Intelligence Surveillance Act: "We determined that the Crossfire Hurricane team's receipt of Steele's election reporting on September 19, 2016, played a central and essential role in the FBI's and Department's decision to seek the FISA order."[14]

The inspector general's report notes that before the use of the Steele dossier, the FBI general counsel's office and the Justice Department's Office of Intelligence had rejected the idea of seeking a wiretap on Page in August of 2016. There wasn't enough information to support a probable cause finding that Page was an agent of a foreign power.[15] And there wasn't enough information to support a probable cause finding against anyone else associated with Trump, which was why the FBI focused on Page.

Not that the use of Steele's dossier was the only abuse of Carter Page. The government successfully applied for a warrant to spy on him in the fall of 2016 and then persuaded the Foreign Intelligence Surveillance Court to grant a series of renewals. According to the Office of the Inspector General, "We identified significant inaccuracies and omissions in each of the four applications—7 in the first FISA application and a total of 17 by the final renewal application."[16]

The FBI had stacked the deck against Page. The IG reports: "As a result of the 17 significant inaccuracies and omissions we identified, relevant information was not shared with, and consequently not considered by, important Department decision makers and the court, and the FISA applications made it appear as though the evidence supporting probable cause was stronger than was actually the case. We also found basic, fundamental, and serious errors during the completion of the FBI's factual accuracy reviews, known as the Woods Procedures, which are designed to ensure that FISA applications contain a full and accurate presentation of the facts." [17]

More than a year before the Obama-appointed inspector general made this report, then U.S. representative John Ratcliffe said the same thing on the Fox News program *Sunday Morning Futures*. To obtain the warrant to surveil Carter Page, the FBI had only shown the court evidence that bolstered its case, without disclosing facts that called it into question. [18] By then much of the press corps had already decided to buy the narrative from Trump opponents, regardless of the burgeoning evidence of FBI abuses.

Speaking of these abuses, they went far beyond omitting evidence favorable to Carter Page. Not satisfied with hiding the facts, at least one FBI attorney altered exculpatory evidence and made it appear incriminating. Among advisers to the Trump campaign, Page was attractive as a target to the FBI because he did business in Russia and he'd met with some shady characters there. These facts could go a long way toward persuading a judge that Page was a Russian agent—as long as the judge never learned the truth: Page had been working with the CIA. Helping a U.S. intelligence agency collect information on the Russians should have earned Page the thanks of a grateful nation. Spying on Putin's Russia is dangerous work. But the FBI not only never told the court he was assisting the good guys; the bureau falsely presented some of his helpful activities as evidence he was helping the bad guys.

The same falsehood was leaked to the press. "I kept getting these calls from reporters throughout the summer of 2016 asking about these totally false allegations which Fusion G.P.S. and their consultants were doing for the DNC," he says. Were Democrats trying to muddy him up to justify the investigation? "Exactly. Well, really, to muddy then-candidate Trump up," Page concludes.[19]

Some FBI officials no doubt noticed that instead of lawyering up and staying silent, Page was publicly insisting that the claims against him were false. Before the last renewal for wiretap authority in 2017, after Page had disclosed his actual role in the press, the FBI worked even harder to mislead. An FBI lawyer had received an email from another government agency confirming that Page had indeed served as a source for U.S. intelligence. Inspector General Horowitz reports that the FBI lawyer then "altered the email that the other U.S. government agency had sent" so that it appeared to state that Page had *not* been a source. The inspector general adds that the FBI lawyer then forwarded the doctored email to a supervisor. Shortly thereafter, a supervisor "served as the affiant on the final renewal application, which was again silent on Page's prior relationship with the other U.S. government agency."[20]

The FBI lawyer who altered the record is named Kevin

Clinesmith. He's among a number of anti-Trump staff who later joined the Mueller investigation and then left after the exposure of a series of texts demonstrating extreme bias against Donald Trump and his supporters. After the Trump victory in the 2016 election, Clinesmith had texted a colleague, "viva la resistance."[21]

The falsifying of evidence against Page was among the reasons Presiding Judge Rosemary Collyer of the U.S. Foreign Intelligence Surveillance Court issued a public order on December 17, 2019, demanding that the FBI report on what it was doing to ensure accurate applications that include all material facts.[22]

That description certainly didn't apply to the FBI's applications to wiretap Page. Officials never told the court that Clinton and the Democrats paid for the dossier and never fully disclosed Steele's Russian connections. The FBI also falsely suggested that Steele had not been the source of a Yahoo! News report about Page, so the story appeared to corroborate Steele's claims.[23]

From the fall of 2016 until the early summer of 2017, the FBI requested and received a series of surveillance authorizations on Page without telling the court that the thin, misleading evidence it had presented was becoming even less believable.

Steele never told the FBI who had actually collected the information for his dossier. But the FBI did manage to find this person by January 2017 and in the course of conversations over several months learned that the information was garbage. In the language of intelligence, this person was the "Primary Sub-source" who had drawn on a "network of sources"—which may have sounded authoritative, but when the FBI found this person, the source said it wasn't so much a network of sources "but rather friends with whom he/she has conversations about current events and government relations," according to a footnote from the inspector general's report, which was finally declassified in April of 2020.[24]

Even if one were inclined to believe this anonymous person passing on comments from anonymous friends, it turned out that the whole anonymous crew was being misquoted. In January of 2017, according to the inspector general's office, "the Primary Sub-source told the FBI that he/she had not seen Steele's reports until they became public that month" and indicated that "Steele misstated or exaggerated the Primary Sub-source's statements in multiple sections of the reporting." For example, one story described as "confirmed" by Steele was, in the words of the source, "rumor and speculation."[25]

During a March 2017 interview, "the Primary Sub-source said he/she made it clear to Steele that he/she had no proof to support the statements from his/her sub-sources and that 'it was just talk.'" An FBI agent reported that the Primary Sub-source said the information came from "word of mouth and hearsay," conversations "with friends over beers" and that comments about Trump's alleged sexual activities, were made in "jest."[26] Looking back now in 2020, current Attorney General William Barr observes that "the dossier pretty much collapsed at that point—and yet they continued to use it as a basis for pursuing this counterintelligence investigation."[27]

The Steele information wasn't credible, but it wasn't necessarily the result of fun and games in 2016. U.S. intelligence later reported that Russian intelligence services were aware of Steele's effort to compile his dossier material as early as July 2016.[28] The FBI was warned as early as January 2017 that Russian intelligence appeared to be feeding false information to Steele.

A recently declassified footnote from the IG report states:

A January 12, 2017, report relayed information from [REDACTED] outlining an inaccuracy in a limited subset of Steele's reporting. . . . The [REDACTED] stated that it did not have high confidence in this subset of Steele's reporting and assessed that the referenced subset was part of a Russian disinformation campaign to denigrate U.S. foreign relations. A second report from the same [REDACTED] five days later stated that a person named in the limited subset of Steele's reporting had denied representations in the reporting and the [REDACTED] assessed that the person's denials were truthful. A [U.S. Intelligence Community] report dated February 27, 2017, contained information about an individual with reported connections to Trump and Russia who claimed that the public reporting about the details of Trump's sexual activities in Moscow during a trip in 2013 were false, and that they were the product of [Russian Intelligence Services] "infiltrat[ing] a source into the network" of a [REDACTED] who compiled a dossier of information on Trump's activities.[29]

Essentially the collusion case had collapsed by early 2017, its core evidence exposed as discredited barroom humor or worse. Yet the FBI leadership continued to seek wiretap renewals without telling FISA judges the truth—and continued to feed reporters an empty conspiracy tale.

Despite the collapse of the case as Trump was taking office, former Obama administration officials and Trump adversaries in Congress would spend years misleading the public with televised allegations and dark conspiracy theories even as many of them were admitting privately under oath that they hadn't seen any collusion evidence. A parade of former senior intelligence and law enforcement officials from the Obama administration took turns condemning Trump on CNN and MSNBC. But when the cameras were turned off, their stories changed.

Current director of national intelligence John Ratcliffe was in Congress at the time trying to get to the bottom of the collusion con. In September 2018 he would appear on Fox Business Network to review the history: "More than seventy witnesses appeared before the House Intelligence Committee. All of them were asked the same question, 'What evidence do you have of Russian collusion with Donald Trump, or the Trump campaign? What evidence do you have of conspiracy? What evidence do you have of coordination?' . . . And they all said, 'We don't have any.'"[30]

Yet, until the 2020 release of interview transcripts confirmed this fact, Democrats on the House Intelligence Committee, led by Representative Adam Schiff of California, spent years pretending they were uncovering damning evidence about the president.

If the collusion case was dead by January of 2017, the business of printing dubious collusion stories was alive and well. In fact, 2017 was the year that reporters from the *New York Times* and the *Washington Post* published a series of stories that would receive their industry's most coveted award, the Pulitzer Prize.

Among the prizewinning submissions was a report published on February 28, 2017. The *Washington Post* wrote: "While Trump has derided the dossier as 'fake news' compiled by his political opponents, the FBI's arrangement with Steele shows that the bureau considered him credible and found his information, while unproved, to be worthy of further investigation."[31]

Long before the story was published, the FBI had enough evidence to know that Steele and his dossier were not credible. The *Post* story elaborated that in 2016 "Steele became concerned that the U.S. government was not taking the information he had uncovered seriously enough, according to two people familiar with the situation."[32] Now everyone knows that the government should not have taken his information seriously at all.

Another *Post* story that helped win the prize was the report published on May 22, 2017, that said Trump had asked intelligence officials "to publicly deny the existence of any evidence of collusion during the 2016 election."[33] Trump was asking them to state the plain fact that they had seen no collusion evidence. But according to the *Post* at the time: "Current and former senior intelligence officials viewed Trump's requests as an attempt by the president to tarnish the credibility of the agency leading the Russia investigation."[34] With the benefit of hindsight, it's clear that the FBI deserved to have its credibility tarnished.

The *Post* continued: "Senior intelligence officials also saw the March requests as a threat to the independence of U.S. spy agencies, which are supposed to remain insulated from partisan issues."[35] Is there anything more threatening than a powerful spy agency refusing to be accountable even to the duly elected president of the United States?

The *Post* saw things differently: " 'The problem wasn't so much asking them to issue statements, it was asking them to issue false statements about an ongoing investigation,' " a former senior intelligence official said.[36] It's now clear that the real problem was anonymous former senior intelligence officials issuing false statements implying that there was evidence of collusion. Or perhaps the *Post* was simply misquoting its sources, just as Steele had done with his own anonymous source's anonymous friends at bars.

Among the *New York Times'* prizewinners was a report on April 22, 2017, sharing suspicions about Carter Page's Russia ties.[37] This was after the FBI had secured a third authorization to wiretap him while again failing to disclose to the court his work for the CIA. Two months later the final renewal of the warrant would be enabled by the doctored email concealing his service to the United States.[38]

In 2018, Columbia University president Lee Bollinger

presented reporters from the *Times* and the *Post* with their Pulitzer Prizes. The citation reads: "For deeply sourced, relentlessly reported coverage in the public interest that dramatically furthered the nation's understanding of Russian interference in the 2016 presidential election and its connections to the Trump campaign, the President-elect's transition team and his eventual administration."[39]

The media establishment had essentially congratulated itself for getting duped into supporting a massive abuse of federal power. One of the many sad lessons is that no American can count on even the most celebrated members of the establishment press to shine a light on such abuses.

As for establishment politicians with access to classified intelligence, some chose to back the FBI abuses targeted at Trump associates. "The FBI had ample reason to believe that Carter Page was acting as an agent of a foreign power based on his history . . . ," claimed Adam Schiff in 2018, long after he should have known this was untrue.[40] After being surveilled and damaged in the press for over a year, no charges were ever brought against Carter Page.

In January of that year, Schiff served as the lead author of a memo from intelligence committee Democrats to House colleagues. "FBI and DOJ officials did not 'abuse' the Foreign Intelligence Surveillance Act (FISA) process, omit material information, or subvert this vital tool to spy on the Trump campaign,"[41] the document falsely claimed. The memo moved on to further deceptions, claiming that the "DOJ cited multiple sources to support the case for surveilling Page—but made only narrow use of information from Steele's sources. . . . DOJ told the Court the truth. Its representation was consistent with the FBI's underlying investigative record, which current and former senior officials later corroborated in extensive Committee testimony." [42]

The Court does not agree, and neither does the Obama-appointed inspector general who investigated the matter.

Schiff's whoppers continued in the 2018 memo: "DOJ's warrant request was based on compelling evidence and probable cause to believe Page was knowingly assisting clandestine Russian intelligence activities in the U.S." We now know that the FBI's evidence was falsified when it wasn't hidden. Schiff wasn't finished misleading the public. His memo stated, "DOJ provided additional information obtained through multiple independent sources that corroborated Steele's reporting." [43] This is false and was known to be false at the moment Schiff wrote it.

Yet Representative Schiff was just beginning his campaign of deception. He would continue pretending for years to have seen "more than circumstantial evidence" of collusion while delaying the release of investigative records showing he hadn't found any. In the spring of 2020 he was still claiming that House Intelligence Committee witnesses reported evidence of collusion even after the release of transcripts proved that they hadn't. [44]

Schiff has been warmly welcomed for years to spin his collusion tales on television programs like NBC's *Meet the Press*. Meanwhile, the man who had the collusion scam figured out by early 2018 has received mostly scorn from the anti-Trump media. Devin Nunes, chairman of the House Intelligence Committee at the time, released a memo in February 2018 that noted the key facts: the FBI had misled the FISA court, had relied heavily on Steele's biased and unverified gossip, and had not disclosed that the dossier was paid for by Trump's Democratic opponent and her party.[45]

In March 2018, Nunes accurately summed up the scandal that has poisoned U.S. politics for years, reporting that the Democratic Party and the Clinton campaign had paid people "to collude and interact with Russians to get dirt on President Trump."[46]

"Devin Nunes should get the Presidential Medal of Freedom, and that may happen," Trump tells us now. But the president was not thrilled with all his GOP colleagues during the long series of investigations. He says, "the Republicans don't play a tough game like the Democrats do." During our interview, Trump calls former Speaker of the House Paul Ryan "a disaster. Paul Ryan didn't issue one subpoena on the Russian thing." Trump argues that Ryan's successor "Nancy Pelosi issued 387 subpoenas. She gives 'em out like cookies." As he continued to discuss the issue, Trump downgraded Ryan to "a *f——* disaster." A former aide to Ryan tells us that the former Speaker figured the subpoena process would take too long and that Trump could just order the release of documents.

The only remaining question is when exactly collusion claims became fraudulent. The FBI continued to use its surveillance tools even after it was clear the evidence justifying their use had been debunked. But was this an FBI fraud right from the start, or did top Obama administration officials reasonably suspect at some point that there really could be some sort of Trump-

Putin conspiracy? While Justice's Inspector General Horowitz uncovered a range of abuses as FBI agents hunted for evidence, he concluded that his Obama administration colleagues at the FBI had still acted appropriately in deciding to launch the investigation in the summer of 2016. In the parlance of prosecutors, he was saying that the investigation was reasonably *predicated*, even if it later went off the rails.

As we write in the summer of 2020, the predication story is falling apart. According to the official history from FBI leadership, the bureau launched a full investigation with just a single piece of questionable evidence, and only because it allegedly came from the most trusted of sources: a friendly foreign government, or FFG.

Back in that summer of 2016, the website WikiLeaks had shocked U.S. politics on July 22 with the unauthorized release of thousands of emails exchanged by leading members of the Democratic Party. Among other embarrassing revelations, the emails showed that the leadership of the Democratic National Committee, which is supposed to be neutral, was favoring former secretary of state Hillary Clinton in her presidential nomination battle against Senator Bernie Sanders of Vermont.

For Democrats, the timing could not have been worse. WikiLeaks published the emails on the Friday before the party's nominating convention was scheduled to begin in Philadelphia on Monday. Over the weekend, Sanders supporters were taking to the streets to protest what many considered a rigged game to protect the party establishment. As for Hillary supporters, another Clinton scandal had exploded just as their candidate was scheduled for a political coronation.

Here was a legitimate case of collusion and it threatened a political catastrophe for Democrats and their nominee. The story could split the party if Sanders supporters refused to unify behind Team Clinton.

Maria arrived that weekend to host live Fox coverage inside the convention venue. As workers were completing the final decorations inside Philadelphia's Wells Fargo Center, party officials were in a state of panic, wondering if their week in the national spotlight would be dominated by the story of the Clinton machine appearing to fix the nomination.

On Sunday, Democratic National Committee chairwoman Debbie Wasserman Schultz, who had been exposed in the emails with her thumb on the scale for Team Clinton, said that she was immediately resigning her post. Avoiding the polarizing embarrassment of Wasserman Schultz at the podium would be helpful, but Democrats would still be answering questions all week about how party bosses had sabotaged the Sanders campaign.

And then all of a sudden something changed. On the day that Wasserman Schultz announced that she would not be presiding at her own convention, Democrats were aggressively feeding media people a story of Russian hacking. Standing at the convention site, it seemed that in the blink of an eye every Democratic lawmaker or political operative was now brushing aside Wasserman Schultz's comments in the emails and stoking speculation that their publication was the result of Donald Trump working with the Russians.

Something was wrong with this new picture, and not

because the Russian government doesn't try to interfere in our democratic process. Russian governments have been attempting to disrupt and discredit free societies for much longer than we've been alive. It was just rather convenient—a perfectly timed, smooth transition Democrats and their media allies made to the creation of a new narrative of Russian support for Trump.

It would take nearly four years for the public to learn many of the essential details of the story. In the spring of 2020 the Trump administration declassified a volume of documents related to the collusion investigation. The House Intelligence Committee subsequently released, among other items, its transcript of sworn 2017 testimony from the DNC's cybersecurity contractor. Under oath he admitted that his firm did not have direct evidence that the Russians took the emails off the DNC server.[48] And of course it had no evidence at all that the Republican presidential candidate had anything to do with it. But in July 2016 much of the credulous media was happy to start running with the theory of a Trump-Russia conspiracy.

While the 2016 Democratic convention was occurring in the United States, Australian diplomat and Clinton admirer Alexander Downer requested an urgent meeting at the U.S. embassy in London. Downer was Australia's high commissioner to the United Kingdom—in other words, the Aussie ambassador to the UK. He told a U.S. diplomat about a conversation he'd had two months earlier with a young man who had recently joined the Trump campaign as a volunteer adviser. Downer said that the new Trump adviser, George Papadopoulos, had suggested over drinks that Russia had damaging information about Hillary Clinton that it might release during the campaign.

Just days after the Downer report, on July 31, 2016, the FBI launched its "Crossfire Hurricane" Trump campaign investigation. The inspector general would report more than three years later that the launch of this historic investigation was based solely on the report from the friendly foreign government: "We did not find information in FBI or [Justice] Department [electronic communications], emails, or other documents, or through witness testimony, indicating that any information other than the FFG information was relied upon to predicate the opening of the Crossfire Hurricane investigation." [49]

Over and over again, the inspector general's report would refer to the FFG, the friendly foreign government, as the source of the report that triggered the investigation, and FBI officials would cite the fact that it came from an FFG as their justification for doing what they did. Bill Priestap, who was then the assistant director of the FBI's counterintelligence division, authorized the opening of Crossfire Hurricane. The inspector general reports of Priestap: "He told us that the FFG information was provided by a trusted source—the FFG—and he therefore felt it 'wise to open an investigation to look into' whether someone associated with the Trump campaign may have accepted the reported offer from the Russians." [50]

But it wasn't really a report from a friendly foreign government. More precisely, it was an unofficial claim from someone who worked at a friendly government. Remember, this was the only evidence used to start an unprecedented surveillance effort targeting participants in a U.S. presidential campaign. The details matter. And the detail of why George Papadopoulos was invited to a wine bar in London to meet Alexander Downer deserves attention. It will strike some people as odd that the issue of Russia's damaging information about Hillary Clinton allegedly came up in this meeting between people who hardly knew each other.

Among the first to notice a problem with the details was Representative Nunes. While serving as the chairman of the House Intelligence Committee in April 2018, Nunes told Maria, "Now this is really important to us because counter-intelligence investigation uses the tools of our intelligence services that are not supposed to be used on American citizens . . . So we've long wanted to know: Well, what intelligence did you have that actually led to this investigation?" Then Nunes answered the question: "We now know that there was no official intelligence that was used to start this investigation." [51]

But how could this be? Less than four months earlier, in one of the *New York Times* stories for which the paper would be handed a Pulitzer prize, reporters had claimed that the information came from "one of America's closest intelligence allies." [52]

It did not come from Australian intelligence. Nunes described the "Five Eyes" agreement through which the intelligence allies Australia, Canada, New Zealand, the United Kingdom, and the United States share intelligence. "We are not supposed to spy on each other's citizens, and it's worked well," he said. "And it continues to work well. And we know it's working well because there was no intelligence that passed through the Five Eyes channels to our government."[53]

It turned out that Downer had already told his story to his own government in May 2016 and the Australian government had *not* passed it on to the United States. Two months later Downer broke protocol, ignored the trusted intelligence-sharing process among the five friendly governments, and told the story himself to American diplomatic staff.

In June 2018 our colleague Kimberley Strassel elaborated on the dangers of this approach: "The Five Eyes agreement provides that any intelligence goes through the intelligence system of the country that gathered it. This helps guarantee information is securely handled, subjected to quality control, and not made prey to political manipulation. Mr. Downer's job was to report his meeting back to Canberra, and leave it to Australian intelligence." Instead, noted Strassel, Downer's story ended up with Elizabeth Dibble "who previously served as a principal deputy assistant secretary in Mrs. Clinton's State Department."[54]

In case anyone was still tempted to swallow the *New York Times* version of events, Malcolm Turnbull, Australia's prime minister in 2016, writes in his new memoir of Downer's report: "He had no authority from Canberra to do this, and the first we heard of it in Australia was when the FBI turned up in London and wanted to interview Downer.

"We were very reluctant to get dragged into the middle of the US presidential election," Turnbull continued, "but agreed to Downer being interviewed on the basis it was kept confidential and any information he provided was not circulated beyond the FBI."[55]

With one glaring exception in Alexander Downer, it seems the Australian government was more protective of the rights of U.S. citizens than our own government was.

But wait, there's more. Even though the officials at the top of the Obama FBI managed to persuade the inspector general to view the Downer claim as a report from a friendly foreign government, it's clear that Downer did not characterize it that way—and the FBI knew it. In May of 2020, the government watchdog group Judicial Watch obtained via the Freedom of Information Act a redacted copy of the official July 31, 2016, FBI electronic communication that created the Crossfire Hurricane case targeting the Trump campaign. While most names are redacted, the document includes an email from a U.S. official in London sharing Downer's story and noting that the "information was provided through informal diplomatic channels." The email says that "extraordinary efforts should be made to protect the source of this information" until it could be obtained "through formal channels."[56] It was clearly not an official intelligence report from a friendly foreign government.

Perhaps one reason the Aussies didn't bring it to their Five Eyes allies is because it was a vague report and didn't include anyone claiming the Trump campaign was actually colluding with Russians. Also, given the many scandals related to Clinton Foundation fundraising, including violations of conflict-of-interest rules adopted when Hillary Clinton became secretary of state, people with damaging information about the Clintons were not exactly rare.

It's worth reflecting on the Obama FBI's conspiracy theory to assess whether FBI leadership was acting in good faith at the start. Neither at the opening of Crossfire Hurricane nor at any time during the campaign did the FBI ever tell Donald Trump about its investigation. When questioned later by the inspector general, senior FBI officials would justify their decision to keep the candidate in the dark by claiming that they couldn't know who in the campaign might potentially be involved in wrongdoing. We're supposed to believe they sincerely thought not only that Donald Trump might be colluding with Russians but also that he would share details of the plot with a twenty-something volunteer who had just joined his campaign.

As for the young newcomer to the Trump campaign, Papadopoulos says that he doesn't remember sharing the story with Downer.[57] But Papadopoulos says he did indeed hear the claim about Russia having information on Hillary Clinton. He says he heard the story from a Maltese professor named Joseph Mifsud who was introduced to him after Papadopoulos had signed on with the Trump campaign. Papadopoulos says it was all a setup to create a pretext for the FBI to go after Trump. The inspector general found no record of Mifsud as a confidential human source for the FBI[58] and Papadopoulos ended up spending eleven days behind bars after striking a plea agreement for lying to the FBI about the timing and extent of his interactions with Mifsud. He says it was entrapment.

But before you dismiss Papadopoulos as paranoid or not credible, it should be noted that the inspector general found that, beginning in the fall of 2016, the FBI did send a number of confidential informants wearing wires to engage Papadopoulos in conversation and record his comments. Asked several times about the idea of getting help from Russians to put out damaging information on Hillary Clinton, Papadopoulos was recorded repeatedly rejecting the idea as wrong, illegal, treasonous, and not something anyone on the Trump team would do. He directly contradicted the FBI's probable cause claim by saying that, to his knowledge, no one associated with the Trump campaign was collaborating with Russia or with WikiLeaks or with any other group in the release of emails. These recorded comments were never disclosed to the FISA court. This exculpatory evidence is among the material U.S. Attorney John Durham is examining in his criminal investigation of FBI abuses committed during the Russia inquiry.

In the series of applications for Carter Page wiretaps, judges were told the Downer story about Papadopoulos to bolster the FBI's collusion narrative. As with Carter Page, significant exculpatory information about Papadopoulos was never shared with the court. After the FBI began interviewing him in 2017, Papadopoulos again rejected the FBI's collusion tale, and some comments from these interviews were included in later renewal applications, but the judges were never told that he had repeatedly rejected the FBI's Russia story in 2016 in a series of conversations recorded without his knowledge.[59]

"The person that bags your groceries at the supermarket has the same number of contacts with Russia and the Russian government as Mr. George Papadopoulos, which is zero," said then-congressman John Ratcliffe in 2018 as he was investigating FBI abuses. He added, "One of the troubling things that came out of my questioning is why, if I have seen classified documents that lend support to Mr. Papadopoulos's contention that he had no knowledge or intent to collude with the Russians or anyone on the Trump campaign having that, why he hasn't seen those documents or why his lawyers haven't seen those documents, or why the judges at the Foreign Intelligence Surveillance Court haven't seen those documents?"[60]

Papadopoulos suspects that the series of confidential sources the FBI admits deploying against him is just the tip of the iceberg. He believes the government was seeking to create evidence against him via a series of bizarre characters who made contact with him overseas. The FBI acknowledges using confidential sources to engage Papadopoulos in what appeared to be intriguing international business ventures as a way of creating situations where he would feel comfortable speaking candidly. One case agent said the hope was that Papadopoulos might "feel a little freer to talk outside the confines of the United States" and perhaps repeat the comments attributed to him by Downer. The strategy involved plying Papadopoulos with drinks and encouraging discussion about politics.[61]

Among the strange interactions the FBI hasn't claimed as its own—at least not yet—was a trip to Israel after Papadopoulos had begun talking to the FBI in 2017. Papadopoulos says "there had been a lot of discussion with the FBI during my first interview with them about the Israelis and my connections to the Israelis and what I was up to in the energy business over there." Sometime after this conversation with the FBI, Papadopoulos says that an "individual who describes himself as an Israeli-American businessman wants to talk to me about the energy business" and "I go to Israel with him and then all of a sudden he's dropping ten thousand dollars in cash in my hands." Papadopoulos says he has no idea why the man discussing possible business was suddenly giving him a stack of U.S. currency but adds that he found it suspicious enough that he quickly turned the money over to lawyers representing him. Then his story gets even more disturbing: "And as I'm flying back to the United States I am basically, you know, I was grabbed by seven FBI agents looking for money." Papadopoulos adds, "I thought it was a set-up."[62] This may sound like a scene from a movie in which he plays some sort of secret agent. That's exactly how the FBI wanted FISA judges to think of him and Carter Page.

But did anyone at the FBI ever really believe it? If not, the case goes down as the greatest violation of First Amendment rights in the long, disturbing history of the FBI. If there wasn't a sincere belief that these men might really be working with Russia to fix an election, then they were simply targeted for surveillance and persecuted for their political beliefs.

For anyone who wants to give every benefit of the doubt to the people who ran the FBI during the Obama administration, it's very difficult to explain how the government treated Joseph Mifsud. This is the Maltese professor who Papadopoulos says told him the story about Russia having damaging information on Hillary Clinton. Mifsud is the man at the very origin of the collusion story. Special counsel Robert Mueller and the FBI say that on April 26, 2016, at a breakfast meeting at London's Andaz hotel, Mifsud told Papadopoulos the Russians had "dirt" on Hillary Clinton in the form of emails.[63] Ten days later Papadopoulos would have his famous meeting with the Australian diplomat Downer that triggered the creation of the Crossfire Hurricane case at the FBI. So, according to the official history, the Mifsud meeting is what started it all.

In a 2017 interview with the FBI, Mifsud admitted meeting Papadopoulos but said he didn't have any inside knowledge about emails or Russian information on Clinton or offering to share it with the Trump campaign. He added that Papadopoulos must have misunderstood him, since at one point they were discussing cybersecurity and hacking generally. Mifsud's denials were not shared with the FISA court, which is appalling given that the FBI's Papadopoulos story was at the heart of the probable cause section of all four of the Carter Page FISA warrant applications.

But there's an even larger problem with the Mifsud story as U.S. citizens consider FBI actions in the collusion saga. Both Mueller and the FBI say they don't believe Mifsud. Mueller and the FBI say that text and email evidence shows that Mifsud told FBI agents falsehoods about the timing and extent of his interactions with Papadopoulos.[64] Yet the Justice Department has never seemed particularly interested in pursuing Mifsud.

According to the official history from Mueller and the FBI, Mifsud is the man who triggered the entire collusion investigation and then made false statements about it to the FBI. And the government has never charged him with *anything*. At special counsel Robert Mueller's July 25, 2019, appearance before the House Intelligence and Judiciary Committees, Representative Jim Jordan (R-Ohio) tried to get an explanation:

JORDAN: *Director, the FBI interviewed Joseph Mifsud on February 10th, 2017. . . . He lied three times. You point it out in the report. Why didn't you charge him with a crime?*

MUELLER: *I can't get into internal deliberations with regard to who or who would not be charged. . . .*

JORDAN: *A lot of things you can't get into. . . . [Y]ou can charge all kinds of people who are around the president with false statements but the guy who launches everything, the guy who puts this whole story in motion, you can't charge him. I think that's amazing.*

MUELLER: *I'm not certain I—I'm not certain I agree with your characterizations.*

JORDAN: *Well I'm reading from your report. Mifsud told Papadopoulos, Papadopoulos tells the diplomat, the diplomat tells the FBI, the FBI opens the investigation July 31st, 2016. And here we are three years later, July of 2019, the country's been put through this and the central figure who launches it all lies to us, and you guys don't hunt him down and interview him again and you don't charge him with a crime.*[65]

After reviewing the record of FBI abuses committed against Americans by the FBI in the collusion probe, how *does* one explain the gentle treatment of the foreign actor who, at least according to the FBI, is a dishonest character and the original source of the collusion story? It doesn't seem to make any sense—unless the FBI leadership was more concerned with taking down Trump than with running down leads on Russian activities. Papadopoulos, for his part, believes Mifsud was a "plant" helping the U.S. government create the pretext to target Trump. As of this writing, Papadopoulos doesn't have proof to back up his theory, but the question posed by Jim Jordan still demands an answer.

There are also more questions to answer about the roles played in this drama by the Aussie diplomat Alexander Downer and by a consultant to the U.S. government named Stefan Halper, who met Page and Papadopoulos at various points in 2016.

Speaking of Downer, Maria asked Attorney General Barr about the FBI launching Crossfire Hurricane based on Downer's vague unofficial report. Barr says, "That is the official version of what happened—that that comment in a London wine bar was what the basis really was for going forward. And I've said that I felt that was a very slender reed to get law enforcement, intelligence agencies involved in investigating the campaign of one's political opponent." [66]

When we asked whether Joseph Mifsud has worked with Western intelligence services, Barr responded, "No, I can't get into that." When asked for more detail on Mifsud, the attorney general said, "No, but I'll just say that one of the things that takes time is that Mr. Durham is trying to look at all the various allegations and concerns that have been raised. So he has been looking at things pre-July [2016] and trying to run those down. And so there's a lot to look at throughout this whole episode, both before and after the election. And he's diligently looking at everything." [67]

In response to a question about the alleged Papadopoulos wine bar conversation that officially started the investigation in July of 2016, Barr said, "It's significant also that the dossier was initiated before July." [68]

There certainly seems to be more to learn about the FBI's use of confidential sources to target the Trump campaign. "They sent in multiple confidential human sources wearing wires," says Senator Ted Cruz (R-Tex.). "One of the things that's so offensive—it's clear these guys assumed Hillary would win, which would mean there'd be no accountability at all. They could get away with this because no one would check." [69]

One thing we can check already is the disparate treatment among those accused of making false statements to the FBI. Trump supporter Papadopoulos was prosecuted but Mifsud was not. Also not prosecuted was Andrew McCabe, the FBI deputy director who played a central role in managing the Russia investigation. Inspector General Horowitz concluded he repeatedly and knowingly made false statements to FBI agents about his leaks to the *Wall Street Journal*. Despite a criminal referral, McCabe's never been charged. Given that the two of us have both written for the *Journal*, we're not going to say it's a bad place to send unauthorized exclusives. But we can still recognize a double standard when we see one in the treatment of people who aren't candid with FBI agents.

Also not charged was former FBI director Comey. When FBI agents showed up at his home after he was fired, he told them he had returned all official documents. But later we learned he had not given up his handwritten notes of meetings with Trump. He saved those for a professor friend to leak and successfully used them to trigger the hiring of a special counsel.

In early 2017 the FBI engineered the prosecution of Trump national security adviser Lieutenant General Michael Flynn (U.S. Army, ret.) even though FBI personnel who interviewed him initially said he didn't lie to them.[70] And the evidence did not support a criminal charge, as America finally learned in 2020 with the release of transcripts of his telephone calls.

In truth, the FBI shouldn't even have been interviewing Flynn. In the final days of the Obama administration the FBI pretended to be investigating him for allegedly violating something called the Logan Act, a 1799 law under which no one has ever been convicted because it would be ruled unconstitutional if ever tested in court. The law purported to make it a crime for citizens to intervene in disputes between the United States and foreign governments.

Specifically, the FBI was trying to claim that Flynn had run afoul of the law while talking on the phone with Russian ambassador Sergey Kislyak during the presidential transition in December of 2016. The idea was to try to call it a crime when an adviser to the president-elect disagrees with the policies of the outgoing administration. "To use this abusive law against the incoming national security adviser was utterly absurd," says George Washington University law professor Jonathan Turley.[71]

Attorney General William Barr agrees and adds: "This wasn't just a private citizen, you know, engaged in negotiations to the detriment of the United States. This was somebody coming into office in a transition—which is an officially recognized function of the United States—and discussing future relations." [72]

No doubt Obama administration officials knew it was a scam that would never fly in court. But they hoped to use the process of investigating this pretend crime to trap Flynn into making an inaccurate statement to the FBI and then prosecute him for that. When the call transcripts were finally released to the public in May of 2020, they didn't reveal some grand conspiracy but simply showed Flynn advocating for America and our friends overseas. He urged the Russians not to throw U.S. diplomats out of Moscow, encouraged cooperation "against this radical Islamist crowd," and thanked Kislyak for the ambassador's offer to help delay an anti-Israel vote at the United Nations. [73]

But Flynn, a decorated military veteran and former head of the Defense Intelligence Agency, fought a years-long legal battle before the Justice Department withdrew its charges in 2020 (though a federal judge has sought to prevent the case from being dismissed). And in what has become a disturbing FBI habit, once again the bureau failed to disclose exculpatory evidence.

Attorney General Barr says that "it's unusual for an outgoing administration, high-level officials, to be unmasking very, very much in the days they're preparing to leave office. Makes you wonder what they were doing. Unmasking used to be fairly rare. It's become more common, but it should be very rare at the higher levels of government." [74]

There were other problems with the Flynn prosecution.

Senator Chuck Grassley (R-Iowa) wrote to Attorney General William Barr in April of 2020: "This is no ordinary criminal case. One of the agents who interviewed Lt. Gen. Flynn, Peter Strzok, was later removed from the Russia investigation after his texts demonstrating animus and bias toward the President were discovered. Additionally, former Director McCabe was fired for lack of candor regarding a leak to the *Wall Street Journal*, and Lt. Gen. Flynn was an adverse witness in a pending sexual discrimination case against Mr. McCabe at the time Mr. McCabe was supervising an inquiry targeting Lt. Gen. Flynn."[75]

Sounds like reason enough for McCabe not to be involved. As for the FBI's Peter Strzok and his texts, many of the most outrageous were shared with FBI lawyer Lisa Page, with whom he was having an extramarital affair. Such affairs are particularly dangerous in counterintelligence work because they increase the risk of blackmail by hostile foreign powers.

What's dangerous for liberty is to have powerful law enforcement officials driven by political motives. While investigating Hillary Clinton for her mishandling of classified information, Page and Strzok seemed to have decided to pull their punches, lest the FBI attract Clinton's ire along with that of its parent agency, the Department of Justice. The following text exchange occurred in February of 2016:

> PAGE: *She might be our next president. The last thing you need us going in there loaded for bear. You think she's going to remember or care that it was more doj than fbi?*
> STRZOK: *Agreed . . .*[76]

In August of that year, the tone was very different when the two texted about Donald Trump:

> *PAGE: He's not ever going to become president, right? Right?!*
>   *STRZOK: No. No, he won't. We'll stop it.*[77]

Another text exchanged between the paramours suggested the problem of politicized law enforcement did not just involve FBI officials. In September 2016, Page texted Strzok that "potus wants to know everything we're doing."[78] It's not clear to which case or cases she was referring, but POTUS is the federal acronym for the president of the United States. Barack Obama owes the country an explanation. So does then–FBI director James Comey.

And, of course, so do Strzok and Page, who have been allowed to evade responsibility with the help of a friendly media. So opposed is the press corps to Donald Trump that many media folk now reflexively reject his arguments regardless of the merits. Consider the following "fact check" feature published by the Associated Press in May of 2020:

> *TRUMP, on the 2016 election: "I'm fighting the deep state. I'm fighting the swamp. . . . They never thought I was going to win, and then I won. And then they tried to get me out. That was the 'insurance policy.' She's going to win, but just in case she doesn't win we have an insurance policy."—interview aired Sunday on "Full Measure with Sharyl Attkisson."*

THE FACTS: He's repeating a false claim that there was a conspiracy afoot to take him out if he won the 2016 presidential race, based on a text message between two FBI employees.

Trump has repeatedly depicted the two as referring to a plot—or insurance policy—to oust him from office if he beat Democrat Hillary Clinton. It's apparent from the text that it wasn't that.

Agent Peter Strzok and lawyer Lisa Page, both now gone from the bureau, said the text messages reflected a debate about how aggressively the FBI should investigate Trump and his campaign when expectations at the time were that he would lose anyway.

Strzok texted about something Page had said to the FBI's deputy director, to the effect that "there's no way he gets elected." But Strzok argued that the FBI should not assume Clinton would win: "I'm afraid we can't take that risk." He likened the situation to "an insurance policy in the unlikely event you die before you're 40." He has said he was not discussing a post-election plot to drive Trump from office.[79]

But if Strzok was not willing to accept the risk of the outcome of a free election, and instead favored "an insurance policy" in a discussion among FBI officials investigating Trump and his associates, doesn't that sound exactly the way Trump described it?

Strzok was fired first by special counsel Robert Mueller and later by the FBI for his texts displaying animus against Trump.

Given Strzok's extreme bias, some could argue that it taints all his work on the Russia investigation. Certainly it calls into question the motivations behind this unprecedented intervention in U.S. politics by a law enforcement agency using the surveillance tools designed for use against foreign enemies.

This brings us back to the official start of the collusion investigation in July of 2016. The many abuses that followed are now a matter of public record. But at its beginning, was the investigation justified? Was it appropriately *predicated*?

Let's now consider the formal moment of creation of the Crossfire Hurricane case on July 31, 2016. A copy of the FBI electronic communication that started it all was obtained in the spring of 2020 via a Freedom of Information Act request filed by the government watchdog group Judicial Watch.[80]

Kevin Brock, former assistant director of intelligence for the FBI and principal deputy director of the National Counterterrorism Center, wrote upon the document's release:

> First, the document is oddly constructed. In a normal, legitimate FBI Electronic Communication, or EC, there would be a "To" and a "From" line. The Crossfire Hurricane EC has only a "From" line; it is from a part of the FBI's Counterintelligence Division whose contact is listed as Peter Strzok. The EC was drafted also by Peter Strzok. And, finally, it was approved by Peter Strzok. Essentially, it is a document created by Peter Strzok, approved by Peter Strzok, and sent from Peter Strzok to Peter Strzok.
>
> On that basis alone, the document is an absurdity, violative of all FBI protocols and, therefore, invalid on its

face. An agent cannot approve his or her own case; that would make a mockery of the oversight designed to protect Americans.[81]

Peter Strzok of all people seems to agree. "I can assure you . . . ," said Strzok at a House judiciary committee hearing in 2018, "at no time in any of those texts, did those personal beliefs ever enter into the realm of any action I took." Then he said:

"Furthermore, this isn't just me sitting here telling you. You don't have to take my word for it. At every step, every investigative decision, there are multiple layers of people above me—the assistant director, executive assistant director, deputy director, and director of the FBI—and multiple layers of people below me—section chiefs, supervisors, unit chiefs, case agents and analysts—all of whom were involved in all of these decisions. They would not tolerate any improper behavior in me any more than I would tolerate it in them. That is who we are as the FBI."[82]

What happened to all those layers when Strzok created the Trump investigation? Perhaps if Strzok had included agents on the ground in the discussion, they might have told him he had no case. Brock notes other significant problems with Strzok's infamous document:

The Crossfire Hurricane case was opened as a Foreign Agent Registration Act (FARA) investigation. A FARA investigation involves a criminal violation of law—in this case, a negligent or intentional failure to register with the U.S. government after being engaged by a foreign country to perform services on its behalf—that is punishable by fines and imprisonment. It is rarely investigated.

In a normal EC opening a FARA case, we should expect to see a list of reasons why the FBI believes individuals associated with a U.S. presidential campaign had been engaged by the Russian government to represent and advocate that government's goals.

This, however, was no normal EC. Try as we might to spot them, those reasons are not found anywhere in the document.[83]

Strzok's electronic communication doesn't get any more compelling once it gets into the report from the Australian diplomat Downer, which is the heart of the document. Brock notes:

Downer claims Papadopoulos "suggested" to him that the Trump team had received "some kind of suggestion" of assistance from Russia regarding information damaging to Hillary Clinton and President Obama. In other words, a suggestion of a suggestion.

Strzok apparently took this nebulous reporting by Downer and then leapt to the dubious conclusion that Papadopoulos and unnamed others were engaged by the Russians to act as foreign agents on Russia's behalf. This, despite Downer also offering two exculpatory statements in the same email: 1) It was "unclear" how the Trump campaign might have reacted to the Russian claims and

2) the Russians likely were going to do what they were going to do with the information whether anyone in the Trump campaign cooperated with them or not.

Strzok then concludes the EC by moving the goalposts. He writes that Crossfire Hurricane is being opened to determine if unspecified "individual(s)" associated with the Trump campaign are "witting of and/or coordinating activities"—also unspecified—"with the Government of Russia." He doesn't even mention Papadopoulos.

Ultimately, there was no attempt by Strzok to articulate any factors that address the elements of FARA. He couldn't, because there are none. Instead, there was a weak attempt to allege some kind of cooperation with Russians by unknown individuals affiliated with the Trump campaign, again, with no supporting facts listed.[84]

For someone not accustomed to reading such documents, what is perhaps most striking in Peter Strzok's electronic communication is the acknowledgment that no one knows if the information that someone claims the Russians might be willing to release includes "material acquired publicly" or "through other means."[85]

The FBI can launch full investigations of Americans participating in election campaigns based on a mere suggestion that a foreign government might release information that is *already public*? If the bar is set this low, the FBI could investigate American citizens for participating in politics during every election cycle.

This would be fundamentally incompatible with the rule

of law on which our liberty and prosperity depend. Deploying intelligence and law enforcement assets against the political opposition is a hallmark of dictatorships, not free and open societies. To prevent a new normal of politicized and corrupt policing, the Justice Department must hold the collusion investigators to account.

The FBI standards applied to Trump associates were clearly not applied to Trump's opponents. In 2016, many of the same FBI officials, and most notably Director James Comey, were also involved in the investigation of Hillary Clinton's mishandling of classified information while serving as secretary of state.

Several Clinton associates were given immunity from prosecution even though they did not help the FBI make a criminal case against anyone. In the spring of 2016, Comey began drafting a statement closing the case and exonerating Hillary Clinton while FBI agents were still conducting the investigation—and before they had even interviewed more than a dozen key witnesses, including Clinton herself.

There have been no reports of the FBI doctoring emails or hiding exculpatory evidence or misleading federal judges or promoting fact-free rumors in an effort to snare Team Clinton. To the contrary, the FBI downplayed the investigation, referring to it only as a "matter" at the request of Obama administration attorney general Loretta Lynch. Three days before Hillary Clinton's interview, Lynch met Bill Clinton on the tarmac at an Arizona airport and both would later claim to the Justice Department's inspector general that they had discussed golf and grandkids but not the Hillary Clinton investigation.

According to the inspector general, Lynch's staff recognized the problem even if she didn't: "The Deputy Chief of Staff said that they quickly realized that the meeting was problematic, because Clinton was not just the former president but was also the husband of someone who was under investigation. The Deputy Chief of Staff said that she felt 'shocked,' and that they all 'just felt completely . . . blindsided.' " [86]

Given the friendly treatment of Hillary Clinton, perhaps no one ended up being shocked that Clinton was never prosecuted by the Justice Department. Senator Chuck Grassley would later find that, during the drafting of Comey's July 2016 statement announcing no charges against Clinton, the description of her conduct as "grossly negligent," which carries a criminal penalty, was changed to read "extremely careless," which does not. [87]

Looking back now, current attorney general Barr says, "I do believe there were two standards of justice during that period of time toward the end of the Obama administration. And all I can do about it is apply one standard of justice, the right standard of justice and make sure we apply it to everybody equally. And that's what I'm trying to do." [88]

Did President Obama direct the investigation against Trump? Maria recently put the question to senior Obama adviser Valerie Jarrett, who responded, "That's not how it works. That's not how our investigations work. We leave that to the intelligence community to bring forward information and the dossier I would imagine would be one piece of a much bigger puzzle." [89]

"Well, you'll notice she didn't answer your question," Sen.

Ron Johnson (R.-Wis.) told Maria after watching an excerpt of the Jarrett interview. "She just talked about in general what the process should be. That's not the process they followed. It is very clear that there was corruption at the highest levels of certainly the FBI. We have evidence of it."[90]

As voters assess President Trump's record in office, they should consider the cost that this double standard imposed on his presidency—and could impose on the country if left unreformed.

As for the target of the FBI's abuse, Trump tells us, "President Obama spied on my campaign. . . . If this were the other way around, every single person involved would be in jail for fifty years and it would have started two years ago." When asked who masterminded the collusion investigation, Trump mentions FBI director Comey and former CIA director John Brennan, but returns his focus to one particular government official: "Obama knew everything. He knew everything."[91]

TIMELINE:
THE COUP THAT FAILED

The full story of the Obama administration's collusion investigation has still not been told, and in the months and years ahead we may learn much more. For the health of our republic, we believe it's essential for Americans to learn who exactly ordered or encouraged the use of federal surveillance tools against the party out of power—and promoted the use of such tools even in the absence of evidence. Abuses by the FBI and perhaps other government agencies are now themselves the subject of federal investigation. As we write, it's impossible to say exactly where such investigations will lead, and the possible strands extend well beyond the material covered in chapter two. Given the number of possible leads, readers may find it helpful to retain the following chronology of events and possible players in this drama, which includes issues that could not be fully explored at this writing but may loom larger as more information is disclosed. Everyone mentioned below and involved in this story deserves the presumption of innocence. Americans also deserve a full accounting of how powers normally reserved for targeting terrorists and foreign adversaries were turned against U.S. citizens participating in politics.

June 2015

Donald Trump announces campaign for president.

August 2015

General Michael Flynn (ret.), former head of Pentagon's Defense Intelligence Agency, meets Donald Trump.

September 24, 2015

Stefan Halper awarded contract valued at $244,960 to study Russia and China by Pentagon's Office of Net Assessment.

February 2016

London Centre of International Law Practice contacts George Papadopoulos on LinkedIn after he leaves Ben Carson presidential campaign. London Centre subsequently hires him.

March 2016

Papadopoulos accepts offer to join Trump campaign as a volunteer foreign policy adviser. Before he leaves London Centre, he is invited by Arvinder Sambei to Rome and there is introduced to Joseph Mifsud by former Italian prime minister Vincenzo Scotti.

April 26, 2016

Mifsud meets Papadopoulos in London. According to Papadopoulos, Mifsud tells him that Russia has potentially damaging Hillary Clinton emails. Special counsel Robert Mueller later reports that Mifsud denied saying any such thing in an FBI interview; Mueller alleges that Mifsud provided false answers under FBI questioning.

May 10, 2016

Papadopoulos meets with Australian diplomat Alexander Downer at a London wine bar. Two months later Downer reported to U.S. embassy in London that Papadopoulos reported hearing that Russians had potentially damaging information on Hillary Clinton. Papadopoulos doesn't recall telling this to Downer.

June 2016

Former British spy Christopher Steele hired by Fusion GPS, an opposition research firm employed by the Clinton campaign and the Democratic National Committee via the Perkins Coie law firm to investigate Trump's possible ties to Russia.

July 2016

Carter Page first meets Stefan Halper after receiving an invitation to an overseas seminar from Steven Schrage. Halper would continue contacts with Page in succeeding months.

July 31, 2016

FBI official Peter Strzok formally opens counterintelligence probe known as "Crossfire Hurricane" into the Trump campaign.

August 2016

FBI learns from another government agency—but never tells the FISA Court—that Carter Page served as an operational contact for U.S. intelligence.

August 8, 2016

Strzok and FBI attorney Lisa Page communicate via text message:

Page: [Trump's] not ever going to become president, right? Right?!

Peter Strzok: No. No, he's not. We'll stop it.

August 15, 2016

Strzok texts Page: "I want to believe the path you threw out for consideration in Andy's office—that there's no way he gets elected—but I'm afraid we can't take that risk. It's like an insurance policy in the unlikely event you die before you're 40."

August 16, 2016

FBI opens "Crossfire Razor" probe into General Flynn.

August 17, 2016

FBI provides "defensive briefing" used as "cover" to monitor and assess candidate Trump and General Flynn, according to handwritten notes of FBI agent Joe Pientka.

August 29, 2016

Stefan Halper emails Trump campaign cochairman Sam Clovis; they meet in the Crystal City neighborhood of Arlington, Virginia, a few days later.

September 2016

Papadopoulos invited by Stefan Halper to London. Halper introduces Papadopoulos to person known as Azra Turk. Halper records conversation in which Papadopoulos says colluding with Russia would be treason and neither he nor anyone on the Trump campaign would ever do such a thing. Government never discloses this evidence to the U.S. Foreign Intelligence Surveillance Court (FISC, or FISA [Foreign Intelligence Surveillance Act] Court).

September 19, 2016

Christopher Steele gives FBI report that will play "a central and essential role" in the FBI's and Justice Department's decision to seek a FISA warrant, according to a 2019 report by the Obama-appointed inspector general of the Justice Department. Inspector general also reports that in warrant application officials never told the court that Clinton and the Democrats paid for the dossier and never fully disclosed Steele's Russian connections, among other omissions.

September 26, 2016

Stefan Halper awarded Office of Net Assessment contract valued at $411,575 to study China's economy.

October 18, 2016

Top Department of Justice official Bruce Ohr, whose wife worked on the anti-Trump project for Fusion GPS, gives one of many briefings to FBI officials on Steele's collusion allegations.

October 21, 2016

FBI secures the first FISA warrant application to surveil Carter Page.

November 2016

FBI dismisses Steele as a confidential source after he breaks protocol by disclosing his work and his relationship with the FBI while serving as an anonymous source for a magazine article. But FBI doesn't stop promoting his claims as reliable with other agencies and the FISA Court.

November 8, 2016

Trump is elected president.

November 18, 2016

Trump names General Flynn his national security adviser.

December 15, 2016

Strzok texts Page: "Think our sisters have begun leaking like mad."

December 23, 2016

Flynn phone call with Russian ambassador Sergey Kislyak.

December 29, 2016

Another Flynn call with Kislyak.

December 2, 2016

Director of National Intelligence James Clapper requests Flynn's identity be unmasked.

December 14–15, 2016

John Brennan and James Comey request Flynn's identity be unmasked.

January 4, 2017 (morning)

FBI agents draft document to close Flynn probe named "Crossfire Razor."

January 4, 2017 (afternoon)

Strzok texts agents not to "close Razor yet" and "7th floor involved," meaning senior FBI leadership is ordering that case be kept open.

January 5, 2017

At Oval Office meeting, Justice Department's Sally Yates, Comey, Brennan, and Clapper brief President Barack Obama, Vice President Joe Biden, and National Security Adviser Susan Rice. They discuss plans for Comey to brief Trump on parts of dossier. Handwritten notes taken around that time by Strzok depict Comey saying that the Flynn calls with Kislyak "appear legit," Obama saying he wants "the right people on it," and Biden raising the subject of the Logan Act.

January 6, 2017

Comey briefs President-elect Trump on parts of Steele dossier.

January 10, 2017

CNN reports on Steele dossier; BuzzFeed publishes dossier.

Jan 12, 2017

First leak of Flynn-Kislyak phone calls published by David Ignatius at the *Washington Post*. Ignatius suggests Flynn may have violated the "spirit" of the Logan Act. Biden requests Flynn's identity be unmasked.

FBI receives U.S. intelligence report warning of an inaccuracy in Steele dossier and assessing that the material was "part of a Russian disinformation campaign to denigrate U.S. foreign relations."

FISA warrant application, still relying largely on Steele dossier and without disclosing key reasons to doubt it, is renewed.

January 20, 2017

Moments before leaving the White House for the last time as national security adviser, Rice sends herself an email about the January 5 Oval Office meeting, claims that Obama wanted everything done "by the book."

Trump is inaugurated.

January 24, 2017

Comey sends FBI agents Strzok and Pientka to talk to Flynn at the White House and try to catch him in a lie. Agents do not tell him he is the target of an investigation.

January 24–26, 2017

FBI interviews Steele's primary sub-source, Igor Danchenko, who tells them he could not corroborate dossier claims. Danchenko indicates that dossier misstated or exaggerated many of his claims, and in any case some of his reports included "rumor and speculation."

January 25, 2017

House Intelligence Committee led by Chairman Devin Nunes (R-Calif.) announces investigation into Russian interference in the 2016 election.

February 9, 2017

Washington Post reports Flynn misled Trump officials about Kislyak call and says nine anonymous sources confirm the Flynn leak, which was from a classified transcript.

February 13, 2017

Flynn resigns, stating he "inadvertently briefed" Trump administration "with incomplete information."

March 2017

FBI meets again with Danchenko, who reports that he never expected his statements to be presented as facts, saying it was "just talk." Adds that information came from "word of mouth and hearsay" expressed in conversation "with friends over beers" and the most salacious claims were made in "jest."

March 2, 2017

Attorney General Jeff Sessions recuses himself from the Russia investigation.

March 20, 2017

At a House Intelligence Committee open hearing, Comey announces the FBI is investigating Russian election interference and possible coordination between Russia and the Trump campaign. At this hearing Representative Adam Schiff reads Steele dossier allegations into the *Congressional Record*.

March 22, 2017

On MSNBC, Schiff tells Chuck Todd he has "more than circumstantial evidence" of Trump associates colluding with Russia.

April 7, 2017

FISA warrant application to surveil Carter Page renewed for the second time. Dossier used again as evidence of collusion.

May 9, 2017

Trump fires Comey.

May 17, 2017

Deputy Attorney General Rod Rosenstein appoints Mueller to investigate alleged Russia collusion.

June 19, 2017

FBI attorney Kevin Clinesmith alters U.S. government email, makes it appear Carter Page was not a source for U.S. intelligence.

June 29, 2017

FISA warrant application to surveil Carter Page renewed for the third time.

Summer 2017

Papadopoulos invited to travel to Israel on business and is surprised to be handed $10,000 in cash. Travels to Greece, gives money to attorneys.

July 27, 2017

Papadopoulos arrested upon landing at Washington Dulles International Airport for lying to the FBI. Agents search him for cash.

December 1, 2017

As his son is threatened with legal jeopardy, Flynn pleads guilty to making false statements to the FBI.

February 2, 2018

House Intelligence Committee chairman Nunes releases four-page memorandum on FBI abuses, laying out many reasons the FBI had to doubt the dossier in 2016—reasons not shared with the FISA Court.

February 14, 2018

FBI's draft talking points for a Senate Intelligence Committee briefing include numerous claims the FBI knew to be false. FBI document maintains dossier primary sub-source "did not cite any significant concerns with the way his reporting was characterized in the dossier" when in fact he had cited numerous such concerns in direct communication with the FBI.

March 22, 2018

House Intelligence Committee votes to release its Russia investigation report, revealing that none of the dozens of witnesses the committee interviewed presented any evidence of Trump or his associates colluding with Russia.

December 4, 2018

Prosecutors recommend no prison time for Flynn.

January 16, 2019

Senator Chuck Grassley (R-Iowa) requests Department of Defense inspector general review Office of Net Assessment contracts with Stefan Halper. Halper's associate Schrage would later tell Maria he never saw anyone receive such lucrative contracts for academic reports.

April 18, 2019

Mueller reports finding no collusion by Trump campaign—or any American.

July 24, 2019

Mueller testifies to the House Judiciary Committee and House Intelligence Committee. He appears disoriented and unfamiliar with the details of his own investigation, and claims not to know what Fusion GPS is.

October 25, 2019

Flynn files motion to dismiss the case against him.

December 2019

Department of Justice inspector general reports "at least 17 significant errors or omissions" in the Carter Page FISA warrant applications, among other problems, with the Crossfire Hurricane investigation.

December 17, 2019

Presiding Judge Rosemary Collyer of the FISA Court issues a public order demanding that the FBI report on what it is doing to ensure accurate applications that include all material facts.

January 14, 2020

Flynn files motion to withdraw his guilty plea.

March 2020

FISA Court effectively bans FBI agents involved in the Trump campaign wiretap abuses from appearing before it on any other matters.

May 7, 2020

Department of Justice announces decision to drop Flynn case.

2020: Office of the Director of National Intelligence (DNI) declassifications:

April 15: Declassified footnotes from the Horowitz report on Crossfire Hurricane (*Review of Four FISA Applications and Other Aspects of the FBI's Crossfire Hurricane Investigation*)

May 7: All witness transcripts from U.S. House of Representatives Permanent Select Committee on Intelligence's Russia investigation

May 12: List of officials who sought to unmask Flynn between November 6, 2016, and January 31, 2020

May 19: Unredacted Susan Rice CYA email

May 29: Declassified transcripts of the Flynn-Kislyak calls

June 11: Annex A of ICA

July 23: Pientka briefing to Trump, notes, and emails on FBI efforts to use briefings to gather evidence

3

American Business Unleashed

We're not in the habit of giving stock tips or making market calls. But after spending years reporting on business and finance, we were convinced that, on the night of November 8, 2016, the conventional market wisdom was way off target.

As the night wore on and equity traders began to grasp that Donald Trump would become president of the United States of America, stock markets around the world started selling off. In the U.S., trading in S&P 500 futures would eventually be halted after a 5 percent decline. After midnight, Paul Krugman of the *New York Times* opined: "If the question is when markets will recover, a first-pass answer is never." [1]

We didn't see it that way. For years we'd been hearing anguished people at companies large and small bemoan the growing federal burden of taxes and regulations. Now the United States would have a president who intended to reduce this hardship and prioritize economic growth.

When Maria sat down around 10:30 on election night for a Fox News panel discussion, Dow futures were down about 700 points. Markets like certainty; it was understandable that some investors were selling. Trump seemed to present more uncertainty than Hillary Clinton, who was essentially promising a continuation of the Obama administration. Trump's talk about ripping up the North American Free Trade Agreement (NAFTA), for example, created big unknowns and potentially significant risks. That night we were focused on the policy differences between the candidates. Trump wanted to cut taxes and regulation. Hillary wanted to raise taxes. Trump wanted to open the spigot on energy. Hillary wanted to spend money on big government programs. It seemed obvious to conclude this would be a great buying opportunity, which is what Maria told colleagues Bret Baier and Megyn Kelly while the markets were selling off.

In fact, the election night selloff turned out to be a huge buying opportunity. Companies had been sitting on cash—not investing or hiring. Complying with the federal health law known as Obamacare was a nightmare for many business owners. It made them wonder what other big idea from Washington would haunt them in the future. Clinton was likely to increase business costs further, while Trump had vowed to reduce them. Even in the middle of the election night market panic, the implications for corporate revenue and earnings growth seemed obvious.

The next morning, with the Trump victory confirmed, Maria told her colleague Martha MacCallum that she'd be "buying the stock market with both hands." Investors began doing the same. The Dow Jones Industrial Average surged almost 29 percent, and U.S. stocks added trillions of dollars in value in the twelve months following Donald Trump's surprise election victory. Investors around the world wanted in on America's new growth story.

It wasn't just an American story. The entire world benefits when its largest economy is healthy, and the new leader of the U.S. economy was a businessman elected on a promise to restore prosperity.

Trump had specifically promised a campaign against federal bureaucracy, and did America ever need one. As if taxes hadn't been high enough, the U.S. government in 2016 forced Americans to spend an eye-watering $1.9 trillion just to comply with federal regulations. That's according to a 2017 report from Clyde Wayne Crews of the Competitive Enterprise Institute. "If it were a country, U.S. regulation would be the world's seventh-largest economy, ranking behind India and ahead of Italy," Crews said. He added that America's regulatory tab had grown nearly as large as the total pretax profits of corporations.[2]

Crews has become one of the most hated men in Washington by tabulating the annual hidden costs—those not counted in direct federal spending—that politicians and bureaucrats impose on the American economy. And nobody imposed more than Barack Obama. According to the Crews annual scorecards, the yearly cost of federal regulation soared by more than $700 billion in nominal dollars from 2008, the last full year of the Bush administration, through Obama's final full year of 2016. "Adjusting for inflation, you can call Obama the $600 Billion Man."[3]

One measure of the amount of red tape spewing out of Washington is the number of pages of proposed and final rules printed in the *Federal Register*. "Of the top 10 all-time-high *Federal Register* page counts, seven occurred under President Barack Obama," noted Crews. Businesspeople can only hope that Obama's last record, "set on his final lap in 2016, will never be broken. Mr. Crews reports that the register 'finished 2016 at 95,894 pages, the highest level in its history and 19 percent higher than the previous year's 80,260 pages.'"[4]

As for the additional $600 billion in annual regulatory burdens added during the Obama years, it's real money. Based on the April 2017 Consumer Expenditure Surveys from the federal Bureau of Labor Statistics, this hidden tax added up to more than twice what American consumers spent each year on gasoline and more than three times what we spent on electricity. It's more than we spent on dining out. This bureaucratic tax also amounted to roughly nine times what American consumers spent on alcoholic beverages, and perhaps there's a connection.[5]

If business owners weren't driven to drink, they were certainly driven to set aside cash for compliance, legal fees, and other regulatory costs. That money could have been used to fund projects that strengthened their companies.

President Trump charted a new course, prioritizing the removal of red tape and rolling back regulations through executive orders. Trump *says* red tape becomes "beautiful" when it is eliminated, and people who manage businesses certainly agree. U.S. firms don't need to have the lightest burden; they only need one that's competitive with the rest of the world. As former representative Jeb Hensarling (R-Tex.) told us, when Washington simply "stops the beatings," growth happens on its own.[6]

Stephen Schwarzman is chairman and CEO of the investment firm Blackstone Group, which manages more than $500 billion of assets for institutions around the world. In 2017 he described the problem Trump was trying to solve as "a regulatory overload." During an appearance on *Mornings with Maria*, Schwarzman said, "You know it was hard for the financial system to extend credit. It was hard for people to borrow." Speaking of U.S. infrastructure projects, he said, "One of the biggest issues isn't just the money. It's the fact we seem to be able to approve almost nothing to get done." Schwarzman added, "In the United States, it's more than [red] tape . . . It's Elmer's Glue. You just can't get stuff done. And in Canada and Germany, it takes two years to approve whole projects that take us 10 to 15 years."[7]

By the end of 2017, eleven months after Trump took office, it was clear that he had driven a significant change during his rookie year as the nation's chief executive. The number of those infamous pages in the *Federal Register* dropped by 35 percent in 2017, to the lowest level in more than twenty years. And the number of final rules described in those pages was the lowest since the 1970s. In the years ahead Trump's government would continue to issue historically low levels of red tape.

Trump's stats are even better than they appear, because

many of the Trump rules repealed earlier rules, meaning they not only didn't add new burdens but actually reduced federal red tape. The nonpolitician was proving to be the only recent president capable of taming the bureaucratic beast.

A 2017 editorial in the *Wall Street Journal* explained: "Ten days after his inauguration, Mr. Trump issued an executive order directing his departments to scour the books for rules they could rescind or repeal without damaging the law. He also directed that for each single regulation issued, agencies should identify at least two for elimination . . . through Sept. 30 the Trump Administration had taken 67 deregulatory actions but only three new significant regulatory actions. That's a 22 to 1 ratio . . . since fall 2016 more than 1,500 planned regulatory actions have been withdrawn or delayed."[8]

Nothing offends most of our colleagues in the press corps like limited government. But some media folks couldn't decide whether to cast the Trump deregulatory effort as empty talk or a monumental threat to all they hold dear. According to a *New York Times* report: "'We are just getting started,' Mr. Trump said, speaking from the Roosevelt Room of the White House. He described progress so far as the 'most far-reaching regulatory reform' in United States history, a claim he did not back up."[9]

Bloomberg, too, cast doubt on whether the Trump campaign against red tape really amounted to much, and labeled the president's comments on the subject "overblown claims of sweeping deregulation." Bloomberg oddly argued that much of his success simply involved halting the implementation of Obama-era initiatives, which was perhaps a point in Trump's favor.[10]

Meanwhile, over at the *Daily Beast*, there was talk of a "Trump revolution" leaving no part of the government untouched as it destroyed "critical regulations" protecting public health.[11]

NBC News for its part published a screed claiming that "American consumers took it on the chin in 2017" due to the Trump regulatory reform.[12]

But American consumers are also creators and earners, and they noticed that the American economy was accelerating.

Back in the 1980s, President Ronald Reagan described the moment he realized his policy mixture of deregulation and tax cuts was increasing American prosperity. "I could tell our economic program was working when they stopped calling it Reaganomics," he used to say with a chuckle.[13]

By this standard, Trumponomics was an immediate success. Not only did Democrats refuse to slap the Trump brand on the nation's economy; one of them offered a competing claim of paternity. *Newsweek* reported in December 2017: "The American economy's success comes down to environmental policies put in place during the Obama administration, said former President Barack Obama during a speech Tuesday as he jokingly thanked himself."[14]

A week later a *Washington Post* "fact checker" opined that "Trump's economy owes largely to trends started in the Obama era."[15]

An Associated Press story was perhaps the most aggressive yet in lauding Obama for America's rising prosperity in the period after he left office. "Trump Claims Credit For What Is Still Mostly Obama's Economy," argued the AP headline. Here's how the news service made its case: "President Donald Trump relentlessly congratulates himself for the healthy state of the U.S. economy, with its steady growth, low unemployment, busier factories and confident consumers.

"But in the year since Trump's inauguration, most analysts tend to agree on this: The economy remains essentially the same sturdy one he inherited from Barack Obama.

"Growth has picked up, but it's not yet clear if it can sustain a faster expansion." [16]

In fact, growth had picked up even a little bit more than Trump had predicted. During Obama's final year in office in 2016, the U.S. economy expanded by 1.6 percent. After taking office in 2017, Trump issued his first federal budget proposal in May of that year. The Trump budget predicted that for the full calendar year 2017 the U.S. economy would post real growth—that is, after adjusting for inflation—of 2.3 percent. The actual number turned out to be 2.4 percent.

That 2017 Trump budget proposal also estimated that real growth in 2018 and 2019 would average 2.55 percent per year. The actual average annual growth rate for those years turned out to be 2.6 percent. The Amazing Trumpkin? Media "fact checkers" like to point out inaccurate statements from the president—or sometimes just comments with which they disagree—but perhaps they should give him some credit for correctly forecasting some of the most important numbers in the world.

The rookie president from the world of business and his advisers had a solid read on the economy. The contrast with his predecessor is striking. From 2010–2016 the Obama White House's multiyear forecasts had overestimated annual economic growth by more than 70 percent.[17]

In the Trump era, growth remained solid until the 2020 coronavirus shutdowns by state and local governments. A key ingredient in that solid growth was that Trump was not embarrassed to support politically incorrect but valuable American industries. Over the course of a few weeks in the summer of 2019, Trump instructed the U.S. Agriculture Department to end a Bill Clinton ban on logging in a large swath of Alaska and then flew overseas and defended America's oil and gas industry.

As for the Clinton logging ban on government-owned land, "it should never have been applied to our state, and it is harming our ability to develop a sustainable, year-round economy for the Southeast region, where less than one percent of the land is privately held," Senator Lisa Murkowski (R-Alaska) told the *Washington Post*. "The timber industry has declined precipitously, and it is astonishing that the few remaining mills in our nation's largest national forest have to constantly worry about running out of supply."[18]

Not long afterward, Trump was in Biarritz, France, delivering a message that virtually no one in his audience wanted to hear. At a press conference with French president Emmanuel Macron following the G7 summit, President Trump described his thoughts on restricting traditional energy production. Here's an excerpt from the White House's official transcript:

Q: Mr. President, there was a significant talk at the summit about climate change. I know in the past you've harbored some skepticism of the science in climate change. What do you think the world should be doing about climate change? And do you still harbor that skepticism?

PRESIDENT TRUMP: I feel that the United States has tremendous wealth. The wealth is under its feet. I've made that wealth come alive. . . .

We're the number one energy producer in the world. . . . It's tremendous wealth. And [liquefied natural gas] is being sought after all over Europe and all over the world, and we have more of it than anybody else. And I'm not going to lose that wealth. I'm not going to lose it on dreams, on windmills—which, frankly, aren't working too well. I'm not going to lose it. . . .

I want clean air. I want clean water. I want a wealthy country. I want a spectacular country with jobs, with pensions, with so many things. And that's what we're getting. So I want to be very careful.[19]

Trump doesn't apologize for the fact that prosperity for Americans is his priority. And he has a conviction that his war on Washington bureaucracy is critical to the success of Americans who work outside of Washington. The results have been striking. By the end of 2019 he was setting yet another new annual record for the fewest number of final rules published in the *Federal Register* since such records began being tallied in the 1970s. (That's when agencies were required to disclose their activities in a standard format.) "It is a notable achievement that all three of the lowest-ever annual rule counts belong to Trump," observes Wayne Crews.[20]

Results for American workers have also been striking. Wage gains were especially strong among the non-rich.

"Rank-and-File Workers Get Bigger Raises" was the headline on a December 27, 2019, story in the *Wall Street Journal*. Eric Morath and Jeffrey Sparshott reported, "Pay for the bottom 25% of wage earners rose 4.5% in November from a year earlier, according to the Federal Reserve Bank of Atlanta. Wages for the top 25% of earners rose 2.9%. Similarly, the Atlanta Fed found wages for low-skilled workers have accelerated since early 2018, and last month matched the pace of high-skill workers for the first time since 2010."[21]

Finally, after a long era of stagnation, wages for workers were rising as fast or faster than the pay of their bosses. The *Journal* reporters added: "Labor Department data paint a similar picture. Average hourly earnings for production and nonsupervisory workers in the private sector were up 3.7% in November from a year earlier—stronger than the 3.1% advance for all employees—implying managers and other nonproduction workers saw a 1.6% wage increase in the past year. The department doesn't produce separate management pay figures."[22]

Beyond wages, Morath and Sparshott also noted that the labor market had lately been especially good for the least-educated workers: "The labor market for skilled workers is always tighter, but it hasn't improved as substantially in recent years. The unemployment rate for high school dropouts fell to 5.3% last month from 7.8% three years earlier. The rate for college grads is down to 2% from 2.4% in November 2016, and is slightly elevated relative to the late 1990s and early 2000s."[23]

A little more than a month later, and one day before his vindication in the Senate impeachment trial, President Trump gave his State of the Union address. Some people may remember the night for Speaker Nancy Pelosi's theatrical shredding of the speech text the president had just presented to her. But she might have reflected on some of its contents. "From the instant I took office, I moved rapidly to revive the United States economy— slashing a record number of job-killing regulations . . . ," said Trump. "Our agenda is relentlessly pro-worker, pro-family, pro-growth, and, most of all, pro-American. . . . We are advancing with unbridled optimism and lifting high our citizens of every race, color, religion, and creed. . . ."[24]

Assessing the results of the Trump deregulation effort today, a bank CEO tells us that his industry hasn't seen any yet but adds that "there has been reform in a lot of other industries. And if you speak to other industry CEOs, they'll tell you, 'Yes, it's been quite a dramatic thing.' And I think we still need more. We've burdened ourselves with too much—I mean, I hate to call it regulation, because it sounds like it's a good thing. It's nothing but politics, corruption, stupidity, red tape, bureaucracy. Take ten small businesspeople to lunch or dinner. And ask them what they have to go through. Forget big companies.

I'm talking about people who own one store, two stores, or three stores. And they'll start telling you about federal audits, state audits, OSHA, workers' comp, insurance, litigation, the ability to get licenses, how long it takes, how many multiple licenses you need."

The bank CEO continues: "And that's a form of corruption. That's not because they were just stupid. It's also that a lot of jobs rely on, you know, not getting permits done quickly. I mean, talk to any real estate person about how long it takes to get a certificate of occupancy. In New York it took 12 years to get the 49 permits required to rebuild a bridge that was basically broken. It could have dropped and killed people. Twelve years. And think of the cost of that, by the way. The Army Corps of Engineers had to come in four times. Four times!"[25]

The Trump administration recently issued a final rule to speed approval of infrastructure projects. The president tells us that projects that in the past might have waited for a decade or more for approval will now receive action within two years. "That's one of the biggest things I will have done. You watch," he adds.

Trump tells us he made deregulation a priority "because I went through, you know, years and years . . . to get approvals" while running a business. "I understand the system. It's a consultant system. The consultants go up to Albany or they go down to Washington and they make it very tough. So you have to hire consultants and pay them millions of dollars to get a simple approval. No, I know that business."[26]

• • •

Beyond Speaker Pelosi, it turns out there's at least one prominent Democrat who might not wish to shred the entire Trump deregulatory agenda. Former president Obama may still be claiming credit for the success of the Trump economy prior to the pandemic. But in an ironic twist, Obama seems to be among the many Americans who are benefiting from Trump's war on Washington red tape. That's because the former president is currently seeking to build the Obama Presidential Center on the South Side of Chicago.

Among the opponents of the massive Obama construction project is Charles Birnbaum, head of the Cultural Landscape Foundation. Birnbaum says that the City of Chicago is using "a Trump-era policy position" to argue that the federal government can't put up any new obstacles to the Obama plan.[27]

As president, Obama famously told America's entrepreneurs, "You didn't build that."[28] He meant to say that business founders benefited from lots of government services and therefore had not really succeeded on their own. Now, thanks to Trump, it seems that Obama may finally be able to build that presidential center.

Will he now agree with Trump that red tape becomes beautiful when it's cut?

4

Trump's Tax Revolution

Is Donald Trump Serious?" asked a *New York Times* headline on September 29, 2015. The story by columnist Joe Nocera began: "As part of his ongoing effort to make a mockery of the American political process, Donald Trump released his tax plan on Monday morning." [1] Candidate Trump's most egregious offense against conventional media wisdom was his proposal to slash the U.S. corporate income tax rate from 35 percent to 15 percent.

The real mockery was the damage the tax had been inflicting on American competitiveness and American workers. When combined with state and local taxes, the total U.S. tax rate on corporate income amounted to nearly 40 percent, the highest in the industrialized world. Also, if an American company brought home the profits made in a foreign market, the

Internal Revenue Service taxed those profits, too—even if they had already been taxed by another government overseas. So U.S. companies had an incentive to keep the money offshore instead of investing it in their U.S. factories.

The IRS tax bite on business was so large that numerous U.S. firms were opting for a so-called corporate inversion, merging with a foreign company and locating the new combined business outside the United States. During the final years of the Obama administration, the Treasury Department issued a flurry of notices intended to prevent American companies from fleeing the country—or at least to make it extremely costly and difficult to leave.

After the rookie Republican presidential candidate announced his plan for reform in 2015, Nocera charged that "Trump's proposed 15 percent corporate tax rate is so low that companies wouldn't need to leave to enjoy drastically lower taxes."[2]

Imagine that: a policy that doesn't chase business overseas. Candidate Trump correctly diagnosed that the broken U.S. tax system was chasing wages overseas, too. Trump's big idea was that a lower tax burden would encourage businesses to invest more in the United States. This business investment would buy more tools and technology for U.S. workers to use on the job and allow them to be more productive. And if workers could get more work done each day, they could demand higher wages.

While the media and political establishment reacted in horror to the idea of a lighter business tax burden and treated Trump's proposal as outrageous, it was hard to argue with him on the merits. Even the economic team at the Obama White

House had acknowledged the benefits to workers of a lower corporate tax rate.

Not that Team Obama ever did anything about it, but they did acknowledge the truth in the 2015 *Economic Report of the President*: "When effective marginal rates are higher, potential projects need to generate more income if the business is to pay the tax and still provide investors with the required return. Businesses will therefore limit their activities to higher-return projects. Thus, all else equal, a higher effective marginal rate for businesses will tend to reduce the level of investment, and a lower effective marginal rate will tend to encourage additional projects and a larger capital stock. Increases in the capital available for each worker's use, also referred to as capital deepening, boost productivity, wages, and output."[3]

In a footnote to that passage Team Obama recognized the work of an economist named Kevin Hassett.[4] Along with his colleague Aparna Mathur, Hassett had been studying the impact of corporate taxation on worker wages for nearly a decade. Hassett and Mathur were trying to figure out who really ends up paying corporate income taxes. They were curious if such taxes are like sales taxes. A lot of economic research has found that consumers carry most of the burden of sales taxes, because when such taxes increase, companies usually don't cut their prices to offset the tax hike. The consumer gets stuck paying the tab.[5]

In an August 2016 op-ed in the *Wall Street Journal*, Hassett and Mathur explained their work: "We applied a similar method to study the impact of corporate taxation on the wages of blue-collar workers. If a higher corporate tax reduces the return to capital, then capital may move abroad. This outflow could reduce the productivity and compensation for domestic workers, who are relatively immobile. So just as a sales tax might have an impact on the final goods price, a higher corporate tax might have an impact on wages. If wages go down when corporate taxes go up, the worker is left holding the tax bag."[6]

And that's exactly what was happening, especially to workers in the U.S. "Our empirical analysis, which used data we gathered on international tax rates and manufacturing wages in 72 countries over 22 years, confirmed that the corporate tax is for the most part paid by workers," the economists wrote.[7]

Hassett and Mathur also noted that they weren't the only ones confirming this phenomenon: "In a 2007 paper Federal Reserve economist Alison Felix used data from the Luxembourg Income Study, which tracks individual incomes across 30 countries, to show that a 10 percent increase in corporate tax rates reduces wages by about 7 percent. In a 2009 paper Ms. Felix found similar patterns across the U.S., where states with higher corporate tax rates have significantly lower wages. . . .

". . . Harvard University economists Mihir Desai, Fritz Foley, and Michigan's James R. Hines have studied data from American multinational firms, finding that their foreign affiliates tend to pay significantly higher wages in countries with lower corporate tax rates."[8]

Hassett and Mathur concluded that there was a clear path to higher wages: "One need only cut corporate tax rates. Left and right leaning countries have done this over the past two decades, including Japan, Canada, and Germany. Yet in the

U.S. we continue to undermine wage growth with the highest corporate tax rate in the developed world."[9]

Not for long. Trump was elected that fall on a promise of tax reform and took office on January 20, 2017. The need for reform of the tax code wasn't recognized just by academic economists but most of all by the executives who had to operate under it. Four days after Trump's inauguration, FedEx chief executive officer Fred Smith appeared on *Mornings with Maria* and explained that a person with a high school education needs "a bulldozer or a tractor or a truck or a plane or something, a piece of capital equipment to allow them to make more money, to have a good income. So our real problem is our tax code is punitive towards capital investment." Smith added that if "you fix the tax code to incent investment in the United States, you'll see a lot of these blue-collar jobs that the president talked about so much during the campaign, come back."[10]

Trump kept saying the same thing as president, instructing his economic team to draft a plan to slash the corporate income tax rate to the 15 percent he had promised and to provide relief for small- and mid-size firms, not just large corporations. Not that the captain of Trump's economic team had to be persuaded. The president had selected Kevin Hassett to chair his Council of Economic Advisers. Now Hassett would get to apply his research to solving America's competitiveness problem. Hassett's colleague Aparna Mathur would join the team later in the Trump administration.

The evidence for lowering corporate tax rates to raise worker compensation continued to pour in. At Canada's University of Calgary, Kenneth McKenzie and Ergete Ferede showed the impact in Canadian dollars of increasing the regional corporate income tax (CIT) on businesses up north: "We calculate that for every $1 in extra tax revenue generated by an increase in the provincial CIT rate, the associated long-run decrease in aggregate wages ranges from $1.52 for Alberta to $3.85 for Prince Edward Island. Applying our estimates to the recent 2 percentage point increase in the CIT rate in Alberta we calculate that labour earnings for an average two-earner household will decline by the equivalent of approximately $830 per year, which amounts to a $1.12 billion reduction in aggregate labour earnings for the province."[11]

There's an argument that the appropriate corporate tax rate is zero—and not just to benefit workers. Corporate income taxes represent multiple taxation because shareholders had to pay taxes on the money they earned before investing it in the business and they will be taxed again if they take profits out of the business via dividends and again if they sell at a gain.

Trump wasn't arguing for a repeal of the corporate income tax. He wasn't even trying to match Ireland's 12.5 percent rate, which had lured businesses from the U.S. and continental Europe to set up shop on the Emerald Isle. The fast-growing Irish economy was an impressive model, but in the United States, Trump simply wanted to transform the highest rate in the developed world into a competitive one. "When it comes to the business tax, we are dead last. Can you believe that? So this cannot be allowed to continue any longer. America must lead the way, not follow from behind," the president said in August 2017 during a speech at the Loren Cook Company in Springfield, Missouri. ". . . We have totally surrendered our competitive edge to other countries. We have totally surrendered. We're not surrendering anymore," he added.[12]

Treasury Secretary Steven Mnuchin told Maria in September: "We have to create economic growth and that's what this is all about."[13] In October the President's Council of Economic Advisers released a short but important paper summarizing the voluminous research showing the connection between low corporate income tax rates and rising wages for workers.[14] Thanks to the work conducted for years by Hassett, Mathur, and many others, the academic debate was no longer about whether heavy taxation of business holds down compensation for employees but about *how much* it hurts employees.

The October report compared the ten developed countries with the highest corporate income tax rates and the ten with the lowest. In 2016, workers in the high-tax locales eked out average wage gains of just half a percent. Meanwhile in the low-tax countries, wages surged by 4 percent.

"We're going to give the American people a huge tax cut for Christmas," said the president before a meeting of his cabinet on November 20, 2017. He added that "our tax plan will return trillions of dollars in wealth to our shores so that companies can invest in America again."[15]

Overseas, there was some concern that Mr. Trump and tax reformers in Congress were about to do exactly that. The long-running Cantillon column in Dublin's *Irish Times* newspaper noted that a U.S. House vote to cut taxes "is highly significant" and that most Republicans in America "are united behind reforming the corporate-tax system." The column added: "This is unsettling for Ireland. Addressing the House this week, Paul Ryan—a proud Irish-American—cited the example of Johnson Controls, a company that has had roots in his home state of Wisconsin since the 1880s but is now based in Ireland. The new tax system will help make the United States 'the most competitive place in the world,' he said. Worrying words for Ireland."[16]

Even the Irish were getting worried? This was the corporate taxation equivalent of the New England Patriots suddenly becoming concerned about the competitive threat posed by the Cleveland Browns. Ireland routinely has the fastest-growing economy in the eurozone, so you can imagine how Europe's also-rans felt about the prospect of the U.S. economy suddenly becoming more competitive.

In fact, some Europeans had been urging us for years to get our house in order. An official with the Organisation for Economic Co-operation and Development, a Paris-based association of industrialized economies, coauthored a 2016 diagnosis of the U.S. problem: "The American tax and accounting system has trapped over $2 trillion of deferred taxable income as 'permanently reinvested' offshore. It encourages the acquisition of U.S. headquartered companies by foreign companies, and then allows foreign companies to strip taxable income from the U.S. activities. This system is bad for domestic job creation, penalizes the entire U.S. economy, and needs to be fixed urgently."[17]

Trump was thinking the same thing. Negotiations with Republicans in Congress resulted in a plan to bring the U.S. tax rate down to 21 percent, not all the way to the 15 percent Trump had proposed. Still, it was significant enough for some Democrats to argue that the Trump tax reform would kill people.

You read that correctly. In December 2017, as the Trump tax plan approached a final vote in Congress, The Hill reported: "Rep. Nancy Pelosi (D-Calif.) hammered the Republicans' tax-code overhaul Monday evening as a culture-shaking economic 'armageddon' that would haunt the working class for years to come.

"Flanked by other top Democrats in the Capitol, the minority leader blasted Republicans for championing a tax proposal she equated to 'the end of the world.'"[18]

Were we all going to die? The prospect of a competitive U.S. tax system seemed to be triggering mass Beltway hysteria. Former Obama economic adviser Lawrence Summers was not predicting that the result of a House-Senate tax compromise would inspire a wrathful God to destroy all of humanity. But he did argue that at least some portion of humanity would indeed be annihilated by the pending legislation.

Summers wrote in the *Washington Post*: "I suggested . . . when it became clear that the tax bill would pass that 'thousands would die.' In light of my sharp criticism of other economists' claims regarding the legislation, some have asked whether my statement is well grounded. I think it is, but this should be open to debate," he graciously conceded.[19]

The Summers argument was that, since one provision of the bill repealed the Obamacare mandate to buy health insurance, many people would foolishly choose not to secure coverage and thereby hasten their own demise. Mr. Summers kept warning of a mass-casualty legislative event as the tax debate proceeded.

Perhaps Summers could have lightened up a little if he had simply reflected on his own work showing the value of growth economics. "Wealthier nations are healthier nations," reported a 1996 study he coauthored in the *Journal of Human Resources*. The research found that life expectancy sharply increases and infant mortality sharply decreases along with gains in per capita income.[20]

It was hard to lighten the mood as Democrats chanted "Kill the bill, don't kill us!" in the House of Representatives.[21] But outside the august chamber many Americans were not just avoiding depression over the tax changes; they were eagerly making plans for an expanding economy. Even before Trump signed the historic reform on December 22, 2017, Americans had been getting wealthier as regulatory relief and the expectation of favorable tax reform sent stock prices rising along with business confidence. Companies from Broadcom to Boeing announced they would move overseas jobs back to the United States. American firms were holding nearly $3 trillion offshore and would soon have the opportunity to bring it back to the United States without paying a confiscatory tax rate.

The reform Trump signed not only included the pro-growth corporate income tax rate cut but also relief for individuals up and down the income scale. This led to a surprising exchange on CNN shortly after enactment. The network's Jake Tapper asked Vermont's socialist senator Bernie Sanders, "I understand you're not a fan of the tax bill. You don't like the large corporate tax cut, and you are not happy with the tax cuts for the wealthy. But, according to the Tax Policy Center, next year, 91 percent of middle-income Americans will receive a tax cut.

"Isn't that a good thing?"

"Yes, it is a very good thing," Sanders was forced to acknowledge.[22]

It's hard to argue with the results of Trump's rookie season in office. The year 2017 was an exceptional one for liberty in the United States, and especially for economic liberty. The largest rate cut in the history of the U.S. corporate income tax, along with tax relief for individuals and families, arrived on top of a yearlong effort to reduce America's regulatory burden.

January 2018 brought news of a fourth-quarter surge in U.S. business investment. The *Wall Street Journal* reported, "Just weeks after the federal government adopted the biggest tax overhaul in three decades, the effects are rippling through corner offices and boardrooms, with companies large and small dusting off once-shelved plans, re-evaluating existing projects and exploring new investment in factories and equipment." The *Journal* elaborated on the corporate reaction to reform: "Specialty drugmaker Amicus Therapeutics Inc. has decided to spend as much as $200 million on a new production facility in the U.S. instead of Europe. Kimberly-Clark Corp., maker of Kleenex tissues, is spending hundreds of millions of dollars to put new machinery in one of its U.S. factories. . . ." Fred Smith's FedEx announced higher wages and new U.S. capital projects.[23]

At the end of January, the president arrived at the World Economic Forum in Davos, Switzerland. The White House press pool report from that day captured the scene: "A crowd of Davos attendees gathered three and four people deep around the balcony overlooking the wide staircase Trump was expected to ascend, cell phones held aloft. Some kneeled on the white leatherette bench that hugs the glass-topped balcony, craning their heads over the side.

"When Trump entered the room below, the crowd fell silent except for the sound of cameras clicking and the slightly ominous music that came from an overhead projection that's been broadcast on one wall all week. He wore a long dark coat and his hair shone golden in the stage lighting overhead. As he slowly ascended the stairs, people started to shout questions. 'Are you going to be treated well,' asked one man, most likely a reporter.

" 'You tell me,' the president replied."[24]

The gathering's top-shelf selection of global capitalists, European statists, and nonprofit beard strokers was trying to figure out what "America First" would mean for them. It certainly seemed to mean better times ahead for U.S. workers. How have things worked out since then?

Trump's corporate tax reform was a game changer. Put simply, a better-equipped worker can produce more and therefore demand higher compensation. In February of this year, just before the season of shutdowns, the White House released the president's annual economic report. The document noted that U.S. labor productivity rose faster after the tax reform than it had during the preceding years of the recovery that began in 2009. The report also made the case that the Trump combination of regulatory relief and tax reform was the key to outperforming foreign competitors. U.S. productivity growth was surging relative to other developed-country competitors, putting America on a path to higher living standards.

The president for his part presented the issue in moral terms: "My Administration's focus on economic growth comes from a deep appreciation of the power of work to drive the economy and transform lives. The truth is, jobs do not just provide paychecks; they give people meaning, allow them to engage with their communities, and help them reach their true potential." [25]

The unemployment rate stood at 3.5 percent, the lowest in fifty years. "Since I came into office, labor force participation is up and wages are growing fastest for historically disadvantaged workers, reversing the trends seen under the previous administration. Under my Administration, and for the first time on record, job openings exceeded people looking for work, with 1 million more open jobs than job seekers at the end of 2019." [26] Trump gets criticized for hyping his achievements, but he has every right to take pride in a historically outstanding pre-Covid job market in the United States. "In 2018 alone, 1.4 million Americans were lifted out of poverty, and the poverty rate fell to its lowest level since 2001. For African Americans and Hispanic Americans, poverty rates are at historic lows, and the poverty rate for single mothers and children is falling much faster than the average. Since I took office, food insecurity has fallen and nearly 7 million people have been lifted off food stamps," says the president in his economic report. [27]

Team Trump could also note falling enrollment in welfare programs, more than 4 million jobs created since the enactment of the tax law, and faster economic growth and wage increases than predicted by the Congressional Budget Office. "Contrary to expectations that the expansion would slow as it matured, economic output has accelerated over the past 3 years relative to the preceding 7½ years, with output growth rising from 2.2 to 2.5 percent at a compound annual rate. In the first three quarters of 2019, U.S. economic growth was the highest among the Group of Seven countries," according to the president's report.[28]

Looking back now at the effort to enact tax reform, Trump tells us, "I had a lot of resistance from a lot of people."[29] So was he serious when, as a rookie candidate in 2015, he proposed lowering the corporate income tax rate to 15 percent? Well, now it can be told. He was serious about making the U.S. competitive, but not entirely serious about the precise number.

Trump tells us: "When I said 15, I said 15 because I wanted to get to 21, 22, 20, you know? I loved the 20 number because it was a round number. Does that make sense? You know, but when I said 15 percent, you never get what you ask for, you know? And—especially with these guys. So if I'm asking for 15 percent, I don't expect to get 15 percent. I'd like to get 20 or 21 percent. And I got that. I got it. It was a great negotiation."[30]

Many U.S. workers would agree.

5

Boom Time and Beijing

On a Friday night in February of 2012, the Phoenix Suns of the National Basketball Association suffered through another visit to the Staples Center in Los Angeles. As usual, Kobe Bryant was the reason for their distress. The Lakers star scored 36 points as LA rolled to a 111–99 victory.[1]

A month earlier, Bryant had dropped 48 on the Suns in another Lakers victory. For a time he seemed to enjoy torturing Phoenix more than any other opponent. ESPN's J. A. Adande found the reason: "I don't like them," Bryant said of the Suns. "Plain and simple, I do not like them. They used to whip us pretty good and used to let us know about it, and I. Will. Not. Forget. That."[2]

Bryant used to call himself the Black Mamba to signify his fierce competitiveness. After exacting yet another measure of revenge on that February night in 2012, Bryant was called "Malicious Mamba" by a Phoenix sportswriter.[3]

That may have been taking the metaphor a little too far. But it turned out that there really was a malicious competitor in the Staples Center that night—one who knows something about torturing opponents. Just months before assuming the chairmanship of the Chinese Communist Party, Xi Jinping was wrapping up a tour of the United States by watching an NBA game. Before heading to Los Angeles International Airport for the long flight home, Xi enjoyed the Lakers victory as an honored guest.

The VIP treatment included greetings from local celebrities and some swag to take back to Beijing. According to the Associated Press, the communist strongman "entered the arena on a red carpet and sat above the official scorer's table and the players' benches. Magic Johnson and David Beckham also stopped by the suite to visit him, and mayor Antonio Villaraigosa presented the Chinese dignitary with a Lakers jersey with his name on the back."[4]

Appearing without a tie, Xi seemed relaxed and friendly. His U.S. trip had been a smashing success, presenting Beijing's next boss as a cheerful contrast to his dour predecessors. By all appearances a modernizing China would continue its progress toward creating a more open society. "A prosperous and stable China will not be a threat to any country," Xi said a few hours before the game. "It will only be a positive force for world peace and development."[5]

Xi's polite hosts in Los Angeles probably didn't realize that the man who was about to become the most important player in the Chinese regime was no reformer but an old-fashioned communist determined to reassert party control over every aspect of his country's life. Today Xi has consolidated power and is the first Chinese communist boss since Mao to hold a lifetime term. He has developed the world's most sophisticated surveillance state and currently holds an estimated one million ethnic minorities in concentration camps.[6]

But back in February 2012, civic leaders in Los Angeles weren't the only ones who failed to appreciate the significance of Xi's rise to power. Before arriving at the Lakers game, Xi had spent much of that Friday—and much of his American trip—with Vice President Joe Biden.

Biden and Xi attended a Friday luncheon at a Los Angeles trade forum. Outside, protesters deplored the Chinese government's treatment of religious dissidents. But inside, the two leaders celebrated their burgeoning relationship. According to an AP report, Xi and Biden said "they had developed a close, personal friendship through visits."[7]

Without question, the trade relationship had been growing, and not without benefits for Americans. U.S. consumers were enjoying lower prices on a multitude of products. Earlier in the week, Xi had visited the Port of Los Angeles. Most of the imports coming through America's busiest port were now made in China.[8]

Xi said through a translator that the United States and China had moved from "mutual estrangement to a close exchange with increasingly intertwined interests."[9] It was true, but the fact that the interests of the United States and the Chinese regime were intertwined didn't mean they were the same.

How exactly did America end up moving from estrangement to a close relationship with a communist dictatorship? It's important to understand how we got here before we decide what kind of relationship we want with China in the future. Trump's challenge to the U.S. political establishment's consensus on China has raised important questions about the best ways to ensure American prosperity and peace.

By the 1970s, business leaders in various countries had been dreaming about the potential of the huge Chinese market for centuries. But when U.S. president Richard Nixon decided in 1971 to visit the communist-controlled nation the following year, it had less to do with economics than with grand strategy and politics.

The United States had been refusing to recognize the communist government ever since it seized power in 1949 and unleashed upon its people the most murderous reign in world history. In 1972 it was impossible to make a legitimate case on behalf of the thugs who ran the place, and so the opening to China was presented as a benefit to American interests. Nixon was trying to conclude a peace deal in Vietnam to enable a U.S. withdrawal. He thought China might help persuade the Vietnamese communists to keep their commitments. Nixon also wanted to get reelected in 1972 and craved diplomatic victories to present to voters. And he figured it was easier to confront America's principal Cold War adversary, the Soviet Union, if the United States could encourage a growing rift between the Soviets and their fellow communists in Beijing (then known as Peking in the West). Every Red Army division that Moscow had to deploy on its Chinese border would not be available to face U.S. troops and allies in Western Europe. In the United States, the euphoria about potential commercial opportunities in China came later. At the outset China was seen as a strategic counterweight to the Soviets in Asia.

But Americans don't naturally welcome relationships with tyrants. The cliché holds that only Nixon could go to China, because only a politician who had established a consistent record of strong anti-communism could sell a deal with such an evil regime. That's why California governor Ronald Reagan supported Nixon's plan: because he said Nixon had proven he knew how to deal with communists.[10] Reagan cited as evidence the 1959 "kitchen debate" in which then–vice president Nixon had argued the merits of the U.S. and Soviet systems with Soviet dictator Nikita Khrushchev.[11]

Not everyone was buying. When Nixon flew to China in February 1972, he brought along the usual mainstream media folks but also the conservative magazine editor William F. Buckley Jr. Perhaps Nixon was thinking that if he could win over Buckley, he could win over the right. In a 2008 essay published by the Richard Nixon Foundation, David Stokes wrote, "It didn't work. Buckley didn't budge. In fact, quite the contrary—he was emboldened in his anti-communism."[12] Buckley was especially appalled at one evening event at which Nixon and his hosts began taking turns toasting one another. Nixon ended up raising his glass to leaders who had presided over the murder of millions of their countrymen.

Wrote Buckley: "It is unreasonable to suppose that anywhere in history have a few dozen men congregated who have been responsible for greater human mayhem than the hosts at this banquet and their spiritual colleagues, instruments all of Mao Tse-tung. The effect was as if Sir Hartley Shawcross had suddenly risen from the prosecutor's stand at Nuremberg and descended to embrace Goering and Goebbels and Doenitz and Hess, begging them to join with him in the making of a better world." [13]

Buckley believed that Nixon had received nothing of substance in return for granting China's communists a propaganda coup and a path to normalized relations. As for the United States, Buckley concluded, "We have lost—irretrievably—any remaining sense of moral mission in the world. . . . Mr. Nixon is so much the moral enthusiast that he alchemizes the requirements of diplomacy into the coin of ethics; that is why when he toasted the bloodiest, most merciless chief of state in the world, he did so in accents most of us would reserve for Florence Nightingale." [14]

Buckley was a media outlier, but many conservative members of Congress remained skeptical of the Nixon policy. Later, the Watergate scandal didn't encourage anyone to give Nixon the benefit of the doubt. Official diplomatic relations between the United States and China wouldn't happen for nearly seven years after Nixon's historic visit.

On January 1, 1979, the United States, now led by President Jimmy Carter, recognized the communist People's Republic as the sole legal government of China and withdrew diplomatic recognition from our friends in Taiwan (also known as the Republic of China). [15] The Chinese nationalist government had fled to the island of Taiwan in 1949 as the communists took over the mainland.

Conventional wisdom has long held that Nixon's surprise opening to China was a strategic masterstroke. And in the years since, the progress in China has been amazing, with a more open society and hundreds of millions of people pulled out of poverty. After the death of Mao eventually led to the ascension of Deng Xiaoping in 1978, China's communist government became increasingly open to profit-seeking business activity as a way to enrich the party and the nation.

This was a welcome development in the West, as was China's continuing role as a Soviet rival in Asia. In 1980 the United States granted China most-favored-nation trade status, which minimized U.S. tariffs on Chinese goods and allowed Export-Import Bank of the United States (EXIM) financing of Chinese purchases. American trade with China more than doubled from the previous year.[16] Then, in 1981, the new Reagan administration expanded the list of technologies China could buy from the United States.[17]

But was China's strange marriage of a communist government and an increasingly capitalist economy built to last? Some had their doubts. Writing at the dawn of China's era of market experimentation, the great economists Milton and Rose Friedman wrote:

The intellectual apologists for centralized economic planning sang the praises of Mao's China until Mao's successors trumpeted China's backwardness and bemoaned the lack of progress during the past twenty-five years.

Part of their design to modernize the country is to let prices and markets play a larger role. These tactics may produce sizable gains from the country's present low economic level. . . . However, the gains will be severely limited so long as political control over economic activity remains tight and private property is narrowly limited. Moreover, letting the genie of private initiative out of the bottle even to this limited extent will give rise to political problems that, sooner or later, are likely to produce a reaction toward greater authoritarianism. The opposite outcome, the collapse of communism and its replacement by a market system, seems far less likely, though as incurable optimists, we do not rule it out completely.[18]

Four decades later the communist regime certainly hasn't collapsed. As for the possibility of greater authoritarianism in reaction to private initiative, in recent years there has been increasing pressure on entrepreneurs to embed the Communist Party within their businesses and to comply with burdensome new regulations.[19] Meanwhile state-owned enterprises have been staging a comeback and taking market share from independent firms started by Chinese entrepreneurs.[20] Did the Friedmans predict the rise of Xi Jinping decades before he took power in Beijing?

In another passage with great resonance for our own time, the Friedmans suggest that there are worse things than tariffs, but they also caution against efforts by our own government to set the rules for trading with a communist government. "Tariffs and similar restrictions distort the signals transmitted by the price system, but at least they leave individuals free to respond to those distorted signals. The collectivist countries have introduced much farther-reaching command elements," wrote the Friedmans.

"Completely private transactions are impossible between citizens of a largely market economy and of a collectivist state," they continued. "One side is necessarily represented by government officials. Political considerations are unavoidable, but friction would be minimized if the governments of market economies permitted their citizens the maximum possible leeway to make their own deals with collectivist governments. Trying to use trade as a political weapon or political measures as a means to increase trade with collectivist countries only makes the inevitable political friction even worse."[21]

In the late 1970s and early 1980s, Washington wasn't imposing many rules on the Chinese regime when it came to the treatment of U.S. companies operating there. But many American firms were eager to dive into the formerly closed market anyway. And some firms were happy to sign up for another China adventure even if they'd been badly burned in the past.

Longtime employees at the American financial giant Citibank might have recalled that when the communists seized the bank's assets in 1950, they didn't do so nicely. "When the Communists broke into a bank-owned staff residence in Shanghai, one Asia hand, Ray Kathe, had to roll himself up in an oriental carpet to protect himself from ricocheting bullets," writes Phillip Zweig. Upon taking over Citi's branches, the Chinese demanded that the bank return all deposits at the exchange rate that was in effect at the time they were made. "Because of inflation that would have been disastrous," adds Zweig, and so Citi left China without settling the issue. The new communist regime responded by essentially holding three bank employees hostage, barring them from leaving the country. Citi ransomed two of them for $500,000 and continued for decades afterward to pay the salary of one employee who was a Chinese national.[22]

Given this history one might think that Citibank would have been the last American company eager to reenter the Chinese market. But one would be wrong. In the late 1970s Citi CEO Walter Wriston was so eager to take another crack at China's nearly one billion potential consumers that he was willing to travel there without knowing exactly how he would return—and over the objections of his wife. The couple was in Hong Kong preparing to visit the Chinese mainland when their travel plans got complicated. Zweig reports: "Kathy Wriston had not been enthusiastic about this trip. Iran Air was the only carrier flying out of China and it was then on strike. . . . She said, 'I'll do anything for Mother Bank, but I don't want to go into China with no way out.' Wriston put his foot down. 'We want the Chinese business,' he said."[23]

Wriston got the business, striking a deal with the Bank of China in 1979. The Chinese government paid Citi just 41 cents on the dollar for the assets it had seized nearly three decades earlier. The timing was appropriate. Wriston's triumph of hope over experience occurred at the dawn of an era of global growth, communist retreat, and Chinese revival. Who could avoid becoming an optimist?

By the mid-1980s, the communists were still running China, but the country had budding young entrepreneurs sprouting up all over the place. "In a tiny bedroom that also serves as an office, Hu Peiyi spreads his hands wide and tells friends how he is going to build his fleet of five secondhand cabs into an empire," reported the *Wall Street Journal's* Julia Leung and Vigor Fung from Shanghai in 1985. "Mr. Hu is one of hundreds of ambitious businessmen who are shaping up as China's first batch of capitalists since the Communist takeover in 1949. They are venturing into fields such as property, industry, consultancy and trade." [24]

Reformers within the increasingly permissive regime were hoping the new competitors would force state-owned enterprises to be more efficient. Chinese leader Deng Xiaoping was willing to abandon communist dogma and acknowledge that some of the ideas of Marx and Lenin had become outdated. Encouraging ideological flexibility and pragmatism, he observed that "it doesn't matter whether a cat is black or white as long as it catches mice." [25]

But there were potholes along the way for the aspiring taxi magnate and every other new business owner, "with bureaucratic delays and hostility from orthodox Communists suspicious of capitalism. Also, some Chinese leaders worry that the growth of the private sector will embarrass the state, which is still largely committed to collective ownership," according to the *Journal* report. [26]

Still, regardless of the difficulty of dealing with old-line apparatchiks, the long waits to get telephone service, and the possibility that the regime could once again turn on a dime and seize their assets, the new capitalists were determined to chase their dreams. "This job ages me fast, but nothing is like being your own boss," said one business owner. Another new capitalist, a thirty-nine-year-old woman named Hu Diqing, had quit her job as a newspaper reporter to form a trading and investment company. "Suppressing one's ambitions is the most painful thing on earth," she said.[27]

Entrepreneurial ambition, finally allowed to express itself, was creating the fastest-growing economy on earth. Symbolic of the zest with which subjects of the communist regime were embracing their new freedom to be capitalists, the classic American board game Monopoly became a huge hit in China.[28]

There was just one problem, which foreshadowed the experience of many American companies with the Chinese market. The skyrocketing sales across the Pacific came as news to Parker Brothers, the U.S. maker of the popular game. China's Monopoly boom was being fed by an unauthorized knockoff version produced at a factory in Shanghai by a local company. Questions about rights to intellectual property—and every other kind of property—would be a recurring issue in China.[29]

But for the first time many Chinese were able to build wealth, and millions were being pulled out of poverty. The size of the Chinese economy would more than double during the 1980s, and the world was paying attention.[30] Beijing's formula for success was inspiring admiration in the most unlikely places. Even Russia's prototypical communist government, which had criticized China's deviations from Marxism, began hoping that a little market magic could revive the Soviet economy, too.[31] Mikhail Gorbachev, who had taken over as communist party boss in 1985, began trying to save the Soviet regime by relaxing the iron grip of central planning and allowing some private business activity. Unable to compete any longer against the vibrant, high-tech economy of the United States, Gorbachev was trying to open the communist system to new ideas while avoiding fundamental reform. But he wasn't moving quickly enough, and the captive peoples in Russia and the rest of Eastern Europe weren't going to be satisfied with a slightly less repressive tyranny.

In June of 1987, U.S. president Ronald Reagan traveled to Berlin's Brandenburg Gate and called Gorbachev's bluff. Standing defiantly at the concrete frontier of the Soviet empire, Reagan told a huge crowd of West Germans:

> Behind me stands a wall that encircles the free sectors of this city, part of a vast system of barriers that divides the entire continent of Europe. From the Baltic, south, those barriers cut across Germany in a gash of barbed wire, concrete, dog runs, and guardtowers. Farther south, there may be no visible, no obvious wall. But there remain armed guards and checkpoints all the same—still a restriction on the right to travel, still an instrument to impose upon ordinary men and women the will of a totalitarian state. Yet it is here in Berlin where the wall emerges most clearly; here, cutting across your city, where the news photo and the television screen have imprinted this brutal division of a continent upon the mind of the world. Standing before the Brandenburg Gate, every man is a German,

separated from his fellow men. Every man is a Berliner, forced to look upon a scar.

Beyond the assembled crowd in front of Reagan, no doubt many Germans on the other side of the wall were also able to hear his speech on radio, despite attempts by the communist East German government to block it.

"We hear much from Moscow about a new policy of reform and openness . . . ," Reagan went on to say. He then spoke the words which would shake the foundations of the communist empire. "There is one sign the Soviets can make that would be unmistakable, that would advance dramatically the cause of freedom and peace. General Secretary Gorbachev, if you seek peace, if you seek prosperity for the Soviet Union and Eastern Europe, if you seek liberalization: Come here to this gate! Mr. Gorbachev, open this gate! Mr. Gorbachev, tear down this wall!"[32]

Two years later the wall collapsed as jubilant Germans poured across the border. One after another, communist regimes fell across Eastern Europe. By Christmas Day of 1991, the Soviet Union was no more.[33] "Ronald Reagan won the Cold War without firing a shot," concluded Margaret Thatcher, who served as Britain's prime minister in the 1980s.[34] Worldwide, hundreds of millions of people were liberated from tyranny. Market economies were rising and new democracies were being born.

Communism was failing all around the world. Perhaps Washington policymakers could be forgiven for thinking that it probably wouldn't last much longer in the place that had become conspicuous for its new embrace of capitalism.

But as much as China's communists wanted to benefit from economic growth, they had no intention of surrendering political power. In early June of 1989, just as the communist government in Poland was losing its grip on power and only months before the fall of the Berlin Wall, student demonstrators in the heart of China's capital were standing in front of Mao Zedong's portrait and demanding liberty. The demonstrations had been allowed for weeks, in part because they were originally presented as a memorial to a senior government official who had advocated reform. But the crowd in Tiananmen Square was growing.

Young people demanded an end to corruption and fashioned a "Lady Democracy" monument that looked like a papier-mâché rendering of the Statue of Liberty. The university students in Tiananmen were inspiring protests in other parts of the country. Chinese tyrant Deng Xiaoping, friendly as he may have been to market liberalization, decided that he could not tolerate demands for political freedom. Deng ordered the army to take Tiananmen.

Tanks rolled through the city, over homemade barricades, and into the square. Ground troops joined in the slaughter. "You never forget watching young people, some of the nation's best and brightest, full of passion and idealism, stand up to machine guns—and then in an instant crumple bloody and lifeless on the ground," recalled Nicholas Kristof of the *New York Times* on the thirtieth anniversary of the massacre. In

June of 1989 he was the paper's Beijing bureau chief and witnessed the carnage in Tiananmen. He remembers soldiers "firing not only on the crowds but even on families watching in horror from balconies. Troops fired at ambulances rescuing the wounded." He also recalls rickshaw drivers who bravely pedaled their bicycle carts into the square during pauses in the shooting to retrieve the wounded. Kristof particularly remembers one such driver: "He had a couple of bleeding people on the back of his cart and was pedaling furiously, his legs straining. He saw me and swerved toward me so that I could bear witness to his government's brutality. As he passed, he pleaded with me: *Tell the world!*

"And tears were streaming down his cheeks."[35]

One of the protest leaders, Rose Tang, managed to survive the assault and then make her way to the United States. In 2019 she told the *Wall Street Journal* about the exciting days before the crackdown when protesters believed that their country really was changing: "It was China at its best and freest." She also shared an entry she made in her diary right after the army attack: "From 2 am sat on the front of the monument with others, sang every happy song I could remember, as this is my last moment in my life, I should enjoy every minute of it. . . . When 5 am, tanks broke into the square, crashed down tents and Monument Lady Democracy. . . . It turned to turmoil. . . . We pushed each other. . . . I fell down and was beaten by a soldier. I felt choked, nearly dying. Lucky enough, I went atop a tank, then fled away, with shoes lost, glasses broken. . . . Cry badly, not only for me, but for the whole country. . . ."[36]

Wang Dan, one of the students who initiated the protests,

had urged his fellow demonstrators to leave the square the day before the massacre. Police captured him several weeks later. During his years in prison, he felt tremendous guilt for starting the movement that led to the deaths of so many people.[37]

Exactly how many murders the communist regime committed on June 4, 1989, has been a matter of debate. Estimates of the death toll in Beijing range from the hundreds into the thousands. In 1989 the official line from the Chinese government was that a few hundred people had died following what it called "counter-revolutionary riots," as if the unarmed students were the aggressors. But in December 2017 the BBC cited newly released British government documents reporting that the Chinese army assault had killed at least 10,000 people. "The figure was given in a secret diplomatic cable from then British ambassador to China, Sir Alan Donald," reported the BBC. "The original source was a friend of a member of China's State Council, the envoy says."[38]

In 1989, Wu Renhua was a young university lecturer and a protester at Tiananmen. After surviving the massacre, he returned to his university campus, where some of the victims' bodies were placed on desks in front of a lecture hall, according to a 2019 report in Taiwan's *Taipei Times*. "I heard a voice in my mind as I looked at those bodies," Wu told the *Times*. "It told me I should never forget this. Never forget."[39]

Wu escaped China with help from Operation Yellowbird, a rescue effort based in Hong Kong. Now living in the United States, he has sought to document every detail of the events leading up to the crackdown, as well as the carnage in the square and its aftermath. "Wu also looked into the death toll and said that 2,600, a figure released by the Red Cross Society of China, was credible based on his survey of about 200 hospitals and the more than 100 sites where the troops opened fire in Beijing," the *Taipei Times* reported.[40]

The Chinese communist regime's killing of thousands of protesting students shocked the world. The news from Tiananmen especially horrified Americans who had been watching television images of the idealistic kids with their homemade Statue of Liberty look-alikes. The students were dreaming of a better life and attempting to exercise basic rights enshrined in the U.S. Constitution. Such rights were also included in the Chinese constitution, but—as with all such documents under Marxist regimes—they were just words on paper.

What is perhaps shocking in retrospect is that the United States of America, where those words really mean something, hardly did anything about it. The Soviet empire hadn't fallen yet but it was on the ropes. So it was a logical moment to ask how much barbarity we should tolerate in order to maintain Beijing as a strategic counterweight to Moscow.

But in a press conference on June 5, 1989, just a day after the Chinese communist military assault on civilians in their own capital, President George H. W. Bush made it clear that not much was going to change in the U.S.-China relationship. He condemned the regime's decision to use force, expressed sympathy for the victims, and announced the suspension of some military sales. Then Bush said, "This is not the time for an emotional response, but for a reasoned, careful action that takes into account both our long-term interests and recognition of a complex internal situation in China."[41]

In Bush's defense, he wasn't simply expressing a cold calculation that China was good for business or that Beijing was a useful strategic asset in the Pacific. He believed that continuing U.S. engagement and expanding commercial ties would feed the democracy movement in China rather than starve it. Throughout history, capitalism has generally been a liberating force. But more than three decades after Bush decided he would look past a horrific crime in the hope of advancing the long-term cause of democracy, it's fair to say he made the wrong decision. The communist regime is still in power. And the consequences of Bush's blunder have been both tragic and enormous.

At that press conference in 1989, Bush said that "the budding of democracy which we have seen in recent weeks owes much to the relationship we have developed since 1972. And it's important at this time to act in a way that will encourage the further development and deepening of the positive elements of that relationship and the process of democratization. It would be a tragedy for all if China were to pull back to its pre-1972 era of isolation and repression."[42] Nearly a half century after Nixon went to China, it's still a land of political repression. As for the Bush policy, "by its own lights—the aim of encouraging China to become a more open, democratic, liberal society—the decision to let Beijing get away with murder 30 years ago has been an abject failure," wrote the *Wall Street Journal*'s Gerard Baker in 2019.[43]

The communist government has done its best to erase the bloody history of Tiananmen. When circumstances require the regime to address the massacre, officials have refused to acknowledge any fault.

One can only imagine how history might have turned out differently. Specifically, it's tempting to wonder what might have happened if, in May 1989, Bush had sent a clear message: Military force against civilians would mean the end of U.S. ties to China. In some ways it has become even more painful to consider this possibility as the years have passed. That's because of various reports of dissent within the People's Liberation Army in 1989, including among senior commanders who opposed turning their guns upon their fellow citizens.[44] Even in the immediate aftermath of the massacre, Bush noted "turmoil" within China's military and political leadership, and there was certainly broader opposition to using the army against protesting students. Outside the Communist Party hierarchy and the army, many ordinary citizens had bravely tried to stop the carnage by standing in the way of military units as they headed toward Tiananmen Square.

If the United States had exerted maximum economic, diplomatic, and moral pressure on the regime in the weeks before the attack, perhaps it would have buckled like so many other Marxist dictatorships of that era. Or maybe the Chinese government would have had to allow significantly more freedom in order to stay in power. But Bush was no Reagan when it came to challenging communist tyrants. An experienced China hand, Bush had briefly served as America's top diplomat there in the 1970s. When he looked at the Chinese government, he saw an important and delicate relationship to be managed. He pronounced himself "mindful" of "complexities" on what he thought was a path to democracy.[45] Three decades later, the simple truth is that China is not a democracy and its people can only wonder if they will ever enjoy political freedom.

In the immediate aftermath of the massacre, the Chinese people didn't even enjoy expanding *economic* freedom. One of the communist leaders most tolerant of political reform, who had been shoved aside before the crackdown, had unfortunately also been the driver of market reform. "According to the official propaganda, China's ambitious effort to reform its state-dominated economy is alive and well. Don't believe it," reported the *Wall Street Journal*'s Adi Ignatius. "Almost four months after the Beijing massacre, it's apparent that the hard-line stance that brought in tanks and troops to clear Tiananmen Square also has swept away plans to let market forces play a greater role in the economy. China's economy is likely to be mired in its inefficient, half-reformed state for years to come. Key reform programs begun under the now-purged Communist Party chief, Zhao Ziyang, have been scrapped indefinitely." [46]

Fortunately the cause of economic reform did advance, even if the cause of political liberty never did. But many Western observers continued to believe that political change was inevitable. As the Chinese Communist Party prepared to celebrate its seventieth anniversary in 1991, Lena H. Sun of the *Washington Post* reported that "to many Chinese interviewed around this vast country in recent months, the party is suffering a continuing and unprecedented decline in its prestige and moral authority. With communism in retreat around the world and with daily reports of political change in the neighboring

Soviet Union and Eastern Europe, many people say the party here also is fighting a losing ideological battle with its own people."[47] Despite the hopeful news that people were increasingly rejecting Marxist dogma and instead seeking eternal truth at churches and temples, the *Post* report also noted ominously: "With decreasing ideological support from the rank and file, the party is using traditional instruments of control—the security apparatus, the military and the news media—to sustain its hold on power, analysts say."

Two years later Ms. Sun reported that as China's economy boomed, Marxism was being replaced by a belief in making money and a flourishing entrepreneurial culture. She noted that "market forces are eroding central control and authority" but also noted that, according to Amnesty International, government torture of prisoners was increasing.[48]

In that same year, 1993, a *New York Times* headline proclaimed that booming China was a "dream market" for the West. Investment capital was pouring into the country as U.S. brands from Avon to McDonald's were ringing up huge sales. And the communist bosses who continued to cling to political power were also able to enjoy the creations of American capitalists.[49]

"When President Yang Shangkun, a stocky 86-year-old who praises the virtues of self-abnegation, takes a bath these days, he steps into a $7,000 whirlpool tub made by American Standard Inc.," reported Sheryl WuDunn.

"The Communist Party leader, Jiang Zemin, a rotund fellow who likes to talk about self-sufficiency, installed the same model last year in his own bathroom," WuDunn continued.

"The Communist leaders seem to like them, for they ordered eight more, and even inquired whether they could obtain whirlpool bathtubs in which two people could bathe together."[50]

And so it went for decades as the Chinese economy surged ever upward and enticed Western investors. When Maria was a CNBC anchor for years during the boom, the amazing China growth story sometimes seemed like the *only* story for Wall Street analysts sizing up the business plans of U.S. multinationals. Around the world, China was celebrated as *the* model of turbocharged competitive manufacturing.

But on top of this vibrant economy, the Chinese communist dictatorship remained in power. And it was no model of law or liberty.

6

Eyes Wide Open

It might have seemed odd to return from a long medical leave and resume work at a job in Illinois just two days before attempting to fly to China on a one-way ticket. But in February 2007 no one at Motorola knew that their colleague Hanjuan Jin was planning to leave the United States. It wasn't until a call came into company headquarters in Schaumburg, Illinois, the next day that it became clear something was very wrong. Turns out that Jin, who worked as a software engineer for the American telecom manufacturer for nine years, had been stopped and detained during a random security search at O'Hare International Airport. She was carrying $31,000 in cash and 1,300 confidential Motorola documents—many stored on a laptop, external hard drives, thumb drives, and other devices. In the two days before attempting to flee to

China, she had accessed hundreds of technical documents from Motorola's internal network and was recorded leaving the office late at night carrying various items.

In 2012 Jin was convicted and sentenced to four years in prison and fined $20,000 for stealing trade secrets.[1]

U.S. District Judge Ruben Castillo called Jin's actions "a raid in no uncertain terms. It is a raid to steal technology. You conducted this raid in the dead of night when you knew that there was a lesser chance you'd get caught." At Jin's sentencing, the judge said she also possessed confidential Chinese military documents and was identified as an employee of China-based Sun Kaisens, a telecommunications firm that U.S. government officials say develops products for China's armed forces. Prosecutors later said the secrets she carried included descriptions on how Motorola produces a walkie-talkie communications feature. Motorola estimated the stolen data was worth $600 million.[2]

Motorola also investigated Jin's alleged ties to another company, Lemko Corporation, which in turn had a commercial relationship with rising Chinese telecom giant Huawei Technologies. Motorola reported that a number of its Chinese-born former engineers, including Jin, were working for Lemko, a small cellular technology firm that had set up shop down the street from Motorola headquarters in Schaumburg. Motorola alleged in a lawsuit that the employees were sending confidential information to the chairman of Huawei, Ren Zhengfei. The defendants denied the claims and the parties settled the case with no admissions of liability. But Motorola Solutions CEO Greg Brown joined Maria on Fox Business in December 2018 and discussed the case. "Huawei definitely stole trade secrets," said Brown, "and we sued but we subsequently settled."[3] After the Fox Business interview, Motorola retracted Brown's statement. The settlement's terms prevented such comments. But no legal settlement can conceal the curious fact that right after Motorola agreed to stop suing Huawei, the Chinese government gave Motorola a critical regulatory approval the government had been sitting on for months. Coincidence?

More recently, the U.S. government has charged Huawei, founded by a former member of China's People's Liberation Army and now the world's largest telecom company, with a range of offenses, including fraud and conspiracy to steal trade secrets. The company has denied the charges.

You won't often hear a company operating in China criticize the Chinese Communist Party for fear of retribution. But for decades there has been a long list of charges, lawsuits, and indictments brought against Chinese companies for theft of intellectual property or trade secrets. In an interview with Maria in 2018, former Microsoft CEO Steve Ballmer said 90 percent of companies in China are using the Microsoft operating system, although only 1 percent are actually paying for it. Ballmer said the theft has to end. "I'm a free trader, by nature. . . . [I]t's the best thing for the world," Ballmer told Maria on Fox Business. "This one's a tricky issue because it's absolutely clear that the rules don't apply in China, and the U.S. government needs to do something. . . ."[4]

The impact of theft on tech companies and their investors is significant. "Without any pressure from the U.S. government—we're talking about $10 billion plus, for example, in Microsoft that would go into profit," Ballmer said.[5] Getting appropriately paid for its software in China would increase the company's annual earnings by 25 percent.

More than a decade after the Motorola incident, the Chinese Communist Party's espionage and intellectual property theft campaign seems more aggressive than ever. "The ultimate ambition of China's rulers isn't to trade with the United States. It is to raid the United States," said Attorney General Bill Barr in a July 2020 speech. "If you are an American business leader, appeasing the [People's Republic of China] may bring short-term rewards. But in the end, the PRC's goal is to replace you."[6] Soon after Barr's remarks, the U.S. ordered the closure of Beijing's consulate in Houston to protect U.S. intellectual property. The Chinese government ordered the closure of the the U.S. consulate in Chengdu, Sichuan province, in retaliation.

"I'm not seeking anything with China anymore. I'm not seeking anything. I think China's been a one-way street," President Trump tells us. "I think we made a great trade deal, by the way . . . we get $240 billion worth of purchases a year. That's pretty good."[7] He's talking about the "Phase One" trade deal he signed with China in January, which reduced some tariffs on Chinese goods coming into the United States. In return, Beijing reduced some of its tariffs and promised to buy more U.S. agricultural products. The Chinese government also promised some protection for intellectual property.

But a strong commitment under Chinese law to prevent the theft of U.S. inventions and trade secrets—plus a real opening of the Chinese economy to foreign competition—turned out to be deal-breakers in Beijing. The Phase One deal was signed only after a more comprehensive agreement had been reached by negotiators, but it was then rejected by the Chinese regime.

Trump recalls the moment after negotiators struck the original agreement, which included fundamental reforms of China's treatment of U.S. inventions and companies: "I made a deal with China. It was unbelievable. It opened up China. . . . It was done. . . . And then we got a call that, 'We'd like to see you,' meaning my people. So I sent Mnuchin and Lighthizer," the U.S. Treasury secretary and U.S. Trade Representative.[8]

When the Americans met their Chinese counterparts, the communist officials said they could not accept "three or four points" on which they had earlier agreed. The U.S. team then called the president. Trump recalls: "I said, 'Take a walk from the deal. Immediately walk. . . . You don't have to hear the points. Take a walk. Because I know what the points are going to be. You can't go into China.'"

Trump continues: "So they go into this beautiful room, and they have four, you know, boards, everything done very professionally with these people. And one of the boards said, 'We won't do . . . intellectual property. . . . We won't do opening up.' Little thing like opening up China. Oh, I see. We're not going to open it up anymore, right? So that's when we walked away."

Trump says that his Treasury secretary wanted to keep negotiating. According to Trump: "I said, 'No, you're not staying. Get out. Leave.' So we left." The Chinese side then made several calls to restart negotiations. The president says, "They came back. And then I said, 'What the hell? If they're going to pay $250 billion worth of purchases, why shouldn't I take it?' But now, I don't even care about that. . . . I feel much differently toward China than I used to."

Trump adds: "They renegotiated me. I've been renegotiated all my life, so I understand that. But they renegotiated me, just like a Brooklyn real estate developer would do—and a Brooklyn smart, vicious real estate developer. I said, 'Hey, this is no different than Brooklyn.'" All kidding aside, the president's story carries a lesson about Beijing's priorities. The Chinese government was willing to continue to accept U.S. tariffs on Chinese products rather than eliminate theft as a business model. What's kind of scary is that as much as Xi has consolidated power like an old-fashioned communist dictator, Trump suspects that Xi still has to answer to other senior party officials who are even less willing to embrace reform. "I have a feeling that President Xi was overridden by his board of toughies, you know? I actually think that, because he knew everything in that deal. He was fine with it. But I think he was probably overridden by somebody in China," says Trump.[9]

Senior Department of Justice officials say there has recently been an explosion in cases related to economic espionage and China, often exploiting academic and exchange programs to steal research or dupe U.S. professors into sharing valuable intellectual property.

After the order to close the Houston consulate, Justice and State Department officials described a network of People's Liberation Army associates who concealed their military affiliation when applying for student visas here and are supported through Beijing's consulates in the United States. According to

U.S. law enforcement, Chinese officials at the Houston consulate have been directing confederates at a Texas research institution on the most valuable information to collect.

Last year the Justice Department convicted a Houston businessman, Shan Shi, of trade secret theft. He had been operating a subsidiary of a Chinese company in order to acquire a U.S. company's technology used in offshore oil and gas drilling.[10]

FBI director Christopher Wray said in a speech at the Hudson Institute in July 2020, "The people of the United States are the victims of what amounts to Chinese theft on a scale so massive that it represents one of the largest transfers of wealth in human history." This includes not just products Americans create but also information they create about themselves. "If you are an American adult, it is more likely than not that China has stolen your personal data," said Wray. A federal grand jury in Atlanta this year indicted four members of the People's Liberation Army for allegedly hacking into the computer systems of the credit reporting agency Equifax and stealing the personal data of 150 million Americans. The Chinese government denied the charges. In 2014, China's hackers stole more than 21 million records from the U.S. Office of Personnel Management, the agency that manages the government's civilian workforce. Among the sensitive digital documents stolen were forms containing highly personal information gathered in background checks for people seeking government security clearances, along with millions of fingerprint records. In 2015, the records of tens of millions of Anthem Insurance records were swiped by Chinese hackers.

As for the broader Chinese government effort to seize valuable information in the United States, Wray says, "We've reached a point where the FBI is opening a new China-related counterintelligence case approximately every ten hours."[11]

Wray says that China's government has "pioneered an expansive approach to stealing innovation through a wide range of actors—including not just Chinese intelligence services but state-owned enterprises, ostensibly private companies, certain kinds of graduate students and researchers, and a variety of other actors all working on their behalf."[12] The Department of Justice recently brought indictments against two Chinese nationals charged with hacking into American firms pursuing coronavirus research—one of numerous recent prosecutions aimed at thwarting Beijing's attempts to steal U.S. inventions.[13]

In June 2020, Chinese national Hao Zhang was found guilty of economic espionage, theft of trade secrets, and conspiracy in federal court in California. Zhang was convicted of stealing from two separate companies in the semiconductor industry: Avago and Skyworks. The judge found that Zhang planned to steal secrets for the People's Republic of China.[14]

Hongjin Tan, a Chinese national who stole trade secrets valued at more than $1 billion from his former employer, an Oklahoma petroleum company, was convicted and sent to prison earlier this year.

In January the U.S. government charged the chairman of Harvard's chemistry department with fraud for allegedly concealing his involvement with China's Thousand Talents Program, which develops relationships with U.S. academics who possess technical expertise. Charles Lieber pleaded not guilty and immediately went on administrative leave from Harvard. In June the Justice Department indicted him on two counts of making false statements to federal authorities, and in July a grand jury brought a superseding indictment on two counts of making and subscribing a false income tax return and two counts of failing to file reports of foreign bank and financial accounts with the Internal Revenue Service.[15] Lieber, an expert on nanotechnology, has pleaded not guilty on all counts.

He's not the only one facing charges, as the Justice Department has recently indicted academics at a range of American universities and research institutions for alleged crimes related to work with Chinese projects focused on acquiring U.S. technologies.[16]

The effort to get the Chinese government to play by civilized rules goes back through decades of U.S. administrations, although Donald Trump was the first to impose significant consequences for Beijing's actions. Via higher tariffs and sanctions, Trump has been punishing the broken promises and lack of respect for the rule of law. Under the George W. Bush administration, then–Treasury secretary Henry M. Paulson Jr. led the U.S.-China economic dialogue. A former Goldman Sachs CEO, he considered a number of Chinese leaders his friends and sought to assure them during the 2008 financial crisis that the Chinese would recoup the money they invested in bonds backed by the failing U.S. mortgage firms Fannie Mae and Freddie Mac, which were rescued by U.S. taxpayers.

But even Paulson is now sounding more like Trump, saying in a 2018 speech in Singapore:

> The United States played the decisive role in facilitating China's entry into the World Trade Organization.

Yet 17 years after China entered the WTO, China still has not opened its economy to foreign competition in so many areas.

It retains joint venture requirements and ownership limits.

And it uses technical standards, subsidies, licensing procedures, and regulation as non-tariff barriers to trade and investment.

Nearly 20 years after entering the WTO, this is simply unacceptable.

It is why the Trump Administration has argued that the WTO system needs to be modernized and changed. And I agree. . . .

Trade with China has hurt some American workers. And they have expressed their grievances at the ballot box.

So while many attribute this shift to the Trump Administration, I do not.

What we are now seeing will likely endure for some time within the American policy establishment.

China is viewed—by a growing consensus—not just as a strategic challenge to the United States but as a country whose rise has come at America's expense.[17]

The Chinese Communist Party is waging a "generational fight to surpass our country in economic and technological leadership," according to the FBI's Christopher Wray, "but not through legitimate innovation, not through fair and lawful competition, and not by giving their citizens the freedom of thought and speech and creativity we treasure here in the United States. Instead, they've shown that they're willing to steal their way up the economic ladder at our expense."

Wray pointed out that "we see Chinese companies stealing American intellectual property to avoid the hard slog of innovation, and then using it to compete against the very American companies they victimized—in effect, cheating twice over.

"Part of what makes this threat so challenging is that the Chinese are using an expanding set of non-traditional methods—both lawful and unlawful—blending things like foreign investments and corporate acquisitions with things like cyber intrusions and espionage by corporate insiders. Their intelligence services also increasingly hire hacking contractors, who do the government's bidding, to try to obfuscate the connection between the Chinese government and the theft of our data."[18]

Senator Ted Cruz said on *Sunday Morning Futures* on Fox News that this is the first time we are seeing theft of intellectual property "being used as an actual strategy to win the global race to number one."[19]

The FBI's Wray emphasized that "this threat is not about the Chinese people as a whole, and certainly not about Chinese-Americans as a group."[20] But the Chinese government has encouraged "the rob, replicate, and replace approach," said John C. Demers, assistant U.S. attorney general for national security. "You rob the intellectual property, then replicate the product, and then you replace the company on the Chinese market and if all goes well on the global market."[21]

Senator Lindsey Graham (R-S.C.), chairman of the Senate Judiciary Committee and a member of the Senate Foreign Relations Committee, said Trump has changed American policy toward China. "He made a decision that our engagement policy under Nixon has not worked," Graham told Maria. "They are a rogue nation and we need to treat them that way." [22]

The United States has effectively banned equipment from telecom giant Huawei in U.S. telecom networks and pushed for the rest of the world to do the same. Secretary of State Mike Pompeo has traveled the world telling allies: "If you are using Huawei in your telecom infrastructure, the U.S. will be forced to limit the information it shares with you." [23] Since 2012, Huawei has employed Andy Purdy as the chief security officer for its U.S. business. Before getting the job at Huawei, Purdy was on the White House staff during the George W. Bush administration, where he helped draft the U.S. national cybersecurity strategy. Then he went to the Department of Homeland Security where he helped to launch the National Cyber Security Division and then led the U.S. Computer Emergency Readiness Team. He was essentially the senior cybersecurity official in the U.S. government.

Now working for Huawei, Purdy has joined Maria on Fox Business many times and denied any back doors to China in Huawei infrastructure, saying he would not share information even if the communist government asked: "I do not support it and it's not our understanding that we have to turn over all our technology to the Chinese government. That's not what our leadership says." [24] But what Chinese law says is that the company is required to turn over data demanded by the government. Huawei chairman Ren Zhengfei, a member of the Communist Party, claims that "we would rather shut Huawei down than do anything that would damage the interests of our customers to seek our own gains."[25]

In his 2020 speech, Wray noted that China's laws not only allow the government to compel any Chinese company to provide any and all information it requires, but also that this could include American citizens' data, and that Chinese companies are required to have Communist Party "cells" inside the company to keep them in line.[26]

Former Google CEO Eric Schmidt, who chairs a Pentagon innovation board, told the BBC that Huawei appears to be used by the Chinese government to spy. But he still argues that the answer is to compete economically, not to cut off engagement.

"There's no question that Huawei has engaged in some practices that are not acceptable in national security," Mr. Schmidt said. "There's no question that information from Huawei routers has ultimately ended up in hands that would appear to be the state. However that happened, we're sure it happened." Nonetheless, he didn't want to cut off, or "decouple," our tech networks from theirs. "Once you diverge these global platforms, you don't get them back," he observed. "We benefit from having a common platform of interchange . . . and I worry that by building these platforms separate, the countries will understand each other less.

"China's going to dominate whether we couple or decouple. They have the resources, they have the money, they have the technology. The question is do they operate on global platforms or do they operate on their own platforms?

"The more segregated the platforms are, the more dangerous it is."[27]

Concerns about the Chinese government's role in technology
have given way this year to concerns about its role in the spread
of infection. Back in January, just two days after the United
States and China signed the Phase One trade deal, the Trump
administration learned details of a new deadly virus from China
that had escaped its borders and was bound for America—if it
hadn't arrived already.

The Chinese government initially downplayed the coronavirus, failing to tell the world what had happened for critical
weeks. The Chinese Communist Party arrested the Wuhan
doctor who sounded an early warning. Arkansas senator Tom
Cotton questioned the origins of the virus from the start,
because the only level 4 superlab in all of China is located in
Wuhan, not far from the wet markets blamed for the virus.
In that virology lab scientists study coronaviruses along with
other deadly diseases. "Look, they knew in China early on,
probably as early as the early days of December, that this virus
was both highly contagious among humans and it was very
deadly for certain people. Yet they wanted to save face. . . .
They wanted to make sure . . . once they realized this virus
was going to cripple their own economy, that it did not
remain limited to China," he said of the Chinese regime on
Sunday Morning Futures on May 10, 2020.[28]

White House trade adviser Peter Navarro said that, along

with lying about the coronavirus and denying the U.S. Centers for Disease Control entry into China to investigate Covid-19's origins, the Chinese Communist Party also attempted to corner the market on protective gear like masks and gloves while the rest of the world was in desperate need of these items, which are largely made in China. "China has a plan to take us over and take the world over. That's not hyperbole. All you need to do is look at what they're doing," according to Navarro.[29]

The Trump administration called out the reliance on China's manufacturing and prioritized moving supply chains to other countries. Attorney General William Barr said, "We've already seen during the pandemic what it means when they have some leverage over manufacturing of things we need."[30] It was during the coronavirus that many Americans realized that 70 percent of the active ingredients in many prescription drugs are made in China. "We have to address our supply chains in China and move manufacturing back here," said Barr. "But this is even more fundamental than our supply chain. If all our industrial practices and our manufacturing practices are built on a platform that they dominate, they will have ultimate leverage over the West. So, this is a competition for the future."[31]

While the world was dealing with the deadly coronavirus, the Chinese Communist Party seized the opportunity to dominate its region and intimidate its neighbors. In early May, Chinese soldiers killed twenty Indian soldiers in a disputed area along the Himalayan border. Meanwhile the Chinese regime was also breaking the promises it made to allow the people of

Hong Kong to maintain the liberties they have long enjoyed. After months of threats from China, the Communist Party introduced a new security law in Hong Kong that destroyed the city's autonomy and tradition of free speech and forced Hong Kongers to live under the same tyranny as the people of mainland China.

In 1997 the United Kingdom transferred control of Hong Kong to China, on the promise from Beijing that Hong Kong would maintain separate governance and economic systems from China for fifty years. It was called "One country, two systems." Secretary of State Mike Pompeo said on *Mornings with Maria*, "The Chinese Communist Party had entered into an agreement . . . that they would allow Hong Kong to have autonomy for fifty years. Halfway through it or so, they've now broken those commitments, those promises that they made to the world. The United States had a series of preferences. We treated Hong Kong more favorably than we did China for all those years because of that treaty. The Chinese Communist Party has now broken its promise."[32]

Maria called billionaire businessman and democracy activist Jimmy Lai in Hong Kong. The founder of New Digital in Hong Kong was on the front lines of the daily protests. "Xi Jinping is just taking advantage of the pandemic to deal aggressively with the world, especially to deal with the Hong Kong rebellion. He thinks this time the whole world is in a crisis— that he can have the space and room to take Hong Kong without other countries reacting to it. We are fighting a war for freedom. We are fighting your war. Please help us," said Lai.[33]

He was arrested and jailed several times after her first interview with him.

In 2019 Hong Kongers took to the streets every day for months to push back on China's authoritarianism. "After the three-month confrontation with the government, we know that the Beijing government is not going to give us any room for freedom," Lai stated. "They are trying to take away our freedom, our rule of law, the way of life that we have had, and the only way we can do is to go on and persist, to fight for it. Or whether we can win and eventually get a universal suffrage, we don't know. But what we know is if we don't—if we don't fight—we will lose all we have and we will lose the freedom, the rule of law, the way of life, all that we have. We have no way but to fight."[34]

Lai noted that things got much harder when Xi Jinping was promoted to dictator for life. Lai expects the Chinese government to continue tightening the screws on Hong Kong. "It is a cold war. It's a war of opposing values. Let's look at the world twenty years from now. Do we want our children to live in the dominance of the Chinese dictatorship values, or do we want to continue the values we have enjoyed? Because definitely, in twenty years, China is going to be the biggest economy in the world if we don't stop them and try to let them learn that the authority to earn from moral force is a much greater force than you earn from using the barrel of gun."[35]

The regime is also abusing the rights of people within the borders of China. Pompeo has called out the Communist Party for the more than 1 million Uighurs, Muslim Chinese citizens, locked up in internment camps in the Xinjiang region: "There are also enormous humanitarian concerns we've seen, as they continue to collect information and use it in ways that are antithetical to what you and I understand about how human beings are to be treated. . . . These million Uighurs . . . are in these terrible situations in these camps in one of the provinces. . . . The complete absence of political freedom inside of this country is something that the American people need to continue to see. . . . They are not allowing these people to move freely." The regime has spent decades repressing another religious minority, the Buddhists in Tibet.[36]

Many in Congress have introduced legislation to try to hold China accountable. Senator John Kennedy (R-La.) said on *Sunday Morning Futures* in July, "What the Chinese Communist Party has done to the Tibetans and the Uighurs is despicable. All the Tibetans and the Uighurs want to do is practice their religion. And the Communist Party of China says, 'Your religion is the Communist Party of China' "[37]

Outside its borders, the regime is claiming for itself international waters of the South China Sea, seeking to dominate a sea lane which carries much of the world's trade. According to retired U.S. Army General Jack Keane, "What you see going on in the South China Sea—harassment, intimidation, they want to call that piece of water theirs. They have no international right to it whatsoever, they planted some artificial islands, and now they claim that's part of China."[38]

Around the world, the Chinese Communist Party is also pursuing a more subtle campaign to exert influence and control by offering countries attractive financing and low-cost infrastructure. Representative Nunes told Maria that "they're moving in . . . first with leverage, like loaning money, building infrastructure . . . And my warning to a lot of our allies in the countries that I meet with is, 'Look, there's nothing for free.'"[39]

Keane added of the Chinese communists, "They are building a deep water port in Pakistan. Why is that? For their navy to impose influence and control on India and the Indian Ocean. They have a navy base at Djibouti. Why is that? To impose influence and control in the Middle East, where 62 percent of their oil passes through the Gulf of Hormuz. . . . So yes, China's influence is economic, to be sure, but it's also becoming a global military power."[40]

The administration has urged corporate America in particular to think beyond the prospect of selling to a billion people and instead focus on the the risks of working with a communist dictatorship. "The American business community has been a big part of the problem because they're willing ultimately, many of them, to sacrifice the long-term viability of their companies for short-term profit so they can get their stock options and move into the golf resort. That's what's driving some of this. They're not taking the long-term view and the national view," Attorney General William Barr told Maria in an interview in May 2020.[41]

But for decades we have spoken to many CEOs and managers of global businesses who have looked to grow their businesses by selling to this huge emerging market with its vast population, climbing the economic ladder. One investor told us: "I'm not political. It's not my role to call out good guys and bad guys. The growth is in China and that's where I want to invest."[42]

Upon hearing the comment, Barr responded, "Well, you know what? We're not speaking German today because American business in the past didn't think that way. It stood with the United States and all the privileges and the benefits and the stability. And the rule of law and the ability to profit as they do, both as companies and individuals, comes from the strength of this country. But we are clearly cracking down on researchers and others that are sent over here to get involved in our key technological programs. And this is not just weapons systems." Barr told us the theft is happening across the U.S. innovation landscape. "This is agriculture. This is medicine. This is robotics. This is artificial intelligence. And so it's the whole gamut of important technologies going forward. Chinese efforts run the gamut from more traditional espionage of recruiting people to work for them explicitly to cultivating relationships that they've been able to use. And the people frequently are not completely attuned to the fact that they are being used as essentially stooges for the Chinese. So it runs the gamut of things. And sometimes some of these high-sounding programs are used to the advantage of the Chinese. So the American business community—we need their understanding of the nature of the problem right now."[43]

An operator of a giant U.S. hedge fund who does business in China tells us that "there are not laws in the same way in China. In other words, who knows what it is? It's like: You do what you get away with and you can't do what you can't get away with."

The hedge fund operator adds of China, "I think it's a big threat but I think it's a natural evolution, if you look at rises and declines of empires. You know, Germany was a threat to the UK. Japan was a threat to the world. The Dutch were a threat to the Spanish. And so there is a rise and of course there is a threat. Right now time is on China's side. Time is against the United States."

There are efforts in the White House and Congress to stop big investor pools of money, such as federal retirement plans, from investing in Chinese companies, such as those under U.S. sanctions, are building weapons for the Chinese military, or will be used to surveil the Uighur community. The Pentagon has compiled a list of companies with ties to China's military, including two groups listed on the New York Stock Exchange, as part of an effort to make it harder for China to secure U.S. investment and sensitive technologies. President Trump stopped the main U.S. government pension fund, which holds the retirement money for military personnel past and present, from investing in Chinese companies that may be building weapons for the Chinese military. The twenty companies spotlighted by the Pentagon include Huawei and Hikvision, which supplies surveillance technology to the detention camps for the Muslim Uighurs. A Hikvision representative has stated that "all our business is required to align with the company's compliance policy."[44] The fund had earmarked 10 percent of its $600 billion in assets under management (AUM) to invest in the Morgan Stanley Capital International index, but the president stopped it because of the inclusion of the Chinese companies in that index. White House economic adviser Larry

Kudlow and National Security Adviser Robert C. O'Brien then sent a letter to the U.S. Railroad Retirement Board warning its managers against investing in Chinese companies on behalf of railroad workers' retirement benefits, saying the trust it oversees is exposing investors to undue economic risk and endangering U.S. national security because it invests in certain Chinese companies. James spoke to Kudlow a few days later. "I certainly don't want American investors to invest in the Chinese military," Kudlow said.

The letter, dated July 7, 2020, was the latest action the Trump administration has taken to curtail U.S. investment in China, specifically companies building weapons for the Chinese military. Those companies, by the way, do not follow the same accounting rules as American companies, something Florida senator Marco Rubio and Senator John Kennedy pushed to change. Kennedy introduced a bill, cosponsored by Senator Chris Van Hollen (D-Md.) and Senator Kevin Cramer (R-N.D.), to force Chinese companies to follow the accounting rules of this country or be prevented from trading on U.S. exchanges. The bill, which passed in the Senate, would give the Chinese companies three years to comply.

When we spoke with President Trump in July, after more than 100,000 Americans had died of coronavirus and the country was facing a severe contraction with millions of Americans out of work, the president was way beyond the niceties displayed at that Mar-a-Lago dinner three years earlier.

"It's a hostile country. It's a country that's taken advantage of the U.S. for many years," President Trump said of China. He was speaking to us on the telephone in July 2020. Chinese buyers had begun dramatically increasing their purchases of U.S. corn and soybeans, but Trump wasn't celebrating. He suspected that recent attempts to fulfill the promises of his "Phase One" trade deal signed with China in January are only occurring because "they know that I'm on the verge of saying, 'Go f—— yourself and I don't want your G-damn trade deal.'"

After the Chinese regime repeatedly lied about the deadly virus it had loosed upon the world—and the United States had sacrificed trillions of dollars trying to contain it—Trump professed no interest in communicating with Chinese dictator Xi Jinping. "I don't speak to him much anymore. I purposely don't want to speak," says the president. "You know, I don't want to be the schmuck that talks to him: 'How is everything? How's the world?'"

Trump's language is crude but he was no doubt expressing the views of countless others in this miserable year of pandemic. And he has mobilized much of the U.S. government to counter the Chinese Communist Party's myriad hostile actions, which are the true obscenity.

There's a media cliché that dismisses Trump policy as ignorant populism for factory workers in Middle America. But what's clear now is that the president has won the intellectual argument on China by exposing the failure of a policy pursued by both parties for nearly half a century. This doesn't mean he's won the argument for tariffs generally or for more government intervention in cross-border commerce. But he's forced the U.S. political and business elite to acknowledge that a communist dictatorship pursuing theft as a business model is not free trade. Trump has also forced an acknowledgment that economic engagement has failed to bring democracy and liberty to the Chinese people or security to China's neighbors.

A CEO of a large U.S. financial institution tells us that by changing American policy and imposing tariffs on China, the president got results. "I would not have done that myself, but it worked. And anyone who says it didn't work is not being fair," says the CEO. "Trump brought them to the table with tariffs. And I was told that by top Chinese people: 'He got us to the table.'"[45]

For decades, U.S. business leaders have feared reprisals from the Chinese government if they explain how badly the regime treats their companies. American CEOs also didn't want to buck the Washington–Wall Street consensus that engagement with China was virtually an unmitigated benefit for business growth and economic vitality. Many business leaders talked about inventions and trade secrets getting stolen in China—but only in private.

Says the financial CEO: "President Trump has been talking about it for quite a long time. I think a lot of people kind of ignored it for too long. We should have been much tougher on China, like going way back to Clinton."

As a presidential candidate in 1992, Bill Clinton certainly talked a big game about confronting the communist regime in

Beijing. He accused the incumbent, President George H. W. Bush, of sending "secret emissaries to raise a toast with those who crushed democracy" in Tiananmen Square.[46]

After Clinton's election as president, the tough talk continued, at least for a few months. Writing in 1998, Carl M. Cannon of the *National Journal* reviewed the sad history of Clinton's attempts to hold China's communists to account: "In March of 1993, Clinton dispatched a letter to Beijing listing 14 areas in which he wanted to see improvement in return for his Administration's support for continued Most-Favored-Nation trading status for China. Incensed, Chinese leaders fired back a letter listing seven areas in which they wanted to see changes in American policy." In May of that year, Clinton announced that he would extend MFN for another year even though his conditions hadn't been met.[47]

The following year Clinton again made a series of requests tied to the renewal of China's most-favored-nation trading status. China's communist regime rejected those, too, but once again Clinton approved the trade relationship. Cannon observed: "A pattern had been established for the Clinton era. Washington gives Beijing a shove, Beijing shoves back, harder. Washington says: Let's shake hands and be friends."

By 1996 the relationship had gotten scandalously friendly when a Chinese arms dealer named Wang Jun attended a fundraising coffee with Clinton at the White House. Clinton later blamed the White House vetting system, and Democrats had to return various illicit contributions tied to the People's Republic.

After a 1998 visit to China, Clinton imagined or pretended—like so many other U.S. politicians from both parties—that democracy and freedom were just around the corner in China: "I visited a village that chooses its own leaders in free elections. I saw cell phones and computers carrying ideas, information, and images around the world. I had the opportunity to talk directly to the Chinese people through national television about why we value human rights and individual freedom so highly. I joined more than 2,000 people in worship in a Beijing church. I spoke to the next generation of China's leaders at Beijing University; to people working for change in law, academia, business, and the arts; to average Chinese during a radio call-in show."[48]

What now seems an especially bitter irony is that Clinton was sharing his happy talk about his visit to the Chinese mainland in a place that is currently being relentlessly pulled under the yoke of Beijing's tyranny. The president said, "Here in Hong Kong we end the trip where I hope China's future begins, a place where free expression and free markets flourish under the rule of law."[49]

Clinton also had plenty of kind words for the Chinese leadership and their wisdom and intellect. A year later a declassified version of a top secret report from the U.S. House Select Committee on U.S. National Security/Military Commercial Concerns with the People's Republic of China was released. The report from Chairman Christopher Cox's committee reads in part:

> The People's Republic of China (PRC) has stolen design information on the United States' most advanced thermonuclear weapons.

The Select Committee judges that the PRC's next generation of thermonuclear weapons, currently under development, will exploit elements of stolen U.S. design information. . . .

The stolen U.S. nuclear secrets give the PRC design information on thermonuclear weapons on a par with our own. . . .

The stolen information also includes classified design information for an enhanced radiation weapon (commonly known as the "neutron bomb"), which neither the United States, nor any other nation, has yet deployed. . . .

The W-88, a miniaturized, tapered warhead, is the most sophisticated nuclear weapon the United States has ever built. In the U.S. arsenal, it is mated to the D-5 submarine-launched ballistic missile carried aboard the Trident nuclear submarine. The United States learned about the theft of the W-88 Trident D-5 warhead information, as well as about the theft of information regarding several other nuclear weapons, in 1995.[50]

After all the misplaced hopes about China among U.S. politicians over the years, the United States fortunately remains in a strong competitive position. JPMorgan Chase chairman Jamie Dimon's firm serves clients in more than one hundred countries. In December 2019 the Chinese government gave JPMorgan Chase permission to hold majority ownership of its Chinese securities business. U.S. banks will receive more freedom to operate there if the Chinese government honors the Phase One deal it signed with Trump. Dimon cautions against overstating the challenge presented by China, telling us, "We should want China to grow peacefully and for it to prosper. It's good for the world and good for China's people if they do succeed. But keep in mind, and I don't say this disrespectfully, that they don't have enough food, water, or energy right now. They don't have our transparency. They don't have our financial markets. There is a significant amount of corruption. They don't have our peaceful neighbors and the security of the Atlantic and Pacific oceans. Their neighbors are very, very tough and complicated, including Afghanistan, Kazakhstan, Vietnam, Pakistan, India, Russia, Japan, North Korea, Mongolia. Their demographics are tough."

On this last point he's referring to China's rapidly aging citizenry. The regime brutally enforced a one-child-per-family policy for decades in an attempt to control its population. The result is that China's working-age population peaked several years ago and will continue to decline.

Is he concerned about Chinese banks stealing JPMorgan Chase's tech and taking market share? "The Chinese banks will be global competitors. They're around the world now. But banks like ours still lead in terms of capability—the ability to move money, research, technology, advice, [artificial intelligence], machine learning. But as long as the Chinese compete fairly, I think that that's fine. I'm one of those people who thinks America shouldn't be afraid of the competition from China or anywhere. It makes us all better."

Dimon adds, "Our infrastructure, our schools, our military, our economy—this country is far ahead in terms of innovation, growth, and capability; it's staggering. Of course, they want to catch up, and we shouldn't fear that. The only thing that's going to hurt us is us. And when I look at what's hurt us the most, it's our own bad policy: regulatory, tax, legal, infrastructure, inner-city schools and education, health care. That's what has hurt us the most. Not the Chinese."[51]

Clearly there will be costs to using economic tools to counter the Chinese Communist Party. Technology investor Dan Niles notes that U.S. multinational companies have a love-hate relationship with China, because they're often forced to share their technology, but feel they need to be selling to Chinese consumers. "Because they're the number one buyer of personal computers in the world. They're the number one buyer of smartphones in the world. They're the number one buyer of autos in the world. You know, you go down the list, they're number one in a lot of categories." Niles adds that virtually all large U.S. companies "to some extent or another do count on China for growth."[52]

A leader of one American multinational, speaking on background, offers a recommendation on dealing with China: "I would just very maturely tighten the noose through tariffs, [a trade agreement with other Pacific countries], doing better treaties with the UK and Europe and Japan and Korea. And basically tell the Chinese: 'These are the new terms of trade. You can be part of the trading system or you don't have to be part of the trading system. You pick.' Also, I think a lot of companies on their own are going to be making changes to have more resilience in supply lines and not rely just on one supply line. . . . I think America should be very tough on the standard of [intellectual property] and anything that makes unfair competition at this point—but maturely. You know, China doesn't want to be cut off from trade with the rest of the world." The CEO notes that the U.S. has a strong advantage in rallying other countries to counter Beijing: "The world wants America. For however much we've pissed people off, when we reach our hands out to, you know, Europeans or Asians, it's like, 'Thank God.' America has been the beacon of hope—for all our mistakes—the beacon of hope. The true blue."

The CEO adds, that "if we think Huawei is a legitimate national security issue—and all of the national security people say absolutely—then we should take legitimate national security actions. Like we've done. That's all. You don't have to breathe too hard over that one."

And if the government of China misbehaves? "Get tighter and tougher," adds the CEO. "And punish 'em. If they do cyber stuff, I hope we're doing it back. I hope we're doing it back to Russia, too. And my view with China and Russia would be 'Hey, if you do it here, buddy, whatever you do here, we'll do it three times there.' And I mean three times. Fight fire with fire a little bit. But I don't want to overdo it. I think that, for the most part, they are rational actors in the world. They are very long term. They're very strategic. They want their rightful place in the world. There's nothing wrong with that. They have a very tough road ahead of 'em. Much tougher than you think. And dominating America is, you know, in my view, unless America is completely stupid—which we are of course sometimes—there's no chance. Not in the lifetime of any American . . ."[53]

Meanwhile from the White House, Trump told us that "a decoupling is not the worst thing in the world."[54]

7

The Media's Trump Boom

In August 2016, Jim Rutenberg wrote in the *New York Times* that if you're a journalist who believes the worst about Donald Trump, "you have to throw out the textbook American journalism has been using for the better part of the past half-century" and "move closer than you've ever been to being oppositional."[1] That line must have gotten a chuckle out of the paper's few remaining conservative readers—as if the *Times* had always played it straight until Trump came along. But it was a watershed moment because it was a front-page story acknowledging—and excusing—biased coverage against a candidate whom the majority of reporters had deemed unacceptable.

Mr. Rutenberg then devoted several paragraphs to the possibility that Trump would start a nuclear war. The article also oddly appealed to the authority of MSNBC host Joe Scarborough, who "said he was concerned that Mr. Trump was becoming increasingly erratic, and asked rhetorically, 'How balanced do you have to be when one side is just irrational?' "[2]

The story was controversial when it was published and would be even harder to defend today. With the benefit of hindsight we know that the hysteria about Trump as a warmonger was unfounded and that the greatest federal abuse of the era was committed *against* Trump, not *by* him. At the time that Rutenberg was working on his story, FBI officials were throwing out the textbook of American law enforcement and being "oppositional" to a presidential candidate and the rule of law.

According to the inspector general of the Department of Justice, August of 2016 was the month the FBI started collecting exculpatory evidence on Trump supporter Carter Page that would not be shared with the Foreign Intelligence Surveillance Act (FISA) court—neither in the government's initial application to wiretap him in October 2016 nor in any of the three renewals.[3]

On the day that Rutenberg's story appeared on the front page of the *New York Times*, the following text exchange occurred between two FBI officials:

> Lisa Page: "[Trump's] not ever going to become president, right? Right?!"
> Peter Strzok: "No. No, he's not. We'll stop it."[4]

Were the FBI paramours at the center of the Crossfire Hurricane case perhaps inspired by the *Times* to abandon the standards of their own profession? One thing we know is that the *Times* argument carried the day among the press corps. Whether inspired by Mr. Rutenberg or not, reporters and producers covering Trump generally agreed to cast aside traditional notions of fairness and objectivity. So began an era of commercial success and journalistic failure in the American media.

Five months after the *Times* and FBI officials raised the question of abandoning their standards in order to stop Trump, their trade hadn't yielded much of a return. Trump had won a stunning election victory. And despite an aggressive surveillance campaign involving confidential sources secretly recording Trump associates and numerous misrepresentations to the FISA court, the FBI had not only come up dry; it was collecting many reasons to doubt the claims in the Steele dossier—the heart of its probable cause argument—and mounting exculpatory evidence for the Trump associates it had targeted for investigation.

The early weeks of January 2017 were officially part of the presidential transition between the Obama and Trump administrations. But they can also be seen as the period when the Obama administration, having failed to generate evidence of collusion, referred the case to friends in the U.S. media, where evidentiary standards were lower and even a failed investigation could be used to damage the new president.

The deceptions inflicted on the FISA court would be rivaled by those FBI director James Comey inflicted on Donald Trump. By October 2016, Comey's FBI had heard from another government agency—but did not share with the FISA court—that Carter Page had served as an operational contact for U.S. intelligence. This undermined the central Steele claim that Page was at the center of some kind of conspiracy between Russia and the Trump campaign.[5] The FBI had learned from Steele himself that a key sub-source for his claims was a "boaster" who "may engage in some embellishment."[6] The FBI had also learned that Steele had falsely claimed to them that he only shared his reporting with the FBI and Fusion GPS, his client funded by Democrats. The FBI also knew—but again did not share with the FISA court—that Carter Page had been recorded without his knowledge telling a confidential source that he had never met a number of the people Steele claimed that he had.[7]

Then in early November 2016 the FBI dismissed Steele as a confidential source after he broke protocol by disclosing his work and his relationship with the FBI while serving as an anonymous source for a magazine article. The outlet was the left-wing publication *Mother Jones*.[8]

But the FBI still wanted to use Steele's claims to maintain the bureau's anti-Trump surveillance. After the FBI fired Steele, he was able to continue feeding the bureau his anti-Trump material via Department of Justice attorney Bruce Ohr, whose wife had worked for Fusion GPS, the firm which had been paid by Democrats to get dirt on Trump and had hired Steele for this purpose.[9]

At a meeting in November of 2016 with FBI officials overseeing the Crossfire Hurricane investigation, Ohr specifically told them that Steele's material was going to the Hillary Clinton presidential campaign. Ohr also reported that Steele was "desperate that Donald Trump not get elected and was passionate about him not being the U.S. President." [10]

In November and December of that year the FBI interviewed overseas contacts who had worked with Steele in the past and received mixed reviews, including specific references to Steele's "poor judgment." [11]

But even though the FBI could not corroborate any of Steele's key claims, continued to collect evidence contradicting them, continued to learn reasons to doubt his motivations and his judgment, and had fired him as a confidential source, the leadership of the FBI would not stop promoting his dossier.

Having misled the FISA court, the bureau then sought to place Steele's claims at the center of the U.S. intelligence community's upcoming assessment of Russia's role in U.S. elections. In December the FBI disseminated Steele's material across the U.S. intelligence community, and senior FBI officials sent notes to colleagues at other agencies calling Steele "reliable." [12]

In a December 17, 2016, memo to a number of bureau colleagues, FBI director James Comey reported that the previous night he had told Director of National Intelligence James Clapper that the FBI thought it was "important" to include Steele's claims in the intelligence report and that Steele "appears to be a credible person with a source and sub-source network in position to report on such things, but we could not vouch for the material. (I said nothing further about the source or our efforts to verify.)" [13] Was it too much to ask that Comey at least mention that the FBI was no longer willing to do business with this source that it kept promoting as reliable?

It makes sense that Comey didn't want to say anything further about Steele or the FBI's verification efforts. To say anything more would have made it nearly impossible to maintain the position that the reporting was credible. For years since, Comey has continued to not want to say anything further. When questioned about Steele—the man whose dubious work Comey had sold to the chief of U.S. intelligence—at a 2018 joint executive session of the House Judiciary and Oversight Committees, Comey would present himself as only vaguely aware of Steele, his work, and his funders.[14]

But back in December of 2016, Comey's FBI was attempting to make Steele's unverified claims the consensus view on Trump and Russia. The CIA dismissed Steele's claims as "internet rumor" but Comey's FBI deputy director Andrew McCabe took the lead in insisting that they be included in the intelligence community's assessment on Russia and U.S. elections that would be presented to President Obama and President-elect Trump in January.[15] Faced with skepticism from others in the U.S. intelligence community, the FBI accepted a compromise in which the dossier material was not included in the main body of the report but appeared in an appendix.[16]

One can only imagine how skeptical the intelligence community, not to mention the judges of the FISA court, would have been if the FBI had shared all its evidence contradicting Steele. The bureau had already collected more than enough information to dismiss the claims as internet rumor or worse.

The point is that the Steele dossier was injected into public discussion only after it had become untenable as the basis for legitimate surveillance. People in our industry like to think that investigative reporting by media organizations shines a light on hidden abuses. But the press corps was about to become the last-ditch tool for the abusers after all of their other tools had failed to deliver their politically desired result.

At the start of 2017, Steele's claims weren't the only ones that could no longer be sustained. Another element of the anti-Trump case was also collapsing. We now know that by Wednesday, January 4, 2017, FBI agents had drafted an order closing the case on Trump's national security adviser, retired lieutenant general Michael Flynn, after finding no evidence to support any charges against him. We know that they were ordered not to close the case by FBI leadership. And we know that according to notes taken by the FBI's Peter Strzok around the time of a White House meeting the next day—Thursday, January 5, 2017—Comey knew there was nothing incriminating in Flynn's recent telephone calls with the Russian ambassador.

Strzok's notes also show Vice President Joe Biden raising the idea of using the Logan Act against General Flynn, essentially proposing a stunning abuse of power. The law, more than two centuries old, is never enforced because it is likely unconstitutional. It was enacted way back in 1799 after George Logan, a Pennsylvania physician and farmer, conducted his own personal diplomacy in an effort to broker a peace agreement between the United States and France. His political opponents in Washington drafted the law, which purported to make it a crime for a private citizen to communicate with a foreign government to influence its conduct in a dispute with the United States. It has long been recognized as a clear violation of the First Amendment's guarantee of free speech. This is why no one has ever been convicted of violating it. Even in its own time the law was widely viewed as a paranoid overreaction to Logan's peace initiative. Pennsylvania issued its own verdict on the matter by electing Dr. Logan to the U.S. Senate in 1800, the year after the law's enactment.

If Strzok's notes are accurate, there's no excuse for Biden's conduct—suggesting an unconstitutional criminal prosecution of the incoming White House national security adviser on the grounds that he didn't agree with the policies of the Obama administration. But the Logan Act abuse seems to have helped keep the Flynn investigation alive. The FBI ended up fooling General Flynn into having a discussion about his recent calls with the Russian ambassador without telling Flynn he was the target of an investigation. Comey would later brag that he probably wouldn't have gotten away with sending FBI agents into the Flynn investigation in a more organized administration. The government then prosecuted Flynn, claiming that he lied in suggesting to the FBI that he hadn't discussed sanctions with the Russian ambassador, even though FBI agents said at the time they didn't think he had lied.

In truth it was none of the FBI's business what policies the incoming national security adviser chose to discuss with foreign officials. And the 2020 release of the call transcripts showed that Flynn appeared to be mainly discussing the expulsion of diplomatic personnel, not the sanctions that had been announced around the same time. The Justice Department dropped the charges in 2020.

But back on January 5, 2017, as Strzok's records make clear, the FBI had no reason to investigate General Flynn and senior officials *knew* they had no reason to investigate him. By then the Steele dossier had also been exposed as unfounded gossip or worse. The collusion case was dead. What happened next may be viewed as FBI director James Comey converting the anti-Trump investigative campaign into an anti-Trump media campaign.

That same day Comey and the intelligence chiefs briefed President Obama on their assessment of Russian activities related to the 2016 U.S. elections. The next morning, January 6, 2017, the group briefed congressional leaders on the same subject and then in the afternoon visited Trump Tower in New York to share the assessment with the president-elect.

After the briefing, the intelligence chiefs left, but Comey stayed behind and told Trump about outlandish Steele tales involving alleged Trump sexual activities. Now, why would Comey choose that moment to share dubious Steele claims with the president-elect? Trump had been elected in early November. In the two months since, the FBI had found nothing to corroborate the stories and numerous reasons to doubt them. Do agencies typically withhold information from the president until they can be confident it's false?

According to an email Comey sent to colleagues after the meeting, the material he described to Trump was "inflammatory stuff." He added that a news organization "would get killed for reporting straight up from the source reports." The inspector general notes, "In testimony before Congress, Comey has described this part of his email as communicating that 'it was salacious and unverified material that a responsible journalist wouldn't report without corroborating in some way.'" Comey told the IG "that he informed President-elect Trump that the FBI did not know whether the allegations were true or false and that the FBI was not investigating them."[17]

This last part was false. The FBI had indeed been trying to confirm the Steele claims and found only reasons to doubt them. But Comey was being honest about one thing: he clearly understood that no responsible journalist would publish Steele's unverified material unless there was some concrete government action justifying coverage—such as intelligence briefings to the president and president-elect.

Four days after Comey met with Trump, CNN reported that the intelligence assessment included the Steele rumors in the addendum. The same day, January 10, 2017, a website called BuzzFeed published the Steele dossier. BuzzFeed's Ben Smith admitted the information was unverified but justified publication on the grounds that the material was the subject of discussion among government officials.[18]

CNN merely described the dossier without publishing it but the network used the same excuse as BuzzFeed. "CNN would not have done a story about the dossier's existence if it hadn't learned that intelligence officials had considered it so important that [they] told Trump about it, the network's Wolf Blitzer said," according to the Associated Press.[19]

As the FBI well knew, Steele had been spreading his tales to media people for months, but major outlets had chosen not to publish or broadcast them because they couldn't be corroborated. Comey's email to colleagues makes clear that he also knew the media establishment would steer clear—unless somebody like him gave them a related event they could use as an excuse to run the salacious rumors.

CNN's dive into the dossier made clear that the news they were reporting was that the rumors had been shared along with the intelligence assessment. As would be true for years, the story was not that anyone had actually found evidence of collusion or Trump being compromised by the Russians—they hadn't and never would. But it was enough for CNN and others that important people in government were discussing the possibility. The story was the investigation itself rather than the underlying substance, which the FBI already knew didn't amount to much.

On January 10, 2017, CNN's Jake Tapper stated explicitly that "a lot of these allegations have been out there before. We haven't reported on them. We haven't discussed them, but what changed is the fact the intelligence officials, these senior intelligence officials brought them to this level of saying, hey, President-elect Trump, you should know about this." [20]

While CNN did note that the claims were uncorroborated, the network's Jim Sciutto stated, "Let's be clear here. You have U.S. intelligence agencies. They have not corroborated this, but are not dismissing these allegations, right? They are not, in effect, treating them as fake news." [21]

In fact the CIA had already dismissed them as "Internet rumor." [22] But by this point why would anyone expect an anonymous leak to CNN to be more honest than a FISA warrant application? The CNN report continued with a discussion between the network's Tapper and Evan Perez:

TAPPER: And, Evan, some of this information was floated last year. Then–Senate Majority Leader Harry sent a blistering letter in October to the FBI director saying that he possessed explosive information about communications between the Trump campaign and the Russian government. Today, now-retired senator Harry Reid said that his statements speak for themselves. What changed? Why is this now elevated?

PEREZ: Well, we now know that Harry Reid is saying this is exactly what he was talking about when he sent those letters. We know the FBI has been busy looking at allegations, including the allegations that there have been surrogates of the Donald Trump campaign who were in touch with intermediaries of the Russian government. Now, none of this has been proven. None of this has gone anywhere, in part because of the election. The FBI had to put a lot on hold and on simmer so to speak until after the election.[23]

A casual viewer might have been fooled into thinking that the report was some sort of vindication for Harry Reid, because he, too, had been flogging the same unfounded rumors. A casual viewer would also have been misled if he thought the dossier hadn't been confirmed simply because the FBI was somehow prevented by the political calendar from evaluating the Steele claims. In fact the FBI had collected a substantial amount of evidence suggesting they were false. Such evidence either never made it to CNN or the network ignored it.

That night on MSNBC, anchor Rachel Maddow introduced the story as "news broken by CNN tonight and then bolstered later by Buzzfeed." Bolstered? Both organizations admitted they had no idea whether the dossier claims were true or false. Maddow went on to describe the "alleged dirt that the Russians allegedly say they allegedly have on Donald Trump . . . that they allegedly used to allegedly cultivate him as basically a Russian asset who would do what they want because he knew what embarrassing stuff they had on him." Like CNN and BuzzFeed, she also acknowledged having no idea whether the dirt she was promoting was true or not. But she still had fun imagining the possibilities. Said Maddow:

"If it is true, of course, and Donald Trump is a Russian agent and knows he is one that's the story of the century. If it isn't true, it's nevertheless the biggest possible distraction at a time when things are already really wobbly for the incoming administration and this historically unpopular president-elect."[24]

In other words, regardless of the truth, it would be presented as bad news for Trump. According to Maddow, the story meant that he was either a Russian asset or he was a wobbly and unpopular president-elect facing a big distraction. The duly elected president would be damaged in either scenario.

Now that we know he was actually the victim of a partisan abuse of federal law enforcement powers to counteract the will of American voters, isn't *that* the story of the century?

On that night in January of 2017, Maddow interviewed NBC correspondent Richard Engel, who raised the question of why the intelligence community would drop the dossier material "like a bomb on president-elect Trump." Mr. Engel then provided an answer:

"I was told by a senior intelligence source that the reason they did it is the intelligence community is angry, the intelligence community effectively wants to put him on notice saying, look, you are saying all these things about Russia, be careful, there are all these allegations out there. Are any of them true? And I was told, 'We can't help you, Mr. Trump, unless you tell us more. We need more input.'" [25]

Our duly elected president is supposed to prove to officials of the outgoing presidential administration that he's not a Russian agent? Of course, they already knew there was no evidence he was. But leaving aside the corrupt and dishonest machinations of senior Obama administration officials, isn't the role of a free press to blow the whistle on such abuse? Maddow and many of her media colleagues spent the next few years applauding it.

And, in turn, anti-Trump FBI officials were applauding the useful media coverage. On the night the news broke, Peter Strzok texted Lisa Page to report that he was with a colleague watching CNN and added: "Hey let me know when you can talk. We're discussing whether, now that this is out, we use it as a pretext to go interview some people." [26]

If the target is anyone but Trump, how do most media people feel about cops being so comfortable employing leaked rumors against their targets that they put *in writing* that they are using them as a pretext to investigate?

FBI boss Jim Comey, for his part, wasn't done with dossier deceptions. The day after the CNN and BuzzFeed stories, January 11, 2017, Comey emailed Director of National Intelligence Clapper to urge him not to say in a public release, "The

[Intelligence Community] has not made any judgment that the information in [the Steele election reporting] is reliable. . . ." Comey wrote:

> *I say that because we HAVE concluded that the source [Steele] is reliable and has a track record with us of report-ing reliable information; we have some visibility into his source network, some of which we have determined to be sub-sources in a position to report on such things; and much of what he reports in the current document is consis-tent with and corroborative of other reporting included in the body of the main [Intelligence Community] report.[27]*

Washington political operators like Comey are not known for being forthright, but this one could go down in the annals of deceptive bureaucratic memo making. His short note directly contradicted the evidence his own bureau had been collecting for months. That same day Comey wasn't any more honest in a phone call with President-elect Trump. The Justice Depart-ment inspector general notes:

> *They discussed a media report that had disclosed the "sala-cious" information, and Trump's concern about how that had been "leaked." Comey said that, among other things, he remembered telling Trump that the source of the infor-mation was "not a government document, and it's not classified." Comey also remembered telling Trump that to "speak of it as a leak doesn't make sense" because "a lot of people in Washington had [the information]," and Comey*

said he told Trump that he had previously warned Trump that it might soon be published by the media.[28]

As Comey's own correspondence shows, he was well aware that serious news outlets would *not* run with the Steele rumors unless they had a hook—like leaked news that someone like Comey had somehow managed to get unverified rumors added as an attachment to a presidential briefing.

To clarify, this report from the inspector general was not included in his work showing how Comey's FBI abused the FISA court and withheld exculpatory evidence in its anti-Trump surveillance. This material comes from a separate inspector general's report that concluded that "Comey's retention, handling, and dissemination of certain Memos violated Department and FBI policies, and his FBI Employment Agreement."[29] It is also not to be confused with still another report in which the inspector general excoriated Comey for his mishandling of the Hillary Clinton email investigation. Serial abusers of power like Comey keep government watchdogs employed.

Anyway, two nights after CNN and BuzzFeed used the Comey-created news excuse to share allegations about Trump, the *Washington Post*'s David Ignatius showed up on MSNBC and made the preposterous argument that if the intelligence chiefs had not included Steele's unfounded gossip in their assessment, then they could have been accused of violating "standard procedure."[30]

Protocol demands that presidents are briefed on every half-baked conspiracy theory circulating in Washington? This was too much for program host Chris Matthews, who responded,

"But we know what happened, David! You're a journalist. What happened was this gave license to the blog—to the Web site out there to take it. Buzzfeed grabbed this as license. It was a catalyst for them. OK, you're going to give a two-page attachment out, we'll show the whole 35-page dossier."[31]

Ignatius insisted that including the Steele material in the briefing was "appropriate." He probably did not realize that the very day he was making this extraordinary claim, the Crossfire Hurricane team at the FBI was receiving an intelligence report identifying a specific inaccuracy in the Steele reporting and assessing that it was "part of a Russian disinformation campaign to denigrate U.S. foreign relations."[32]

Not that this intelligence assessment or the huge volume of exculpatory evidence on Carter Page would be included in submissions to the FISA court that day as Comey signed the first wiretap renewal application.

The huge unreported story was the abuse of FBI powers, but the next day's *Washington Post* simply provided more assistance to the abusers. David Ignatius, fresh off his MSNBC appearance, called for a "full investigation" of the dossier claims, seemingly unaware that the FBI had been investigating and accumulating mounting evidence of their falsity.[33] Ignatius also wrote about Michael Flynn, the retired Army general preparing to become national security adviser in the Trump White House:

According to a senior U.S. government official, Flynn phoned Russian Ambassador Sergey Kislyak several times on Dec. 29, the day the Obama administration announced the expulsion of 35 Russian officials as well as other measures in retaliation for the hacking. What did Flynn say, and did it undercut the U.S. sanctions? The Logan Act (though never enforced) bars U.S. citizens from correspondence intending to influence a foreign government about "disputes" with the United States. Was its spirit violated? The Trump campaign didn't immediately respond to a request for comment.

Someone in the U.S. government had committed a felony by leaking Flynn's name from a wiretapped conversation. Not as outrageous but highly disturbing was that a newspaper columnist, of all people, would question whether a U.S. citizen had violated the "spirit" of the Logan Act. As noted previously and as Ignatius should have known, the appalling "spirit" of the Logan Act was to criminalize free speech. Only when targeting a Trump associate would a major newspaper consider publishing such commentary.

In his column, Ignatius did raise the possibility that "the Trump team's contacts helped discourage the Russians from a counter-retaliation" and therefore Flynn's phone conversations might have been helpful—as indeed they were. Ignatius also noted the possibility that the dossier material included Russian disinformation—apparently without realizing the FBI had found evidence to that effect and would keep it hidden for years.

In an update to his column, Ignatius wrote that a Trump transition team official "confirmed that Flynn had spoken with Kislyak by phone, but said the calls were before sanctions were announced and didn't cover that topic."[34] Just as Strzok planned to use the CNN report as a "pretext," Strzok and his FBI colleagues would also use the Ignatius column to attempt to prosecute Flynn for the phone conversations that were illegally leaked.

The unfounded theory that Trump and his associates had betrayed the country animated media coverage for years, yet when Trump responded angrily—as anyone might—his reaction was portrayed as an ominous sign of potential authoritarianism or, more charitably, as an oafish reaction by a rookie politician who didn't understand that you don't mess with the press. A *New York Times* story by Glenn Thrush and Michael Grynbaum in February of 2018 said that Trump "has stumbled into the most conventional of Washington traps: believing he can master an entrenched political press corps with far deeper connections to the permanent government of federal law enforcement and executive department officials than he has."[35]

Didn't he know that the duly elected president is no match for the unelected Washington establishment? The Timesmen added that Trump "is being force-fed lessons all presidents eventually learn—that the iron triangle of the Washington press corps, West Wing staff, and federal bureaucracy is simply too powerful to bully."[36]

The story also noted he was against the Washington practice of anonymous media attacks: "I'm against the people that make up stories and make up sources," Mr. Trump said. "They shouldn't be allowed to use sources unless they use somebody's name. Let their name be put out there. Let their name be put out."[37]

Trump was also excoriated for describing purveyors of false information as "enemies of the people." News reports in the *Times* and elsewhere compared his use of the term to its use by murderous dictators like Stalin and Mao.[38] We, too, oppose Trump's use of the term. It also should be noted that many media outlets were busy falsely painting *him* as an enemy of the people.

It's also clear that Trump was never really any threat to a free press, which has thrived as it has gleefully attacked him. CNN continued flogging the collusion story and found it was good for business. Network president Jeffrey A. Zucker said in 2017 that his employees wear insults from the president "as a badge of honor." According to a *New York Times* report, "Once the down-the-middle nerd of the cable news playground, CNN—under the guidance of Mr. Zucker, a former sports and morning show producer with a yen for flood-the-zone programming—is now an elbows-out player in national politics. . . ."[39]

The "elbows-out" coverage would include a series of programs hosted by a non-doctor named Brian Stelter who would host panels of other non-doctors to issue long-distance diagnoses of the president's mental health. It was as if CNN were trying to confirm the accuracy of Trump's attacks on "fake news."

But the collusion story continued to dominate publicly, even as FBI officials kept confidential the fact that the case had fallen apart. Throughout the early months of his presidency, Trump would grow increasingly frustrated that government officials like Comey had found no evidence of collusion but refused to say so in public. The president hosted Comey for dinner at the White House on January 28, 2017. Comey recounted the event in a memo the next day. According to the Justice Department's inspector general:

> *A portion of [the memo written by Comey] summarizes a discussion between Trump and Comey concerning the "salacious" material and Trump's wondering whether "he should ask [Comey] to investigate the whole thing to prove it was a lie." According to [Comey's memo], Comey replied that the decision about whether to initiate an investigation was up to Trump, but that Comey said he "wouldn't want to create a narrative that [the FBI was] investigating him, because [the FBI was] not, and [Comey] worried such a thing would be misconstrued."* [40]

The truth was that the FBI *had* been investigating Trump, and while one can never prove a negative, the bureau already had plenty of material to conclude there were falsehoods in the dossier, some of them likely manufactured by Russian intelligence services in order to smear Trump. Comey was presenting himself as worried about a potential scenario that he had already created. His unfounded investigation was indeed being misconstrued by the press in order to suggest Trump was in league with the Russians.

"Already, Trump has flirted with treason," declared Timothy Egan of the *New York Times* shortly before Trump took office.[41] By July of that year *Times* columnist Maureen Dowd seems to have concluded that the Trump administration had gone fully medieval:

Wicked siblings willing to do anything for power. Secret deals with sworn enemies. The shock of a dead body. A Wall. Foreign bawds, guns for hire, and snakes. Back-stabbing, betrayal and charges of treason. Little birds spying and tattling. A maniacal mad king and his court of scheming, self-absorbed princesses and princelings, swathed in the finest silk and the most brazen immorality, ruling with total disregard for the good of their people.

The night in Washington is dark and full of terrors. The Game of Trump has brought a pagan lawlessness never before seen in the capital.[42]

Some readers were gratified to see a *Times* columnist go on record against pagan lawlessness, but the talk of treason continued. "When the President Isn't a Patriot," read one 2017 *Times* headline. The story now appears online under the headline: "Odds Are, Russia Owns Trump."[43] "The Real Coup Plot Is Trump's" was another 2017 *Times* doozy.[44]

Times columnist Paul Krugman has been peppering his screeds with treason references for years. But instead of simply assailing the president, he prefers to accuse tens of millions of other Americans of being willing to sell out their country.

In a 2017 *Times* blog post entitled, "The New Climate of Treason," Krugman wrote that "essentially the whole GOP turns out to be OK with the moral equivalent of treason if it benefits their side in domestic politics."[45]

In another piece that year the *Times* fixture wrote that his partisan opponents appeared to be willing to betray their country not just for power, but for money as well. In "Judas,

Tax Cuts and the Great Betrayal," Krugman wrote that "almost an entire party appears to have decided that potential treason in the cause of tax cuts for the wealthy is no vice."[46] Perhaps realizing how dishonest and mean-spirited his comment would appear to a reasonable person, Krugman added that he was just barely exaggerating.

We never bought the collusion story advanced by the Comey FBI. In a Fox Business interview in April of 2017, one of us asked President Trump if he had made a mistake in not asking Comey to step down at the very start of the administration and whether it was too late to fire him. The president said it was "not too late" but added, "I want to give everybody a good fair chance."[47] The record shows that Comey had already had more than enough chances to conduct fair and honest investigations. By the next month Trump's patience was exhausted and Comey was fired.

For almost the next two years, as Robert Mueller was engaged in his fruitless search for collusion evidence, much of the press corps continued making outrageous and empty accusations about the president. We focused on the facts. Week after week on *Sunday Morning Futures* on the Fox News Channel and *Mornings with Maria* on the Fox Business Network, viewers heard directly from members of Congress who had received classified briefings, questioned witnesses, and examined the relevant evidence. Viewers also heard from Americans like Carter Page and George Papadopoulos who had been targeted by Comey's FBI. The programs reported numerous important details about the campaign against Trump and the most important was that there was no evidence of collusion. Reporting this fact earned nothing but scorn from many people in our industry, who, sadly, had adopted Rutenberg's view that the traditional standards of journalism should no longer apply.

Speaking of the *New York Times*, columnist Paul Krugman didn't just enjoy hurling treason allegations at the president but insisted on including all kinds of other vicious and unfounded accusations about Trump and his voters:

> *For more than a generation, the Republican establishment was able to keep this bait-and-switch under control: racism was deployed to win elections, then was muted afterwards, partly to preserve plausible deniability, partly to focus on the real priority of enriching the one percent. But with Trump they lost control: the base wanted someone who was blatantly racist and wouldn't pretend to be anything else. And that's what they got, with corruption, incompetence, and treason on the side.*[48]

Treason on the side. Krugman has so thoroughly convinced himself of the wickedness of people who disagree with him that he asserts that one of America's two main political parties "will do anything, even betray the nation, in its pursuit of partisan advantage."

"Trump, Treasonous Traitor" was the headline on a *Times* column by Charles M. Blow in July 2018. Blow wrote:

> *Put aside whatever suspicions you may have about whether Donald Trump will be directly implicated in the Russia investigation.*

Trump is right now, before our eyes and those of the world, committing an unbelievable and unforgivable crime against this country. It is his failure to defend.[49]

The astounding argument was that even if the Russia collusion conspiracy theory fell apart—as it did eight months later with the completion of the Mueller report—it was still reasonable to accuse Trump of treason because his administration was insufficiently tough on Russia, in the estimation of Charles M. Blow. With sledgehammer subtlety, the *Times* columnist added that "America is being betrayed by its own president" and reiterated that "Trump is a traitor."[50]

The media's collusion party was profitable and fun while it lasted, but all bad things must come to an end. Even Robert Mueller's team of anti-Trump prosecutors formally admitted there was no collusion evidence in the spring of 2019, triggering a season of sinking ratings in cable news. Even historically strong viewing for a two-night Democratic presidential debate in June couldn't save MSNBC from a stinker of a second quarter that year.[51]

Business picked up toward the end of 2019 when Representative Adam Schiff led Democrats in a partisan effort to impeach the president without alleging any crime. No House Republicans voted to impeach and a couple Democrats voted against the misguided prosecution, but the case moved to the Senate, where the president was acquitted.

Before the case failed in the Senate, it revealed the lengths some media folk would go in attempting to drive Trump from office. Democrats argued that Trump had abused his office by suggesting to the president of Ukraine that his government examine a lucrative board seat Joe Biden's son Hunter had received from a Ukrainian energy company while the elder Biden was vice president and overseeing Ukraine policy. Hunter Biden had no particular expertise in Ukraine or the energy business. What's more, Joe Biden had withheld aid from the country until the Ukrainian government forced the firing of a local prosecutor investigating Hunter Biden's business associates. The Ukraine gig was similar to other deals the younger Biden had struck in China and Romania while his father was vice president and leading U.S. policy in those countries—lucrative arrangements for which Hunter Biden was manifestly unqualified.

The basic problem for Democrats was that they were arguing it was an impeachable offense for Trump to suggest an investigation of conduct that any reasonable person would agree ought to be investigated. So, in the months leading up to impeachment, the strategy was to focus on Trump and not the underlying Biden conduct.

Trump lampooned the Bidens at an October 2019 campaign rally in Minnesota, making jokes about how Hunter Biden knew nothing about the places and industries where he was collecting large checks overseas.

NBC News simply decided to cut off coverage of the rally. As MSNBC host Nicolle Wallace ended coverage of the Trump event, she told viewers: "We hate to do this, really, but the president isn't telling the truth."[52] The president *was* telling the truth, and it hurt their narrative.

In a tweet the next day, NBC's *Meet the Press* said: "The

president held a campaign rally last night and attacked Hunter Biden. We cannot in good conscience show it to you."[53]

The program's host, Chuck Todd, told viewers, "We aren't going to play the sound. We aren't going to repeat the President's vicious attacks on Hunter Biden. The President of the United States stood in front of a crowd of supporters and character-assassinated a man." Todd added that Hunter Biden is "not a public figure, he isn't running for office, and he's not a campaign surrogate. He's not even on the campaign trail, and he isn't in any way asking for this attention, obviously."[54] Yes, obviously no one seeks attention for being handsomely compensated in situations involving clear conflicts of interest for a relative serving as vice president of the United States.

Todd even admitted the Trump remarks were "newsworthy" but insisted that he couldn't "in good conscience amplify those attacks." Todd didn't claim Trump's comments were untrue but vaguely asserted that they "seemed to cross a line." Then the anchorman instructed, "We all need to play a role in not rewarding this kind of politics—not just the press. This is the job of anyone who has sworn an oath to defend the Constitution."[55] There's nothing in the Constitution preventing people from questioning the way relatives of politicians monetize their proximity to power. In fact, the First Amendment ensures that people *can* raise such questions without fear of government interference.

The effort to bury the story wasn't confined to NBC. "There is no evidence of Joe Biden doing anything wrong . . . ," asserted CNN host Erin Burnett in cutting off discussion of the Ukraine deal.[56]

There's also no evidence that Hunter Biden did anything but rent his famous name and connections. Neither he nor his foreign associates could explain what exactly he had done to deserve the millions of dollars he had collected overseas. In 2019 he quit the Ukraine and China ventures and pledged not to do such things again if his father wins in 2020. Essentially the media was defending Biden conduct that the Bidens were hardly willing to defend. The situation became almost comical when reporters at Hong Kong's *South China Morning Post* attempted to get some answers from Hunter Biden's Chinese associates:

> *BHR (Shanghai) Equity Investment Fund Management Company has grabbed global media attention for its links with Hunter Biden, the son of former United States vice-president Joe Biden, after US President Donald Trump fired a barrage of corruption allegations at him and requested China investigate the Bidens' financial activities in the country.*
>
> *The company has repeatedly declined to elaborate on the younger Biden's role at the firm when contacted by the* South China Morning Post *via phone, mail and visits to the office. But Jonathan Li Xiangsheng, the firm's chief executive and Hunter Biden's partner, has said the company was working on an explanation about the American's role.*
>
> *Li refused to comment on the younger Biden when reached by the* Post *on Monday.*

A recent visit to the firm's registered address in Beijing found a small, plainly decorated office, where a receptionist said she had never seen Hunter Biden.[57]

More than five years after going into business with Hunter Biden, his associates in China were still "working on an explanation" of his role there. If this doesn't arouse the curiosity of a real journalist, it's hard to imagine what would. But the reaction of much of the American media tells us how rare such journalists have become.

The impeachment drama didn't last as long as the collusion saga, although it dragged into February 2020, when perhaps another story coming out of China should have been getting more attention from Washington lawmakers.

As for the collusion story that dominated the news for years, Trump tweeted in May of 2020:

When are the Fake Journalists, who received unwarranted Pulitzer Prizes for Russia, Russia, Russia, and the Impeachment Scam, going to turn in their tarnished awards so they can be given to the real journalists who got it right. I'll give you the names, there are plenty of them![58]

Now that everyone knows the history, some readers may wonder if Trump's tweet was too polite.

8

The Cost of Covid

Covid-19 emerged in China in late 2019 and by the end of July 2020 had killed close to 700,000 people worldwide. During that same time period more than 30 million people in the world died of other causes. The virus has not been as fatal as many feared, yet many politicians keep insisting that it is.

As we write in the summer of 2020, Congress has already spent more than $2.6 trillion in response to the coronavirus. Lawmakers are considering plans to spend trillions more. The federal government is borrowing the money and saddling future generations with more debt. If Americans were forced to pay the Covid bill this year, income taxes would have to more than double. Along with the direct spending, the Federal Reserve has essentially printed nearly $3 trillion of new money, much of which it uses to purchase federal debt. If this binge of money creation ever causes people to lose faith in the U.S. dollar, the cost to America and the world will be many times that amount.

Even now the cost of the virus response is not limited to the burden placed on federal taxpayers. Businesses and opportunities disappear, many never to return, and treatments for numerous other health problems have been postponed or neglected. This year many places in America have shuttered large parts of society for months even though Covid-19 has killed nowhere near the number of Americans who die of heart disease or cancer, which each kill about 600,000 Americans every year.[1]

But Covid mortality does have a connection to those other ailments. A large majority of Covid deaths occur in people older than sixty-five. In Ohio, for example, the median age of a patient dying of Covid-19 is 80.[2] Not surprisingly, given the age of the most vulnerable population, many of the victims are also suffering from other illnesses at the time of death. Doctors call these conditions comorbidities, and in many cases Covid kills people who are likely to die within months of some other cause. The state of New York, for example, has reported that 90 percent of those dying with Covid have at least one comorbidity, such as hypertension, diabetes, coronary artery disease, or cancer. Thousands of Covid deaths in New York have occurred among people who were at least eighty years old and also suffering from dementia.[3]

How many lives and how many trillions of dollars could the United States have saved if the Chinese Communist Party had not lied and suppressed information about the virus in the early days of the epidemic?

President Trump ordered travel restrictions between China and the United States on January 31, 2020. The next day Joe Biden tweeted, "We are in the midst of a crisis with the coronavirus. We need to lead the way with science—not Donald Trump's record of hysteria, xenophobia, and fear-mongering. He is the worst possible person to lead our country through a global health emergency."[4] Under a President Biden, would passengers from Wuhan still be arriving at airports in the United States?

The Chinese regime should have banned international flights weeks earlier, which might have saved the world from the global emergency. Instead of trying to protect lives and halt the spread of infection, the government in Beijing initially focused on silencing people who acknowledged the deadly threat emerging in the city of Wuhan in Hubei province.

A week after Trump's travel order, people all over China were mourning the loss of a heroic young doctor who had tried to sound the alarm. Dr. Li Wenliang was just thirty-three years old when he left behind a wife, a child, and another on the way. In late December 2019, the Wuhan physician had begun warning about a series of pneumonia cases that he initially thought were caused by severe acute respiratory syndrome, or SARS, but later concluded were tied to a novel coronavirus.

Instead of receiving praise for spotting a deadly threat, Dr. Li was interrogated by Communist Party officials. Local police forced him to write a statement blaming himself and pledging to stop spreading "rumors."

"They told me not to publish any information about this online," Dr. Li later told the *Beijing Youth Daily*. "Later, the epidemic started to spread noticeably. I'd personally been treating someone who was infected, and whose family got infected, and so then I got infected."[5]

After his death, the *South China Morning Post* quoted a Wuhan university professor named Tang Yiming: "If the words of Dr Li had not been treated as rumours, if every citizen was allowed to practise their right to voice the truth, we would not be in such a mess, we would not have a national catastrophe with an international impact."[6]

The professor wasn't alone. "On Chinese social media," reported the *Wall Street Journal*'s Jonathan Cheng, "commenters posted tributes to Dr. Li, circulating a quote from an interview he had given just days before his death: 'I believe a healthy society should not just have one voice.'"[7]

At least for a moment the voice of the dictatorship wasn't able to drown out the cries of protest. "The outpouring of grief and anger online has overwhelmed censors battling to repress the most scathing voices and damaging comments," Tan Dawn Wei reported in Singapore's *Straits Times*. "Hashtags like 'we want freedom of speech,' which started trending on Chinese microblogging site Weibo shortly after Dr Li's death, have since been scrubbed clean. But another trend has emerged, featuring selfies of people wearing a face mask with the words, 'bu neng, bu mingbai' (can't, don't understand) written on it. The words refer to a declaration that Dr Li was forced to sign by the Wuhan police, in which he was asked if he could comply with the local authorities and stop spreading 'rumours,' to which

Dr Li wrote, 'can.' He was also asked if he understood that he would face the full force of the law if he continued his 'illegal activities,' to which he wrote, 'I understand.'"[8]

The people of China, held captive by the Beijing dictatorship, still can't exercise free speech. And the United States is still wrestling with the virus that the Chinese Communist Party allowed to attack an unsuspecting world. Appearing on *Mornings with Maria* on April 17, 2020, U.S. secretary of state Mike Pompeo said, "the Chinese Communist Party needs to come clean about what took place there" and noted that the United States was seeking access to a Wuhan virology lab "so that we can determine precisely where this virus began."[9]

It's appropriate to blame the Chinese regime for its lies and cover-ups related to the virus. But many U.S. mayors and governors can also be blamed for overreacting to it. From the moment Covid-19 emerged in the United States and throughout the period of pandemic, the media and political class was largely uninterested in exploring the costs and benefits of potential responses. The consensus was to shut down much of the economy and create massive government programs to clumsily offset the damage. President Trump initially and sensibly avoided endorsing the lockdowns enacted by state and local politicians. But after being told by federal health experts that the alternative would result in the deaths of millions of Americans, he supported the idea of shutting down for several weeks to "flatten the curve."

At the time, it was largely understood that, without a vaccine, some deaths were inevitable. The idea was to force Americans to keep their distance to slow the spread of the virus. Instead of an immediate spike of infections that could overwhelm medical systems as millions of people got sick at the same time, the idea was to turn the spike into a rounded curve so that hospital visits would be spread over a longer period.

But the idea that millions of Americans would die from the virus was just a guess, and its author appeared to abandon his predictions soon after making them. Neil Ferguson is an Imperial College London scientist whose dire virus forecasts helped inspire aggressive measures by the White House and other authorities in both the United States and the United Kingdom. On March 16 of this year he coauthored a widely read report which described Covid-19 as "a virus with comparable lethality to H1N1 influenza in 1918." [10]

According to the U.S. Centers for Disease Control and Prevention, the 1918 virus is estimated to have killed 50 million people worldwide, [11] more than 70 times the number killed by the coronavirus as of the end of July 2020. The 1918 flu was even more devastating in relative terms because the world's population was a fraction of our current count.

But less than ten days after Dr. Ferguson's highly disturbing report, which was being used to justify lockdowns all over the world, he told a committee of Parliament he was "reasonably confident" the country's health service could cope with the peak of the epidemic and that the number of deaths in the United Kingdom might total less than 20,000. [12] He also said that people who would have shortly died anyway "might be as much as half or two thirds of the deaths we see, because these are people at the end of their lives or who have underlying conditions."[13]

We were turning the global economy upside down largely to prevent terminal patients from contracting the coronavirus along with whatever was *already* killing them? Ferguson's stunning testimony was mostly ignored in the United States, where many governors and mayors proceeded to enforce lockdowns that could no longer be justified by any reasonable consideration of benefits and costs. But it seems that President Trump was paying attention because he insisted that the coronavirus cure must not be worse than the disease and soon turned against the lockdowns.

The staggering shutdown expense was just beginning to come into focus. Eric Morath, Jon Hilsenrath, and Sarah Chaney reported in the *Wall Street Journal* on March 26: "A record 3.28 million workers applied for unemployment benefits last week as the new coronavirus hit the U.S. economy, marking the end of a decade-long job growth.

"The number of Americans filing for claims was nearly five times the previous record high," they continued. "Pennsylvania, Ohio and California were among 10 states reporting more than 100,000 claims, leaving unemployment systems overloaded."[14]

Because not everyone suddenly out of work was able to file and because many independent workers didn't qualify, the awful numbers were actually a gross understatement of the damage to American livelihoods. And the numbers would get much worse.

The *Journal's* Marcus Walker would write a few days later: "The coronavirus has produced something new in economic history. Never before have governments tried to put swaths of national economies in an induced coma, artificially maintain their vital organs, and awaken them gradually." [15] And never before had they taken such costly action with so little evidence to support it.

Numerous politicians pretended that economy-crushing shutdown mandates were the only sensible response, rather than focusing on protecting the vulnerable elderly while relying on those at lower risk to exercise good judgment and employ frequent handwashing, social distancing, and other voluntary measures. States like Georgia, South Dakota, and Texas, which largely relied on voluntary measures to fight the spread of infection, would achieve results that were better than many shuttered jurisdictions. By contrast, the governors of New York and New Jersey, among the most aggressive in issuing shutdown orders, would preside over the highest per capita Covid death tolls in the United States—and in fact the highest in the world.

But even in the hardest-hit areas, the damage was not nearly as bad as one might assume from the hysterical media and political reaction. Senate minority leader Chuck Schumer (D-N.Y.) and MSNBC's Joe Scarborough have been among those comparing Covid-19 to World War II. [16] The virus will need to get vastly more destructive to approach the scale of 1940s carnage. The National World War II Museum in New Orleans counts a total worldwide death toll of 60 million for the entire conflict but acknowledges the total might be more like 90 million—more than 100 times the Covid total. More than 400,000 Americans died in World War II, almost all of them young people who lost many more years of life than the elderly who succumb to Covid.[17]

World War II was even more devastating in relative terms because in the 1940s the world had less than a third of its current population, according to the U.S. Census Bureau.[18] Also, many of the civilian deaths and almost all of the battle deaths were young people, denied many decades of life by the horrific conflict.

Even in Italy, where an aging population and a socialized medical system created a perfectly awful storm of suffering this year, total virus deaths to date don't come close to the World War II carnage.

"The current coronavirus disease, Covid-19, has been called a once-in-a-century pandemic. But it may also be a once-in-a-century evidence fiasco," observed Dr. John Ioannidis, professor of medicine and biomedical data science at Stanford University, in March. ". . . Better information is needed to guide decisions and actions of monumental significance and to monitor their impact.

"Draconian countermeasures have been adopted in many countries. If the pandemic dissipates—either on its own or because of these measures—short-term extreme social distancing and lockdowns may be bearable," he noted. "How long, though, should measures like these be continued if the pandemic churns across the globe unabated? How can policymakers tell if they are doing more good than harm?"[19]

Dr. Ioannidis notes the 1918 flu pandemic that killed millions and adds: "One can only hope that, much like in 1918, life will continue. Conversely, with lockdowns of months, if not years, life largely stops, short-term and long-term consequences are entirely unknown, and billions, not just millions, of lives may be eventually at stake.

"If we decide to jump off the cliff, we need some data to inform us about the rationale of such an action and the chances of landing somewhere safe."[20]

Fortunately, Covid is not as deadly as World War II. But shutdowns enacted in response to Covid are similar to warfare in that they ask disproportionate sacrifices from young people. Kids are at little risk of Covid, but they have been forced to bear most of the cost.

If all schools in the country are shut down, we rob America's children of about $1.6 billion per day of education, an expense they will pay over time in reduced earnings. That's according to University of Chicago economist Casey Mulligan, who tells us that additional life lessons learned at school (beyond those that raise earnings) would go on top of the $1.6 billion.[21]

The Goldman School of Public Policy at the University of California Berkeley notes a recent cost-benefit analysis of school closures coauthored by its graduate Rob Moore.[22] The study focuses on the possibility of closing K–12 schools in Ohio for four months this fall. According to Mr. Moore's firm, Scioto Analysis, the shutdown would have a disproportionate impact on kids' future earning potential: "Overall, the cost-benefit analysis found that total costs in lost wages outweigh benefits measured in risk of death reduction by a factor of 14 to 1."[23]

"More than nine out of ten COVID deaths in Ohio are among people age sixty and up . . . ," says Moore. "Meanwhile, the average student loses out on $12,000–$27,000 in lifetime earnings by losing four months of schooling. School closings are in essence an intergenerational transfer."[24] As noted earlier, the state of Ohio reports that the median age of those dying with the virus was eighty.

Some have argued that teachers face too great a risk conducting classes in person this year. One may wonder why they are not considered essential workers, even as states like New York and New Jersey apply the label to the staff at liquor stores. Whether essential or nonessential, teachers aren't at great risk of contracting Covid. In July the *Times* of London reported: "There has been no recorded case of a teacher catching the coronavirus from a pupil anywhere in the world, according to one of the government's leading scientific advisers.

"Mark Woolhouse, a leading epidemiologist and member of the government's [Scientific Advisory Group for Emergencies] committee, told *The Times* that it may have been a mistake to close schools in March given the limited role children play in spreading the virus."[25]

The report created a rather awkward moment for U.S. teachers' unions and their media friends. That's because it arrived just after the New York newspaper called the *Times* (no relation) published an op-ed from a teacher named Rebecca Martinson who opined: "Every day when I walk into work as a public-school teacher, I am prepared to take a bullet to save a child. In the age of school shootings, that's what the job requires. But asking me to return to the classroom amid a pandemic and expose myself and my family to Covid-19 is like asking me to take that bullet home to my own family."[26]

Perhaps a bit overstated? Charlotte Hays of the Independent Women's Forum calls Ms. Martinson's op-ed "An Emotional Plea to Play Hooky" and observes:

"The most prominent fact cited is that 75 'school-based' employees of the New York City Department of Education lost their lives to COVID-19 between March 16, 2020, and June 22. While each of these losses is undeniably tragic, to make these numbers meaningful, we need to know which ones contracted the infection because of their jobs. New York City's public schools began shutting down in mid-March."[27]

The *Times* report from the United Kingdom suggests that the number is zero. The London paper quoted Professor Mark Woolhouse, chairman of infectious disease epidemiology at Edinburgh University, saying that school-age kids are "minimally involved in the epidemiology of this virus." He added that youngsters are "vanishingly unlikely to end up in hospital or to die from it" and "rarely transmit" the virus to others.[28]

The *Times* also reported: "Dr Gabriel Scally, president of the epidemiology and public health section of the Royal Society of Medicine, said that reopening schools should have been one of the top priorities of lifting the lockdown. 'It is a real indictment of our society that we can manage to open pubs and nail bars but we can't open schools,' he said."[29]

The *Times* of London report followed a June statement from the American Academy of Pediatrics that notes the negative impact of lockdowns as well as the relatively small Covid risks faced by children. The organization says it "*strongly advo-cates that all policy considerations for the coming school year should start with a goal of having students physically present in school.* The importance of in-person learning is well-documented, and there is already evidence of the negative impacts on children because of school closures in the spring of 2020. Lengthy time away from school and associated interruption of supportive services often results in social isolation, making it difficult for schools to identify and address important learning deficits as well as child and adolescent physical or sexual abuse, substance use, depression, and suicidal ideation. This, in turn, places chil-dren and adolescents at considerable risk of morbidity and, in some cases, mortality" (emphasis in the original).[30]

When the shutdowns began in the spring, the cost imposed on the mental health of young people was barely considered by politicians and infectious disease experts in their rush to address the Covid risk. "Suicide, help hotline calls soar in Southern California over coronavirus anxieties" was the headline on an April report in the *Orange County Register*. The story noted a more than 8,000% increase in monthly call volume at a Los Angeles mental health crisis line in March. There was also a surge in calls to Riverside County's crisis and suicide helpline.[31]

A commentary in the British medical journal the *Lancet* warned: "Suicide is likely to become a more pressing concern as the pandemic spreads and has longer-term effects on the gen-eral population, the economy, and vulnerable groups." Signed by numerous doctors engaged in mental health research, the article noted: "Loss of employment and financial stressors are well-recognised risk factors for suicide."[32]

Was Washington paying attention? National Institute of Allergy and Infectious Diseases director Anthony Fauci acknowledges that he doesn't study the societal trade-offs involved in his virus recommendations. In Senate testimony in May he made it clear that the economic consequences of shutdowns, which he had previously called "inconvenient," were not his responsibility.[33] Fauci was testifying shortly after the U.S. unemployment rate had hit a post–World War II high.[34]

The government health expert is clear on the fact that Americans should not rely on him to conduct cost-benefit analysis of the policies he promotes. But even within the realm of public health, he's not making the case that continuing to restrict activities will make Americans healthier overall but only that it will, in his opinion, reduce Covid-19 deaths.

Another medical doctor, Senator Bill Cassidy (R-La.), asked at the May hearing about calculating the negative impact of school shutdowns on the health of children compared to the possible benefits of avoiding Covid-19. Dr. Fauci said, "I don't have a good explanation, or solution to the problem of what happens when you close schools, and it triggers a cascade of events that could have some harmful circumstances."[35]

How can a public health official endorse the radical step of closing schools without at least presenting an argument that it would have a net benefit for public health?

To be clear, children have been paying the largest share of the cost of shutdowns, but they're not the only ones. Appearing on *Mornings with Maria* in May, Hologic CEO Steve MacMillan said that in April and early May "we have seen a dramatic drop-off in women going for their mammograms" and pegged the recent decline in U.S. mammogram visits at an astounding 80 to 90 percent. MacMillan warned of potential long-term consequences and said, "The whole key to cancer screening is finding things early." [36]

"With most of the nation still on lockdown, many people are missing regular screenings and checkups with their doctors," Jeff LeBenger and Mike Meyer wrote in the *Wall Street Journal* in May. "Some may be experiencing early symptoms of illness, yet aren't seeking treatment. The effects of a six-week delay are surmountable in most cases, but a six-month delay would lead to much sicker patients and dramatic increases in death rates for major illnesses such as cancer. The number of people who die as a result of these delays could end up rivaling or exceeding deaths due to Covid-19."

The doctors warned: "Much is being written about the potential of Covid-19 to return aggressively in the fall, assuming it recedes during the summer. But there may be a major aftershock that could throw the health system into further crisis: a flood of patients with other illnesses who are much sicker than they would be had they not delayed visits to their doctors for fear of coronavirus exposure." [37]

The panicked reaction of politicians and the press encouraged patients to overreact. Dr. Harlan Krumholz is a professor of medicine at Yale and director of the Center for Outcomes Research and Evaluation, Yale–New Haven Hospital. During the shutdown spring he wrote in the *New York Times* about a bizarre decline in the demand for medical services: "What is striking is that many of the emergencies have disappeared. Heart attack and stroke teams, always poised to rush in and save lives, are mostly idle. This is not just at my hospital. My fellow cardiologists have shared with me that their cardiology consultations have shrunk, except those related to Covid-19. . . .

"And this is not a phenomenon specific to the United States," Dr. Krumholz continued. "Investigators from Spain reported a 40 percent reduction in emergency procedures for heart attacks during the last week of March compared with the period just before the pandemic hit."[38]

Ohio physician Kristofer Sandlund reported, "I am seeing a reluctance amongst my most vulnerable patients to seek medical care of any sort. Patients with stroke symptoms are not calling the EMT's and delays are costly."[39]

The shutdowns also put the health system under extreme financial pressure. Politicians issued draconian orders to prevent the virus from overwhelming hospitals. But according to an April report in the *Wall Street Journal*, "Hospitals have been cutting the elective surgical procedures and routine care that normally pay the bills in order to free up resources."[40]

The nonmedical advice from economist Scott Grannis is to "pray for a speedy reopening of the economy." Mr. Grannis predicts that the shutdown "will prove to be the most expensive self-inflicted injury in the history of mankind."[41]

9

Is Bidenomics Turning Out to Be Bernienomics?

Some Democrats must be wondering why their party asked them to show up and vote in this year's primaries and caucuses. Since last winter Democratic voters nationwide have made it abundantly clear that they do not want a candidate promoting massive structural change in American government and society. But the party leadership seems determined to give them one anyway.

Beginning in South Carolina in late February and continuing through the final months of the nomination contest, Democrats soundly rejected the radical option: Vermont's socialist senator Bernie Sanders. Exit polling data published by the *Washington Post* in March showed that, across the Super Tuesday states, most Democratic voters consider themselves conservative, moderate, or somewhat liberal, while a minority call themselves "very liberal."[1] Most of these Democratic primary voters don't regard income inequality as the most important issue facing the country, and their votes made clear that they aren't seeking the socialist revolution promised by Sanders.

But since the voters had their say, party leaders seem to be systematically ignoring the message. After vanquishing Sanders, former vice president Joe Biden has moved rapidly toward Sandernista positions on the environment, health care, financial regulation, and many other issues.

Perhaps Democrat bosses are revealing their true beliefs, or maybe it's just a panicked response to the usual lack of enthusiasm for Biden. Despite strong polling, Biden doesn't have an enthusiastic following. Kevin Roose reported in the *New York Times* in April: "Joe Biden is very famous, but you wouldn't know it from looking at his YouTube channel. . . .

". . . [T]he virtual crickets that greet many of his appearances have become a source of worry for some Democrats, who see his sluggish performance online as a bad omen for his electoral chances in November.

" 'This video is 2 days old and it's sitting at 20,000 views,' one commenter wrote under a recent video of Mr. Biden's. 'This is a guy that is supposed to beat Trump?' "

A Biden campaign podcast called "Here's the Deal" was a springtime flop.[2]

Biden's sharp left turn on policy may help him secure some enthusiastic young Sanders voters. But since there were demonstrably more Biden voters than Sanders voters, one wonders how many aging non-radicals will come along for the leftward ride in November. After defeating Sanders, Biden decided to start taking the socialist senator's advice and giving him a say in the Biden agenda, and adopting many of his policies.

In the summer, they set about crafting ideas to appeal to party radicals. In *Forbes*, Sally Pipes described the new groups created to draft policies as "a who's who of the progressive elite—and signal that Biden is going to run for the White House on a platform that is further to the left than any Democrat in history.

"His healthcare task force is a haven for advocates of a government takeover of health insurance. . . .

"The highest-wattage name on Biden's climate change task force is New York Rep. Alexandria Ocasio-Cortez. She has made the Green New Deal her signature legislative proposal."[3]

In 2019 the Green New Deal and its potential $100 trillion price tag received not a single vote in the U.S. Senate even though a number of senators, including vice presidential candidate Kamala Harris, had served as cosponsors. But its radical author is helping to craft the Biden plan for governing. In the summer of 2020 Ocasio-Cortez and her radical colleagues joined with Team Biden to publish a long document entitled, *Biden-Sanders Unity Task Force Recommendations.*[4]

The 110-page Biden-Sanders coproduction essentially calls for the political revolution long promised by Bernie Sanders. It says that "Democrats commit to forging a new social and economic contract with the American people."[5] Just like the Sanders campaign—and just like Venezuela's socialist constitution[6]—the new Biden plan recognizes things like housing and health care as rights guaranteed by government.

The plan promises higher wages and affordable financial services. The "new social and economic contract" will also provide policies to address America's alleged history of "economic exclusion and political suppression."[7]

The plan makes clear that the goal is to grow the public sector, not the private economy: "We will invest in the caring workforce, including by directing significant funding to state and local governments to retain and hire more teachers, public health professionals, nurses, home care workers, social workers, and other critical positions. Democrats reject any efforts to privatize public-sector jobs, from our schools to the United States Postal Service."[8]

There's so much more, from Medicaid expansion to a new government-run health plan to free public college and university tuition for most students to applying ancient telephone regulation to the internet to a new Office of Environmental Justice to prosecute business.

"We will set a bold, national goal of achieving net-zero greenhouse gas emissions for all new buildings by 2030, on the pathway to creating a 100 percent clean building sector," proclaims the Biden-Sanders plan. ". . . Democrats will move quickly to reestablish strong standards for clean cars and trucks that consider the most recent advances in technology, and accelerate the adoption of zero-emission vehicles in the United States while reclaiming market share for domestically produced vehicles.

"We will reduce harmful air pollution and protect our children's health by transitioning the entire fleet of 500,000 school buses to American-made, zero-emission alternatives within five years. We will lead by example in the public sector by transitioning the 3 million vehicles in the federal, state, and local fleets to zero-emission vehicles."[9]

"Environmental regulation is shaping up as a defining issue in the presidential race, with President Trump doubling down on his bid to ratchet back government oversight and former Vice President Joe Biden promising to reverse Mr. Trump's regulatory rollbacks,"[10] note Alex Leary and Timothy Puko in the *Wall Street Journal*. In July the presidential campaign rivals "outlined diametrically opposed views. Mr. Trump ordered a streamlining of environmental reviews and said he would keep shrinking the reach of government to help business. Mr. Biden, the presumptive Democratic nominee, released a $2 trillion clean-energy plan he said would spur job growth through investments in new technology. . . . Mr. Trump also took a swipe at Mr. Biden's proposals. 'The American people know best how to run their own lives,' Mr. Trump said. 'They don't need Washington bureaucrats controlling their every move and micromanaging their every decision.' . . . Mr. Biden promised 'historic investments,' invoking language Vermont Sen. Bernie Sanders used during the primaries. Since Mr. Sanders dropped out, Mr. Biden has engaged progressive groups that once had been harsh critics, and his proposals . . . drew rave reviews from them."

The *Journal* report added: "When Mr. Trump came to power in 2017, he and congressional Republicans undid more than a dozen major Obama-era regulations that had yet to take effect, using the Congressional Review Act. . . . The president also has used executive orders during the pandemic to trim or suspend other regulations, allowing truckers to be on the road longer hours and scaling back restrictions on telehealth." [11]

Former vice president Biden has indeed been winning rave reviews from the progressive left for many of the proposals he's recently agreed to promote. But do most Americans think the federal government should decide who qualifies for loans in this country? The Biden-Sanders "unity" document brazenly calls for the political allocation of credit by creating a new government-run credit reporting agency. Right from the start, it would be a huge player in U.S. lending as the document promises:

> All federal lending will accept this credit agency and require that this agency be used. This includes, but would not be limited to federal home lending, PLUS loans (parent loans backed by the U.S. government), other loans that are guaranteed by the U.S. government, as well as any employment through federal agencies or for federal contracts.

> - The private agencies will also be required to provide their data to the federal credit agency.
> - The federal credit agency will also ensure the algorithms used for credit scoring don't have discriminatory impacts, including accepting non-traditional sources of data like rental history and utility bills to ensure credit. [12]

Are credit algorithms discriminatory if they don't yield the financial results the Biden-Sanders team wants?

In July, Jaret Seiberg of the Cowen Washington Research Group reported: "Democrats are advancing a financial policy agenda that is heavy on social justice and reversing years of discrimination." He added that this "will make it harder to stop these policies" because opponents "may fear being labeled as racist."

If Biden wins, Senator Elizabeth Warren of Massachusetts "will have enormous policy influence even if she stays in the Senate," says Seiberg.[13] This likely means new federal regulation of all large corporations, not just financial firms. Today businesses are created under state law. But in an August 2018 op-ed in the *Wall Street Journal*, Senator Warren introduced a plan to require all corporations with more than $1 billion in annual revenue to get a federal corporate charter. "The new charter requires corporate directors to consider the interests of all major corporate stakeholders—not only shareholders—in company decisions," wrote Senator Warren.[14]

"Stakeholders" are people who don't actually own the business but would like to have a say in how it is run. Senator Warren claims that running a business for the actual owners shortchanges workers, customers, and the surrounding community. But of course people who run companies already know they won't be in business very long if they alienate everyone on whom their businesses rely. Serving the long-term interests of shareholders necessarily requires executives to attract and retain a talented workforce, to provide good value for consumers, to deal fairly with suppliers, and to respect the laws and customs wherever a business operates.

Typically the alleged responsibilities of a company to its "stakeholders" who don't own stakes in the business are defined vaguely and often intended to get businesses to push policies that voters have declined to endorse. "The discussions of the 'social responsibilities of business' are notable for their analytical looseness and lack of rigor," wrote Milton Friedman in 1970. ". . . The first step toward clarity in examining the doctrine of the social responsibility of business is to ask precisely what it implies for whom." [15]

The future Nobel Prize–winning economist elaborated: "What does it mean to say that the corporate executive has a 'social responsibility' in his capacity as businessman? If this statement is not pure rhetoric, it must mean that he is to act in some way that is not in the interest of his employers. For example . . . that he is to make expenditures on reducing pollution beyond the amount that is in the best interests of the corporation or that is required by law in order to contribute to the social objective of improving the environment." [16]

The idea of corporate "stakeholders" who don't have a direct stake in the business has been popular for some years at many companies, and various nonprofit organizations are eager to wield influence over other people's property. But given that they are neither owners of the business, nor elected officials, nor regulators, why should such organizations be elevated to the level of the consumer or employee?

Such organizations may soon be given much more power, because Joe Biden is lately sounding a lot more like Elizabeth

Warren. In a July speech in Pennsylvania, the former vice president said: "It's way past time to put an end to the era of shareholder capitalism—the idea that the only responsibility a corporation has is to its shareholders." [17] Investors may now wonder how Biden plans to define the new responsibilities of the businesses they own.

Team Biden may believe that the response to the coronavirus is changing our politics. Is the campaign betting that the lockdown wrecking ball hurled at the foundations of the U.S. economy this year is making government activism more popular? Many unemployed Americans are surely hoping that lockdowns are becoming less popular. As we write this, the economy appears to be on the mend, but the damage has been historic. In April the U.S. unemployment rate hit a post–World War II high of 14.7 percent. What's particularly striking about the Biden candidacy is that the former vice president continues to insist that a historic economic calamity should be addressed with a historically large tax increase.

When Joe Biden announced his campaign for the presidency in 2019, he presented himself as a nonideological defender of the status quo, a leader to prevent President Trump from altering "the character of this nation." A July 2020 tweet from the former vice president suggests that Biden now has something much more ambitious in mind: "We're going to beat Donald Trump. And when we do, we won't just rebuild this nation—we'll transform it." [18]

What would it cost to transform the nation? Biden has

already proposed roughly $4 trillion in tax hikes—more than twice as large as the tax increase promoted by Hillary Clinton in 2016. But the Biden tax surge won't be nearly enough to cover the more than $9 trillion in new spending he's proposed, or all of the policies promoted by his "task force" collaborators. The new taxes and regulations will be inflicted on an economy that is just beginning to heal.

The former vice president likes to say that nobody making less than $400,000 would see their taxes rise under his plan. This is misleading, because along with a series of taxes on afflu-ent individuals, Biden would also significantly raise taxes on businesses, which are not just owned by the wealthy. Given the broad ownership of stocks via 401(k) retirement plans and pension funds, his new tax burdens would threaten the wealth of most American households.

And of course virtually all workers feel the impact of a slowing economy. In April the Tax Foundation reported that the Biden plan would reduce take-home pay for workers up and down the income scale. The Tax Foundation added that "Biden's tax plan would reduce the economy's size by 1.51 per-cent in the long run. The plan would shrink the capital stock by 3.23 percent and reduce the overall wage rate by 0.98 percent, leading to 585,000 fewer full-time equivalent jobs." [19]

Dan Clifton of Strategas Research figures the Biden plan to raise the corporate income tax rate will reduce the earnings per share of the S&P 500 by 11 percent. Mr. Clifton explains: "Dividends are taxed twice: first at the corporate level and then when distributed at the individual level. This is important because Biden is proposing to raise the corporate tax rate from

21 to 28 percent and tax dividends at the ordinary income level for those making over $1mm per year. The tax increases raise the effective tax rate on dividends from 40 to 60 percent." [20]

Mr. Clifton notes other disincentives to operating U.S. businesses: "Just the prospect of the Biden tax plan being implemented will encourage companies to consider the sale of their businesses. Under the Biden plan, the capital gains tax rate is nearly doubled from 20 percent to 39.6 percent. The after-tax rate of return on the sale of the business is much higher this year compared to next year if the tax plan is implemented." [21]

Why does Biden keep moving to the left on economic policy? Not everyone thinks he needs to excite the socialist "Bernie Bros" to get elected. Michael Tesler writes at the website FiveThirtyEight that "while Biden voters may not be all that excited about voting for Biden, they're very enthusiastic about voting *against* Trump" (emphasis in the original). [22]

But the Biden camp clearly believes they need to gin up more enthusiasm for their candidate, or they wouldn't be working so hard to please the activists who swooned over Sanders. That's why Biden rolled out that new $2 trillion proposal to counter climate change, both more expensive and more ambitious in the pace of mandated changes than the plan he backed during the Democratic primaries.

Yet Democratic voters picked him over Mr. Sanders precisely because they did not want revolutionary change. Voters across the political spectrum have been sending the same message ever since. A July CNBC poll found a lead of 10 points for Biden, but also a warning against adopting a radical agenda. Voters who participated in the CNBC survey clearly don't want what Mr. Sanders has been selling. A full 54 percent of them express an unfavorable view of socialism, compared with just 29 percent who view it favorably. Similarly, 54 percent have a favorable view of capitalism, while just 27 percent express an unfavorable view.[23]

Another recent addition to the Biden agenda is an effort to mimic Trump trade policy by reducing imports, at a cost to Americans of $700 billion. Mr. Biden is now promising the costs of trade disputes, but with none of the pro-growth Trump tax and regulatory reforms that resulted in the best job market in American history prior to the virus.

Speaking of Trump tax reform, the corporate income tax rate reduction was a game changer for American competitiveness, but the 2017 law also lowered rates for individuals in every tax bracket. If a new administration repeals the Trump reforms, the people noticing immediately will not just be the wealthy. Phil DeMuth, author of *The Overtaxed Investor: Slash Your Tax Bill & Be a Tax Alpha Dog*, says, "To see what a good deal we have now, let's look at the numbers. A married couple filing jointly shows $78,000 of ordinary income, their current marginal rate is 12%." But if the Trump tax cuts disappear, this couple's marginal rate "will more than double, to 25%," he adds.[24]

The repeal of Trump tax reform would bring especially bad news for retired people. According to DeMuth, "If you receive $30,000 from Social Security and have $36,000 of other income, you will be taxed at a marginal rate of 46%, even while supposedly being in the 25% tax bracket (because of the nutty way Social Security is taxed). In some cases, your tax rate can go as high as 56%. More people will experience rising tax rates throughout retirement—first gradually, following the accelerated required minimum distributions from their retirement accounts, and then suddenly, when the first spouse dies and the survivor has to file as a single taxpayer."[25]

And there are more Trump reforms at risk, says DeMuth; "The Trump tax reform doubled standard deductions, such that far fewer taxpayers still bother to itemize. . . . Remember the Alternative Minimum Tax, which made you do your taxes twice, under two completely different tax regimes, and then pay whichever was greater? That annual ritual has all but disappeared," but it would come back to life without the Trump law. DeMuth adds that "the qualified business income deduction, which lets eligible small-business owners deduct up to 20% of their income," would also go away.[26]

What would be the cost of a Biden presidency? This depends on just how much of the Sanders agenda Biden wants to enact. The tax increases Biden has already announced would collect much more from taxpayers than simply repealing the Trump tax reforms. But if Biden wanted to pay for all the spending Bernie Sanders promoted as a candidate last winter, even adding another zero to the $4 trillion Biden tax hikes still wouldn't cover it.

10

Trump's Unfinished Business

I f it were easy to create the conditions for America's 1980s economic resurgence, then all presidents would be as admired as Ronald Reagan. In recent years the U.S. economy in the pre-Covid Trump era grew faster than it had during the Obama years, but it still didn't approach the sizzling pace of the Reagan renaissance. After the 2017 Trump tax cut ignited a surge in capital investment, business confidence was restrained a bit by the Trump trade disputes with foreign governments.

The Tax Foundation estimates that Trump's enacted and threatened tariffs, plus retaliatory tariffs imposed by other countries in response, offset nearly a third of the additional growth produced by his income tax reform. According to a February 2020 report from the organization's Erica York,

"Tariffs imposed so far by the Trump administration are estimated to reduce long-run GDP by 0.23 percent, wages by 0.15 percent, and employment by 179,800 full-time equivalent jobs.

"The administration's outstanding threats to impose additional tariffs would, if acted upon, further reduce GDP by 0.24 percent, wages by 0.17 percent, and employment by 184,200 full-time equivalent jobs."[1]

A big opportunity for Trump now is to reduce the economic drag from tariffs at least outside of China—keeping the pressure on Beijing while encouraging growth with all our other trading partners. In April 2020, President Donald Trump told James that he plans "a pause on new tariffs" other than ones related to China "for a short while."[2] The president hadn't given up his belief that tariffs can be a valuable negotiating tool and a useful source of government revenue. But he was increasingly focused on encouraging a post-shutdown economic rebound and figured that this is not the moment to engage in new trade fights with allies. The "pause" has exceptions, including the reimposition of an earlier tariff on Canadian aluminum.

As for tariffs on imports from China, Mr. Trump said that, due to changes in the value of the Chinese currency, Chinese producers rather than U.S. consumers have been shouldering the burden. Given the destruction caused by the coronavirus, Beijing shouldn't necessarily expect much progress in future trade discussions.[3]

But a pause on new tariffs outside China is at least a start in setting conditions for a global rebound. Even better would be a concerted effort to reduce tariffs and other trade barriers to zero among friends and allies. This is the bold and beautiful pro-growth idea that the president promoted at a G7 meeting in 2018. The world has never needed it more than right now, given the economic carnage resulting from mandated shutdowns across the globe. To be clear, we are not predicting that if reelected, Trump will stop using the tariff cudgel with countries beyond China. James urges against tariffs given the cost, while Maria views them as leverage that Trump uses to open foreign markets.

Trump may be using this leverage again given that he sees its recent application as a success—for example, when he used a tariff threat to force Mexican action to stem the flow of illegal border-crossers into the United States. In 2018 large caravans of migrants fled Central America, headed north, and attempted to cross into the United States. In June 2019 Trump threatened new tariffs unless Mexico deployed more troops to limit illegal migration through its territory. Trump tells us, "I said, 'If you don't stop the caravans, I'm going to charge you a 25 percent . . . tariff on your cars coming in and . . . all the stuff that you send us. . . . So stop the people. . . .' On a Friday I said, 'It starts on Monday.' And they called, and we negotiated a deal."[4] Mexico agreed to deploy thousands of its National Guard troops throughout the country, and especially on its southern border with Guatemala.

Mexico has honored its side of the bargain and remains a good friend to the United States.

Also, even absent any further governmental action, many

U.S. companies are looking to diversify their supply chains to avoid overreliance on China. Given the destruction caused by Covid-19—and the unconscionable conduct of the Chinese regime in attempting to hide evidence of the virus rather than warning the world—it's impossible to argue that America's medical supply chain should be entirely reliant on China.

Moving production of medical drugs, devices, and equipment will mean added costs, and tariff reductions in other locales can help offset the expenses of renovating supply chains.

The president's playbook of tax cuts, deregulation, and supply chain moves can be a welcome first step toward creating the conditions for the next American surge in capital investment. A campaign to turn his 2018 G7 vision into reality could trigger another Trump jobs boom in the United States and a robust economic rebound worldwide. Nancy Lazar, cofounder of the investment research firm Cornerstone Macro, already sees a powerful trend of "onshoring" production and moving jobs back to the United States. Since the start of 2020 her firm counts more than one hundred companies shifting manufacturing to the United States. "This is the tip of the iceberg," she told Maria, adding that capital spending is the "ugly duckling" of the economy "because it creates a beautiful thing. It creates jobs. When China started to join [the World Trade Organization] in 2001, our capital stock growth deteriorated. That destroyed the breadth of our job growth. That then lowered the prime age labor force participation rate. That then led to an increase in the number of people on disability. That then led to, obviously, a deterioration in real, real family income growth. We're now seeing the reverse of all of that."[5]

Even with the cost of trade fights, the Trump tax and regulatory reforms were so powerful that the pre-Covid Trump job market was still as good as it gets—or at least as good as it has ever gotten since the government began keeping track. In March 2018, the Labor Department released its regular Job Openings and Labor Turnover Survey, better known as the "Jolts" report. The feds reported a remarkable finding about the historic eagerness of businesses to hire. "On the last business day of January, the job openings level increased to a series high of 6.3 million," noted the government.[6]

The *Wall Street Journal*'s Lev Borodovsky wrote, "The ratio of jobs openings to unemployment reached 1.0 for the first time since the government started tracking the data."[7] In sum, the feds had no record of any time when jobs were so plentiful relative to job-seekers.

That same month, the Department of Agriculture reported that fewer people were using food stamps: "Spending for USDA's 15 domestic food and nutrition assistance programs totaled $98.6 billion in FY 2017, 4 percent less than in the previous fiscal year and almost 10 percent less than the historical high of $109.2 billion set in FY 2013.

"The Supplemental Nutrition Assistance Program (SNAP) accounted for 69 percent of all Federal food and nutrition assistance spending in FY 2017. On average, 42.2 million persons per month participated in the program, almost 5 percent fewer than in the previous fiscal year. Reflecting the decrease in participation, Federal spending for SNAP totaled $68.0 billion, or 4 percent less than in the previous fiscal year. This was also 15 percent less than the historical high of $79.9 billion set in FY 2013."[8]

We mentioned in chapter four the stir Trump caused when he arrived at the World Economic Forum in Davos, Switzerland, just after the passage of his tax cut and amid the resulting U.S. boom in business investment. "I'm here to deliver a simple message: There has never been a better time to hire, to build, to invest, and to grow in the United States. America is open for business, and we are competitive once again," Trump said in a speech to the global gathering.[9]

Thanks to the Trump tax and regulatory reforms, U.S. businesses continued their hiring binge. And the record breaking continued. In February 2019 the government's Bureau of Labor Statistics reported that on the last day of December 2018 the number of job openings in the United States hit another record high—surging all the way up to 7.3 million.[10]

The Associated Press added that the total of 7.3 million open positions were "far greater than the number of unemployed, which stood at 6.3 million." According to AP: "Businesses have shrugged off a variety of potential troubles for the economy in the past two months and kept on hiring."[11]

During his 2019 State of the Union address, Trump strayed from his prepared text to call for legal immigration in "the largest numbers ever." [12] At a subsequent cabinet meeting, he once again called for allowing more workers into a U.S. economy that sorely needed them.

"Speaking of jobs, we have to have more people coming into our country," said Trump. He added that "we want to have people come into our country, but we want to have them come in through a merit system, and we want to have them come in legally. And that's going to be happening." [13]

Later in his remarks he returned to the topic of the U.S. worker shortage and one of the obvious solutions: "More people [are] working today in the United States than at any time in the history of our country. We're getting very close to 160 million people. And we've never had anything like that, which tells you that we have to have people come into our country—great people. . . . But we want them to be productive, and they—we want people that are going to love our country and help our country." [14]

Trump may never agree with congressional Democrats on how to address illegal immigration. But as for the legal variety, the possibilities are intriguing—and one of the keys to achieving Reagan-style economic growth above 3 percent per year. The key is welcoming *legally* more people who are eager to love this country and chase the American dream.

In April an inspiring story appeared in the *New York Times*, believe it or not. Amazingly, it managed to show the tough, striving American can-do spirit while exposing the costs of shutdowns and rebutting the claims of immigration opponents all in one fell swoop. The story even managed to highlight the opportunities available in lightly governed South Dakota compared to blue-state alternatives.

Caitlin Dickerson and Miriam Jordan reported on employees at South Dakota's Smithfield pork-processing facility, which the *Times* called, in April 2020, "the nation's largest single-source coronavirus hot spot. Its employees now make up about 44 percent of the diagnoses in South Dakota. . . ."

Given the recent infection at the plant one might have expected the workers to be the most supportive of stay-at-home orders. But according to the *Times* account:

> "I can't wait to go back to work for the simple reason that this is the only thing that supports my family," said Achut Deng, a Sudanese refugee who in six years worked her way up from a "wizard knife" operator paid $12.75 an hour to a shift lead making $18.70. "I do feel sorry for everyone who is going through this, I feel sorry for myself, but it's like, I feel better now so I'd rather go back to work."
>
> . . . [M]any workers said that the grueling work at the plant, before the virus hit, had offered them a life that otherwise would never have been possible as immigrants and refugees. "Honestly, I was able to improve myself," said Yoli Hernandez, a single mother of four from El Salvador, who started at the plant in 1999 and earns $17.30 an hour. "This is the only place where I was able to make a living and raise my kids."
>
> Sara Birhe, whose family arrived in Sioux Falls from

Ethiopia in 2001, said her mother bought a four-bedroom house and sent her children to college on a single income from the plant. "Working at Smithfield, you can provide for your family and not struggle as much as if you were working in California, Chicago, or D.C.," she said.[15]

Once we break out of the Covid-related recession imposed by state and local government lockdown orders, there's every reason to believe that the U.S. economy will be humming again and in need of more workers.

As recently as February of this year, across the country and across industries at businesses large and small, employers were saying they couldn't find enough workers to fill all of their open positions. The Trump economy featured an outstanding job market for workers but also included missed opportunities as employers couldn't staff up to meet demand. And the president recognized this. The *Wall Street Journal*'s Michelle Hackman reported the hopeful news: "The Trump administration plans to allow 45,000 additional seasonal guest workers to return to the U.S. this summer, the highest number since the president took office, according to three administration officials."

Hackman added: "The seasonal worker program, known as the H-2B visa program, enables U.S. employers to hire as many as 66,000 foreign workers a year, with the allotments split evenly between the winter and summer seasons. Congress permits the Department of Homeland Security each year to raise that cap by as many as 64,000 additional visas. In Mr. Trump's first two years in office, DHS raised the cap by 15,000 visas to 81,000, and last year it raised the cap by 30,000 to 96,000. The additional visas will primarily be available to workers who have previously qualified for H-2B visas because the administration has more confidence that they will leave the country once their job assignments end." [16]

There's little argument against admitting people who have already proven they can be productive workers and good guests of the United States.

Also, America can always use productive citizens. There may be a separate opportunity to admit people who can become more than guests. Nick Miroff and Josh Dawsey reported last winter in the *Washington Post*: "Acting White House chief of staff Mick Mulvaney told a crowd at a private gathering in England on Wednesday night that the Trump administration 'needs more immigrants' for the U.S. economy to continue growing, according to an audio recording of his remarks obtained by the *Washington Post*.

" 'We are desperate—desperate—for more people,' Mulvaney said. 'We are running out of people to fuel the economic growth that we've had in our nation over the last four years. We need more immigrants.'

"The Trump administration wants those immigrants to come in a 'legal fashion,' Mulvaney said, according to the recording." [17]

The administration had recently won a Supreme Court case allowing the government to tighten rules to ensure that immigrants do not require public assistance. The Department of Homeland Security's U.S. Citizenship and Immigration Services says: "Self-sufficiency has long been a basic principle of U.S. immigration law. Since the 1800s, Congress has put into statute that individuals are inadmissible to the United States if they are unable to care for themselves without becoming public charges. Since 1996, federal laws have stated that aliens generally must be self-sufficient."[18]

Fair enough. But for those who are ready and eager to work, why not let them make America even greater?

Trump has essentially already fulfilled his signature 2016 campaign promise thanks to the colorful tariff threat, which he described to us in our interview, that resulted in Mexico's deployment of additional troops to stem illegal migration. In 2019, Donald Luskin of Trend Macrolytics commented on the news: "Mexico just agreed to expend its resources to stem the flow of migrants from Central America through Mexico into the United States. In essence, Trump just delivered on the biggest, craziest campaign promise in history. He just used tariffs to get Mexico to agree to pay for the wall."[19]

And at least according to Trump his recent agreement with Mexico is leading to even more cooperation in the region. The *Wall Street Journal*'s Louise Radnofsky reported: "President Trump praised Mexico's efforts to intercept Central American asylum seekers and said that Guatemala was getting ready to sign an agreement that would make it a final refuge for people fleeing poverty and violence in the region."[20]

Trump can now focus on helping the United States enjoy the benefits of legal migration. Long term, as long as the United States maintains pro-growth policies, the worker shortage is going to get worse. In November 2019 the government's National Center for Health Statistics released its final report on 2018 births in the United States: "The general fertility rate . . . for the United States in 2018 was 59.1 births per 1,000 females aged 15–44, down 2% from 2017 (60.3) and a record low rate for the nation. . . . This is the fourth year that the rate has declined. . . ."[21]

Fortunately there's a world of talent eager to come here. Uber's CEO Dara Khosrowshahi received asylum in the United States as a child in 1978 after his family fled revolutionary Iran. According to a 2018 profile by Sheelah Kolhatkar in the *New Yorker*: "Khosrowshahi's family led a prosperous upper-class life in Tehran until the Iranian Revolution threw the country into chaos. A wealthy uncle lived in New York, and the Khosrowshahis, after escaping temporarily to the South of France, where the family had vacationed in the past, immigrated to the United States and moved into a three-bedroom condominium in Tarrytown. Shortly after they arrived in the U.S., fifty-two American diplomats were taken hostage in Tehran, a crisis that lasted more than a year and created a surge of anti-Iranian sentiment in America. The family watched from across an ocean as their manufacturing business, which produced consumer and pharmaceutical goods under brands licensed from Western countries, was nationalized by the new Islamic government."[22]

Ever since, people who have been waiting for the Iranian government to reform have been constantly disappointed. And as Ms. Kolhatkar noted, after the young Dara Khosrowshahi found refuge in the United States, the regime in Tehran wasn't done messing with his family: "When he was in his early teens, his father returned to Iran to take care of his own father, who was ill. He was arrested by the government and detained for six years. Khosrowshahi's mother, left to care for three teenage boys, took a job as a salesperson at a high-end women's-clothing boutique in Manhattan—the sort of store she had previously frequented as a client. 'I think there was this undercurrent within my family, which was that we had lost everything,' Khosrowshahi told me. In his first address to Uber employees, in August, he put it more bluntly: 'There's this chip you have on your shoulder as an immigrant that drives you.' "[23]

U.S. policy should be to import as many chip-on-the-shoulder achievers as we can find. One of Uber's founders, also an immigrant, seems to have been carrying a different type of chip on *his* shoulder, yet it still proved useful to the American economy. Stuart Anderson writes in *Forbes*: "Many people may not realize that one of the founders of Uber, Garrett Camp, is an immigrant from Canada. Camp came up with the idea for Uber after becoming frustrated dealing with taxis while seeing a girlfriend."[24]

Okay, maybe that's not quite as inspiring a tale as the escape from Tehran, but Mr. Camp and his cofounder Travis Kalanick have made life easier for millions of people looking for rides.

Legitimate asylum seekers and Canadian transplants aren't the only people who make great contributions to the United States. And of course some immigrants do much more than found ride-hailing companies. According to Anderson: "Mexican-born immigrant and Medal of Honor recipient

Alfred Rascon was once asked about his courage on the battle-field fighting for America even though he had yet to become a citizen. 'I was always an American in my heart,' said Rascon.

As for the other potential drivers of growth, in an interview with us the president said a June Supreme Court decision gives him a lot of latitude to act administratively without going to Congress.[25] In a 5–4 decision Chief Justice John Roberts sided with the Court's four liberals in preventing the president from rescinding the Obama decision to allow the so-called Dreamers, people brought here illegally as children, to remain in the United States. The baffling decision requires the Trump administration to conduct a long and difficult rule-making process to rescind his predecessor's policy, even though the Obama policy wasn't legal.

The Court found—or invented—a broad presidential ability to entrench federal policies without changes in law. The Obama policy was known as Deferred Action for Childhood Arrivals, or DACA, and Trump seems eager to make the most of the precedent. He told us that "when the Supreme Court ruled on DACA, they gave the President powers the likes of which have never been given to a President. And I always said, 'They can't rule positively on DACA. There's no way they can do it.' . . . And yet for political reasons, they ruled on DACA the way they did. . . . So I'm going to be doing tax cuts and I'm signing them myself. I'm not going through Congress."[26]

Trump pointed out that under the new precedent he has the right to enact other changes along with tax cuts, "like a health care bill, like an immigration bill, like numerous things. They're all being drawn right now. And all I have to do is sign them." He added that he intends to enact a big tax cut for middle-income taxpayers and also wants to knock the corporate income tax rate down another notch to 20 percent from 21 percent.[27]

Speaking of the courts, Trump forecasts in our interview that there will soon be a total of three hundred Trump appointees seated on the federal bench. And he thanks former Senate majority leader Harry Reid (D-Nev.), who in 2013 led his fellow Democrats in abolishing the Senate filibuster for the consideration of potential federal judges. The Reid change meant that a minority of senators could no longer block votes, and, therefore, many more judicial appointments could be confirmed. Reid and his colleagues engineered this break with Senate tradition in order to pack the influential D.C. Circuit with their ideological allies, perhaps not realizing that once in the majority, Republicans could use the same method to approve lots of conservative judges. Before Reid destroyed the judicial filibuster, such an action was known as the "nuclear option," because it represented such a radical shift in Senate process. Now some Democrats regret their decision to detonate, and Trump says this includes current Senate minority leader Charles Schumer (D-N.Y.) The president reports that Schumer frequently says, "The worst thing that ever happened to us was Harry Reid." But of course Trump sees the situation differently: "Thank God we had the nuclear option."[28]

Still, as he closes in on the end of his first term, there are many things about the political process for which the president is not at all thankful. Maria asked him for the biggest takeaway from his time in Washington. "Deep-seated corruption," responded Trump. "People are there and they're protected." [29]

If reelected, Trump will need a growing economy to finance the massive federal debt held by the public, which has ballooned to a staggering $21 trillion. In the area of restraining spending, Trump has failed just like the usual professional politicians. Biden's proposals would increase the debt even faster than Trump's. But if the president is reelected, America needs him to enact spending restraint before interest rates rise back up toward typical levels and servicing the federal debt becomes unbearable.

The other big related challenge is maintaining the value of the dollar and preventing inflation after the Federal Reserve just created nearly $3 trillion of new money to maintain the financial system while the nation's underlying economy was largely shut down.

On this score the president deserves great credit for appointing economist Judy Shelton to the board of the Fed. At her confirmation hearing in the Senate Banking Committee, Ms. Shelton showed her keen understanding that the Fed does not exist to enable ever larger federal budgets. Shelton said:

I keep going back to the fact that the power to regulate the value of U.S. money was granted by our Constitution to Congress. It's in Article 1, Section 8. And in the very same sentence Congress is given the power to define the official weights and measures for our country, because money was meant to be a measure, to be a standard of value. I think that money has to work the same for everyone in the economy, and it's important that it serve that purpose as a reliable measure, so that people can plan their lives.

I don't see how you can have a free market economy if people can't rely on the most vital tool that makes markets work. It's through money that we transmit market signals. And you need clarity of those signals or supply and demand can't figure out what's the optimal solution. . . . [A]t the Federal Reserve is a responsibility to remember that money has to work for everyone and that in a sense it's a moral contract between the government and the citizens.[30]

Credit President Donald Trump with another great hire. If Shelton can help the Fed maintain the value of the dollar, tariff fights ease, and legal migration is allowed to rise, the earlier Trump tax and regulatory reforms can allow America's economy to roar again. The results could be truly historic.

In addition to the president's immigration, tax cut, and further energy deregulation plans, the Trump campaign released a set of principles for a second term. They include creating

10 million new jobs in ten months, developing a Covid vaccine by the end of 2020, providing school choice for students, and continuing to "drain the swamp" by pushing congressional term limits, among other moves.

The administration has also been clear about holding China in check and returning law and order to our cities, partly by fully funding and hiring more police and law enforcement officers.

And if Americans are able to enjoy continued peace and prosperity in a second Trump term, they should also expect that a historically informal method of presidential communication will continue. When we inquired whether he ever asks anyone—for example, First Lady Melania Trump—to review tweets before he sends them, Trump responded, "A little bit. But basically, I do what I do. You know, I'm president. Somebody said, 'Oh, that's not good.' I said, 'Oh, really? Where are we?' 'Sir, we're in the Oval Office.' I said, 'That's right.'"[31]

Acknowledgments

This book builds on our work at the Fox Business Network, Fox News, and the *Wall Street Journal*. We're grateful to the people who allow us to do the jobs we love and helped us to tell this story about an extraordinary period in U.S. political history. We thank Suzanne Scott and Jay Wallace at Fox News, Lauren Petterson at the Fox Business Network, Robert Thomson at News Corp, and Almar Latour and Paul Gigot at the *Wall Street Journal*. We're also grateful to Lachlan and Rupert Murdoch for creating and maintaining the vibrant media competition that helps a free society to thrive.

Speaking of vibrant competitors, we thank our parents, Vinny and Josephine Bartiromo and Neal and Jane Freeman, for teaching us the value of hard work and for all their love and support.

We've also lately been fortunate to have the support of Abby Grossberg and Patrick Michael Ignozzi in conducting research and producing news-making television.

ACKNOWLEDGMENTS

We thank James's kids, Will, Neal, Jane, and Jack, for their good cheer and for often remaining quiet while their father was working.

Thanks are also due to Anthony Mattero, David Larabell, and Andy Elkin of the Creative Artists Agency and to Natasha Simons of Simon & Schuster, who made it happen.

Notes

Introduction

1. "As Mar-a-Lago Resort Opens, How to Make the President's Favorite Dessert That's Served There," *Inside Edition*, Nov. 3, 2017, article and TV segment at https://www.insideedition.com/mar-lago-resort-opens -how-make-presidents-favorite-dessert-thats-served-there-37786.

2. *Mornings with Maria*, hosted by Maria Bartiromo, Fox Business Network, Apr. 12, 2017.

3. Geoff Raby, "How Xi Jingping Got Trumped by Cruise Missile Diplomacy," Opinion, *Financial Review*, updated Apr. 10, 2017, https://www.afr.com/opinion/how-xi-jinping-got-trumped-by-cruise-missile -diplomacy-20170410-gvhjdo.

4. *Sunday Morning Futures*, hosted by Maria Bartiromo, Fox News Channel, Feb. 16, 2020.

5. Chao Deng and Josh Chin, "Chinese Doctor Who Issued Early Warning on Virus Dies," *Wall Street Journal*, Feb. 7, 2020, https://www .wsj.com/articles/chinese-doctor-who-issued-early-warning-on-virus -dies-11581019816.

6. Lev Borodovsky, "The Number of Job Openings Matches the Number of Unemployed for the First Time," *Daily Shot* (blog), *Wall Street Journal*, Mar. 19, 2018, https://blogs.wsj.com/dailyshot/2018/03/19 /the-daily-shot-the-number-of-job-openings-matches-the-number-of -unemployed-for-the-first-time/.

7. "Transcript: Donald Trump at the G.O.P. Convention," *New York Times*,

July 22, 2016, https://www.nytimes.com/2016/07/22/us/politics/trump
-transcript-rnc-address.html.

8. "Full Text: Donald Trump 2016 RNC Draft Speech Transcript," Politico, July 21, 2016, https://www.politico.com/story/2016/07/full-tran
script-donald-trump-nomination-acceptance-speech-at-rnc-225974.

9. *In Re Accuracy Concerns Regarding FBI Matters Submitted to the FISC*,
United States Foreign Intelligence Surveillance Court, Washington, D.C.,
Docket No. Misc. 19-02, Rosemary M. Collyer, Presiding Judge, Order
entered Dec. 17, 2019, https://www.fisc.uscourts.gov/sites/default/files
/MIsc%2019%2002%20191217.pdf.

10. *In Re Accuracy Concerns Regarding FBI Matters Submitted to the FISC*,
United States Foreign Intelligence Surveillance Court, Washington,
D.C., Docket No. Misc. 19-02, James E. Boasberg, Judge, Corrected
Opinion and Order entered Mar. 5, 2020, https://www.fisc.uscourts
.gov/sites/default/files/Misc%2019%2002%20Corrected%20Opinion
%20and%20Order%20JEB%20200305.pdf.

11. Maria Bartiromo, "Dow 24000 and the Trump Boom," *Wall Street Journal*, Dec. 14, 2017, https://www.wsj.com/articles/dow-24000-and-the
-trump-boom-1513294061.

12. James Freeman, "January Jobs Surge," *Wall Street Journal*, Feb. 2, 2017,
https://www.wsj.com/articles/january-job-surge-1486052605.

13. Joe Concha, "CNN Headline Declares 'End of the Internet As We
Know It' After Net Neutrality Vote," The Hill, Dec. 14, 2017, https://
thehill.com/homenews/media/364959-cnn-headline-declares-end-of
-the-internet-as-we-know-it-after-net-neutrality.

14. Glenn Thrush and Michael M. Grynbaum, "Trump Ruled the Tabloid Media.
Washington Is a Different Story," *New York Times*, Feb. 25, 2017, https://
www.nytimes.com/2017/02/25/us/politics/trump-press-conflict.html.

15. Michael D. Shear and Catherine Porter, "Trump Refuses to Sign G-7
Statement and Calls Trudeau 'Weak,'" *New York Times*, June 9, 2018,
https://www.nytimes.com/2018/06/09/world/americas/donald-trump
-g7-nafta.html.

Chapter 1: Morality and Prosperity

1. Doyle McManus, "The Good News: Trump's Ineptitude," *Los Angeles
Times*, Jan. 13, 2019, https://www.latimes.com/nation/la-na-pol-mc
manus-column-20190111-story.html.

2. Justin Wise, "Trump Says 'You Have No Choice but to Vote for Me' at
New Hampshire Rally," The Hill, Aug. 15, 2019, https://thehill.com

/homenews/administration/457653-trump-says-you-have-no-choice
-but-to-vote-for-me-at-campaign.

3. Jake Tapper and Karen Travers, "President Obama Says America Has
Shown 'Arrogance,'" ABC News, Apr. 3, 2009.

4. Karl Rove, "The President's Apology Tour," *Wall Street Journal*, Apr. 23,
2009, https://www.wsj.com/articles/SB124044156269345357.

5. Max Fisher, "Obama, Acknowledging U.S. Misdeeds Abroad, Quietly
Reframes American Power," *New York Times*, Sept. 7, 2016, https://
www.nytimes.com/2016/09/08/world/americas/obama-acknowledging
-us-misdeeds-abroad-quietly-reframes-american-power.html.

6. "Remarks by President Trump to the 74th Session of the United
Nations General Assembly," The White House, Sept. 24, 2019, https://
www.whitehouse.gov/briefings-statements/remarks-president-trump
-74th-session-united-nations-general-assembly/.

7. Ibid.

8. Christopher Orr, "How 'Caddyshack' Explains the Presidential Race,"
Atlantic, Sept. 16, 2015, https://www.theatlantic.com/politics/archive
/2015/09/cinderella-story-outta-nowhere/405547/.

9. Josh Barro, "Donald Trump Is the Guilty-Pleasure Candidate," Business Insider, Mar. 15, 2016, https://www.businessinsider.com/donald
-trump-brand-products-voting-2016-3.

10. "Playback: The Guilty Pleasure President," Politico, May 18, 2016,
https://www.politico.com/video/2016/05/playback-guilty-pleasure
-president-057020?filterVideo=1201016315.

11. Paul Krugman, "Judas, Tax Cuts and the Great Betrayal," Opinion, *New
York Times*, May 12, 2017, https://www.nytimes.com/2017/05/12/opin
ion/judas-tax-cuts-and-the-great-betrayal.html. Paul Krugman, "The New
Climate of Treason," *The Conscience of a Liberal* (blog), *New York Times*,
July 14, 2017, https://krugman.blogs.nytimes.com/2017/07/14/the-new
-climate-of-treason/.

12. *Sunday Morning Futures*, hosted by Maria Bartiromo, Fox News Channel,
Mar. 25, 2018.

13. John Burnett, "Thousands of Cars Line Up at One Texas Food Bank As Job
Losses Hit Hard," Special Series: The Coronavirus Crisis, NPR, Apr. 17,
2020, https://www.npr.org/2020/04/17/837141457/thousands-of-cars
-line-up-at-one-texas-food-bank-as-job-losses-hit-hard.

14. Sarah Chaney and Eric Morath, "April Unemployment Rate Rose to a
Record 14.7%," *Wall Street Journal*, May 8, 2020, https://www.wsj.com
/articles/april-jobs-report-coronavirus-2020-11588888089.

15. Abdi Latif Dahir, "'Instead of Coronavirus, the Hunger Will Kill Us.' A Global Food Crisis Looms," *New York Times*, updated May 13, 2020, https://www.nytimes.com/2020/04/22/world/africa/coronavirus-hunger -crisis.html.

16. David Thomas, CFA, and Chad Wessel, *2019 Emerging Therapeutic Company Trend Report*, BIO Industry Analysis, http://go.bio.org/rs/490-EHZ -999/images/BIO%202019%20Emerging%20Company%20Trend %20Report.pdf?_ga=2.171345888.17682745.1589058506-1285406470 .1589058506.

17. Ian Millhiser, "What Trump Has Done to the Courts, Explained," Vox, updated Feb. 4, 2020, https://www.vox.com/policy-and-politics /2019/12/9/20962980/trump-supreme-court-federal-judges.

18. "Giving USA 2020: Charitable Giving Showed Solid Growth, Climbing to $449.64 Billion in 2019, One of the Highest Years for Giving on Record," Giving USA, June 16, 2020, https://givingusa.org/giving-usa -2020-charitable-giving-showed-solid-growth-climbing-to-449-64-bil lion-in-2019-one-of-the-highest-years-for-giving-on-record/.

19. *The Index of Global Philanthropy and Remittances 2016*, Center for Global Prosperity, Hudson Institute, n.d., https://scholarworks.iupui .edu/bitstream/handle/1805/15876/2016%20IGPAR.pdf?sequence =1&isAllowed=y.

20. "Additional U.S. Foreign Assistance Builds upon U.S. Leadership in the Global COVID-19 Response," Press Statement, U.S. Department of State, Michael R. Pompeo, Secretary of State, May 6, 2020, https://www.state.gov/additional-u-s-foreign-assistance-builds-upon-u-s -leadership-in-the-global-covid-19-response/.

21. *CAF World Giving Index, 10th Edition*, Charities Aid Foundation, Oct. 2019, 4, https://www.cafonline.org/docs/default-source/about-us-publica tions/caf_wgi_10th_edition_report_2712a_web_101019.pdf.

22. Ibid.

23. Ibid., 5.

24. Ibid., 8.

25. *Mornings with Maria*, hosted by Maria Bartiromo, Fox Business Network, May 7, 2020, https://video.foxbusiness.com/v/6154930412001 /#sp=show-clips.

26. Christopher Rugaber, "US Job Openings Jump to Record High of 7.3 Million," Associated Press, Feb. 12, 2019, https://apnews.com/bf2ff7ec 19c74f2a8451f4bf2876e7ee.

Chapter 2: The Coup That Failed

1. *Sunday Morning Futures*, hosted by Maria Bartiromo, Fox News Channel, Mar. 24, 2019.
2. *Sunday Morning Futures*, hosted by Maria Bartiromo, Fox News Channel, June 21, 2020.
3. "Sen. Johnson: Obama Administration Totally Corrupted the Transition of Power," video and transcript of *Sunday Morning Futures*, hosted by Maria Bartiromo, Fox News Channel, May 31, 2020, https://www.foxnews.com/transcript/sen-johnson-obama-administration-totally-corrupted-the-transition-of-power.
4. Ibid.
5. *Sunday Morning Futures*, hosted by Maria Bartiromo, Fox News Channel, June 21, 2020.
6. *Review of Four FISA Applications and Other Aspects of the FBI's Crossfire Hurricane Investigation* (Redacted for Public Release), Office of the Inspector General, U.S. Department of Justice, Oversight and Review Division (20-012), Dec. 2019 (revised), 188, https://www.justice.gov/storage/120919-examination.pdf.
7. "IG Footnotes: Serious Problems with Dossier Sources Didn't Stop FBI's Page Surveillance," web page of Chuck Grassley, United States Senator for Iowa, Apr. 15, 2020, https://www.grassley.senate.gov/news/news-releases/ig-footnotes-serious-problems-dossier-sources-didn-t-stop-fbi-s-page-surveillance.
8. Talia Kaplan, "Former Acting DNI Grenell on Declassifying Russia Probe Docs: 'Transparency Is Never Political,'" Fox News Channel, June 14, 2020, https://www.foxnews.com/media/grenell-on-declassifying-russia-probe-docs-transparency-is-never-political.
9. *Review of Four FISA Applications and Other Aspects of the FBI's Crossfire Hurricane Investigation*, 90–91.
10. Ibid., 195n349.
11. Ibid., 91.
12. Ibid., 186.
13. Ibid., 186n355.
14. Ibid., vi.
15. Ibid., vi.
16. Ibid., 413.
17. Ibid.

18. *Sunday Morning Futures*, hosted by Maria Bartiromo, Fox News Channel, Oct. 14, 2018.

19. *Sunday Morning Futures*, hosted by Maria Bartiromo, Fox News Channel, Dec. 8, 2019.

20. *Review of Four FISA Applications and Other Aspects of the FBI's Crossfire Hurricane Investigation*, 8, 160.

21. Adam Goldman and Charlie Savage, "Russia Inquiry Review Is Said to Criticize F.B.I. but Rebuff Claims of Biased Acts," *New York Times*, Nov. 22, 2019, https://www.nytimes.com/2019/11/22/us/politics/russia -investigation-inspector-general-report.html.

22. *In Re Accuracy Concerns Regarding FBI Matters Submitted to the FISC*, United States Foreign Intelligence Surveillance Court, Washington, D.C., Docket No. Misc. 19-02, Rosemary M. Collyer, Presiding Judge, Order entered Dec. 17, 2019, https://www.fisc.uscourts.gov/sites/default/files /MIsc%2019%2002%20191217.pdf.

23. *Review of Four FISA Applications and Other Aspects of the FBI's Crossfire Hurricane Investigation*, vi.

24. "IG Footnotes: Serious Problems with Dossier Sources Didn't Stop FBI's Page Surveillance."

25. *Review of Four FISA Applications and Other Aspects of the FBI's Crossfire Hurricane Investigation*, 187.

26. Ibid., 188.

27. *Sunday Morning Futures*, hosted by Maria Bartiromo, Fox News Channel, June 21, 2020.

28. "IG Footnotes: Serious Problems with Dossier Sources Didn't Stop FBI's Page Surveillance."

29. Ibid.

30. *Mornings with Maria*, hosted by Maria Bartiromo, Fox Business Network, Sept. 19, 2018.

31. Tom Hamburger and Rosalind S. Helderman, "FBI Once Planned to Pay Former Spy Who Authored Controversial Trump Dossier," *Washington Post*, Feb. 28, 2017, https://www.washingtonpost.com/politics/fbi-once -planned-to-pay-former-british-spy-who-authored-controversial-trump -dossier/2017/02/28/896ab470-facc-11e6-9845-576c69081518_story .html.

32. Ibid.

33. Adam Entous and Ellen Nakashima, "Trump Asked Intelligence Chiefs to Push Back Against FBI Collusion Probe After Comey Revealed Its Existence," *Washington Post*, May 22, 2017, https://www.wash

ingtonpost.com/world/national-security/trump-asked-intelligence
-chiefs-to-push-back-against-fbi-collusion-probe-after-comey-revealed
-its-existence/2017/05/22/394933bc-3f10-11e7-9869-bac8b446820a
_story.html.

34. Ibid.

35. Ibid.

36. Ibid.

37. Matt Apuzzo, Michael S. Schmidt, Adam Goldman, and Eric Licht-blau, "Comey Tried to Shield the F.B.I. from Politics. Then He Shaped an Election," *New York Times*, Apr. 22, 2017, https://www.nytimes .com/2017/04/22/us/politics/james-comey-election.html.

38. *Review of Four FISA Applications and Other Aspects of the FBI's Crossfire Hurricane Investigation*, xi.

39. "The 2018 Pulitzer Prize Winner in National Reporting: Staffs of the New York Times and the Washington Post," The Pulitzer Prizes, n.d., https://www.pulitzer.org/winners/staffs-new-york-times-and-washington -post.

40. "Intel Committee Ranking Member Schiff Releases Democratic Response Memo," Press Release, U.S. House of Representatives Permanent Select Committee on Intelligence, Feb. 24, 2018, https://intelligence.house.gov /news/documentsingle.aspx?DocumentID=358.

41. Ibid.

42. Ibid.

43. Ibid.

44. Editorial Board, "All the Adam Schiff Transcripts," Opinion, *Wall Street Journal*, May 12, 2020, https://www.wsj.com/articles/all-the-adam-schiff -transcripts-11589326164.

45. Letter from Donald F. McGahn II, Counsel to the President, to Devin Nunes, Chairman, House Permanent Select Committee on Intelligence, Feb. 2, 2018, https://www.documentcloud.org/documents/4365338 -Nunes-memo.html.

46. *Sunday Morning Futures*, hosted by Maria Bartiromo, Fox News Channel, Mar. 25, 2018.

47. President Donald Trump, telephone interview with Maria Bartiromo and James Freeman, July 16, 2020.

48. *Interview of: Shawn Henry*, Executive Session, Permanent Select Committee on Intelligence, U.S. House of Representatives, Washington D.C., Tues., Dec. 5, 2017, https://intelligence.house.gov/uploadedfiles/sh21 .pdf.

49. *Review of Four FISA Applications and Other Aspects of the FBI's Crossfire Hurricane Investigation*, ii.

50. Ibid., 53.

51. *Sunday Morning Futures*, hosted by Maria Bartiromo, Fox News Channel, Apr. 22, 2018.

52. Sharon LaFraniere, Mark Mazzetti, and Matt Apuzzo, "How the Russia Inquiry Began: A Campaign Aide, Drinks and Talk of Political Dirt," *New York Times*, Dec. 30, 2017, https://www.nytimes.com/2017/12/30/us /politics/how-fbi-russia-investigation-began-george-papadopoulos.html.

53. *Sunday Morning Futures*, hosted by Maria Bartiromo, Fox News Channel, Apr. 22, 2018.

54. Kimberley A. Strassel, "The Curious Case of Mr. Downer," *Wall Street Journal*, May 31, 2018, https://www.wsj.com/articles/the-curious-case-of -mr-downer-1527809075.

55. David Crowe, "Downer Raised Russia Concerns at US Embassy Without Government Approval," *Sydney Morning Herald*, Apr. 18, 2020, https:// www.smh.com.au/politics/federal/downer-raised-russia-concerns-at-us -embassy-without-government-approval-20200416-p54kho.html.

56. Department of Justice documents obtained by Judicial Watch under the Freedom of Information Act, FOIPA Request No. 1442326, Civil Action No. 19-CV-02743, Subject: The Electronic Communication Which Led to the Initiation of the Counterintelligence Investigation of the Trump Campaign (as Described in the 4/4/18 Letter from Nunes to Wray and Rosenstein), supplied by David M. Hardy, Section Chief, Record/ Information Dissemination Section, Information Management Division, cover memo dated Mar. 17, 2020, https://www.judicialwatch.org/wp-con tent/uploads/2020/05/JW-v-DOJ-reply-02743.pdf.

57. *Review of Four FISA Applications and Other Aspects of the FBI's Crossfire Hurricane Investigation*, 263.

58. Ibid., 51n64.

59. Ibid., 167.

60. *Sunday Morning Futures*, hosted by Maria Bartiromo, Fox News Channel, Oct. 28, 2018.

61. *Review of Four FISA Applications and Other Aspects of the FBI's Crossfire Hurricane Investigation*, ix.

62. *Sunday Morning Futures*, hosted by Maria Bartiromo, Fox News Channel, Oct. 6, 2019.

63. Special Counsel Robert S. Mueller, III, *Report on the Investigation into Russian Interference in the 2016 Presidential Election*, Vol. 1, U.S. Department

of Justice, Washington, D.C., Mar. 2019, 88–89, https://www.justice.gov/storage/report.pdf.

64. Special Counsel Robert S. Mueller, III, *Report on the Investigation into Russian Interference in the 2016 Presidential Election*, Vol. 1, 193.

65. Full Transcript: Mueller Testimony Before House Judiciary, Intelligence Committees," NBC News, July 25, 2019, https://www.nbcnews.com/politics/congress/full-transcript-robert-mueller-house-committee-testimony-n1033216.

66. *Sunday Morning Futures*, hosted by Maria Bartiromo, Fox News Channel, June 21, 2020.

67. Ibid.

68. Ibid.

69. *Sunday Morning Futures*, hosted by Maria Bartiromo, Fox News Channel, Dec. 22, 2019.

70. Letter from Charles E. Grassley, Chairman, Committee on Finance, to William Barr, Attorney General, Department of Justice, Apr. 27, 2020, via electronic transmission, https://www.grassley.senate.gov/sites/default/files/2020-04-27%20CEG%20to%20DOJ%20(Flynn).pdf.

71. James Freeman, "Has Trump Been Too Polite to Comey?," Opinion, *Wall Street Journal*, Apr. 30, 2020, https://www.wsj.com/articles/has-trump-been-too-polite-to-comey-11588263818.

72. *Sunday Morning Futures*, hosted by Maria Bartiromo, Fox News Channel, June 21, 2020.

73. Call transcripts released by Senators Grassley and Johnson, May 29, 2020, https://d3i6fh83elv35t.cloudfront.net/static/2020/05/FlynnTranscripts.pdf.

74. *Sunday Morning Futures*, hosted by Maria Bartiromo, Fox News Channel, June 21, 2020.

75. Letter from Charles E. Grassley, Chairman, Committee on Finance, to William Barr, Attorney General, Department of Justice, Apr. 27, 2020.

76. Texts released by Senate Judiciary Committee, Jan. 25, 2018, https://www.judiciary.senate.gov/imo/media/doc/2018-01-25%20CEG%20Letter%20to%20FBI%20Source%20Texts.pdf.

77. "Abbreviated Timeline of Key Events Related to Crossfire Hurricane Investigation," Senate Homeland Security and Governmental Affairs Committee, Dec. 18, 2019, https://www.hsgac.senate.gov/imo/media/doc/abbreviated%20timeline%20horowitz.pdf.

78. Jake Gibson, "FBI Lovers' Latest Text Messages: Obama 'Wants to Know Everything,'" Fox News Channel, Feb. 7, 2018, https://www.foxnews

.com/politics/fbi-lovers-latest-text-messages-obama-wants-to-know
-everything.

79. Hope Yen, Marilynn Marchione, and Calvin Woodward, "AP Fact Check:
     Faulty Trump Claims on Virus Drug, Vote Fraud," Associated Press,
     May 25, 2020, appearing in U.S. News & World Report, https://www
     .usnews.com/news/politics/articles/2020-05-25/ap-fact-check-faulty
     -trump-claims-on-virus-drug-vote-fraud.

80. Department of Justice documents obtained by Judicial Watch under the
     Freedom of Information Act, FOIPA Request No. 1442326, Civil Action
     No. 19-CV-02743, Subject: The Electronic Communication Which Led
     to the Initiation of the Counterintelligence Investigation of the Trump
     Campaign.

81. Kevin R. Brock, "New FBI Document Confirms the Trump Cam-
     paign Was Investigated Without Justification," The Hill, May 27, 2020,
     https://thehill.com/opinion/white-house/499586-new-fbi-document
     -confirms-the-trump-campaign-was-investigated-without.

82. Paul Waldman, "The Peter Strzok Fiasco Wrecks the GOP's Bogus Con-
     spiracy Theory," The Plum Line (Opinion), Washington Post, July 12, 2018,
     https://www.washingtonpost.com/blogs/plum-line/wp/2018/07/12/the
     -peter-strzok-fiasco-wrecks-the-gops-bogus-conspiracy-theory/.

83. Brock, "New FBI Document Confirms the Trump Campaign Was Inves-
     tigated Without Justification."

84. Ibid.

85. Department of Justice documents obtained by Judicial Watch under the
     Freedom of Information Act, FOIPA Request No. 1442326, Civil Action
     No. 19-CV-02743, Subject: The Electronic Communication Which Led
     to the Initiation of the Counterintelligence Investigation of the Trump
     Campaign.

86. Office of the Inspector General, U.S. Department of Justice, A Review of
     Various Actions by the Federal Bureau of Investigation and Department of Jus-
     tice in Advance of the 2016 Election, June 2018, 209, https://www.justice
     .gov/file/1071991/download.

87. "Clinton 'Grossly Negligent' in Comey's Draft Statement on Email
     Probe," Chuck Grassley, United States Senator from Iowa, Nov. 6, 2017,
     https://www.grassley.senate.gov/news/news-releases/clinton-%E2%8
     0%98grossly-negligent%E2%80%99-comey%E2%80%99s-draft-state
     ment-email-probe.

88. Sunday Morning Futures, hosted by Maria Bartiromo, Fox News Channel,
     June 21, 2020.

89. *Mornings with Maria*, hosted by Maria Bartiromo, Fox Business Network, July 28, 2020.

90. *Sunday Morning Futures*, hosted by Maria Bartiromo, Fox News Channel, Aug. 2, 2020.

91. President Donald Trump, telephone interview with Maria Bartiromo and James Freeman, July 16, 2020.

Chapter 3: American Business Unleashed

1. Paul Krugman, "What Happened on Election Day; Paul Krugman: The Economic Fallout," Opinion, *New York Times*, Nov. 9, 2016, https://www.nytimes.com/interactive/projects/cp/opinion/election-night-2016/paul-krugman-the-economic-fallout.

2. "The $600 Billion Man," by James Freeman, *Wall Street Journal*, May 31, 2017, https://www.wsj.com/articles/the-600-billion-man-1496251287.

3. Ibid.

4. Ibid.

5. *BLS Reports: Consumer Expenditures in 2017*, U.S. Bureau of Labor Statistics, Report 1080, Apr. 2019, https://www.bls.gov/opub/reports/consumer-expenditures/2017/home.htm.

6. Maria Bartiromo, "Dow 24000 and the Trump Boom," *Wall Street Journal*, Dec. 14, 2017, https://www.wsj.com/articles/dow-24000-and-the-trump-boom-1513294061.

7. *Mornings with Maria*, hosted by Maria Bartiromo, Fox Business Network, Apr. 11, 2017.

8. Editorial Board, "The Great Rules Rollback," Opinion, *Wall Street Journal*, Dec. 25, 2017, https://www.wsj.com/articles/the-great-rules-rollback-1514237372.

9. Eric Lipton and Danielle Ivory, "Trump Says His Regulatory Rollback Already Is the 'Most Far-Reaching,'" *New York Times*, Dec. 14, 2017, https://www.nytimes.com/2017/12/14/us/politics/trump-federal-regulations.html.

10. Alan Levin and Jesse Hamilton, "Trump Takes Credit for Killing Hundreds of Regulations That Were Already Dead," Bloomberg Businessweek, Dec. 11, 2017, https://www.bloomberg.com/news/features/2017-12-11/trump-takes-credit-for-killing-hundreds-of-regulations-that-were-already-dead.

11. Jay Michaelson, "The Ten Worst Things Scott Pruitt's EPA Has Already Done," Daily Beast, Dec. 29, 2017, https://www.thedailybeast.com/the-ten-worst-things-scott-pruitts-epa-has-already-done.

12. Herb Weisbaum, "Consumers Were the Biggest Losers of 2017," NBC News, Dec. 28, 2017, https://www.nbcnews.com/business/consumer /consumers-were-biggest-losers-2017-n833081.

13. "The Second American Revolution: Reaganomics," Ronald Reagan Presidential Foundation & Institute, n.d., https://www.reaganfoundation.org /ronald-reagan/the-presidency/economic-policy/.

14. Graham Lanktree, "Barack Obama Thanks Himself for Success of American Economy Since Donald Trump Became President," *Newsweek*, Dec. 6, 2017, https://www.newsweek.com/barack-obama-thanks -himself-american-economys-success-739598.

15. Nicole Lewis, "Comparing the 'Trump Economy' to the 'Obama Economy,'" Fact Checker, *Washington Post*, Dec. 14, 2017, https:// www.washingtonpost.com/news/fact-checker/wp/2017/12/14/compar ing-the-trump-economy-to-the-obama-economy/.

16. Christopher S. Rugaber, "Trump Claims Credit for What Is Still Mostly Obama's Economy," Associated Press, in *Denver Post*, Jan. 20, 2018, https://www.denverpost.com/2018/01/20/donald-trump-takes-credit -for-barack-obama-economy/.

17. Lawrence B. Lindsey, "Judging President Obama on His Own Terms," Opinion, *Wall Street Journal*, Oct. 3, 2016, https://www.wsj.com /articles/judging-president-obama-on-his-own-terms-1475537355.

18. Juliet Eilperin and Josh Dawsey, "Trump Pushes to Allow New Logging in Alaska's Tongass National Forest," *Washington Post*, Aug. 27, 2019, https:// www.washingtonpost.com/climate-environment/trump-pushes-to-allow -new-logging-in-alaskas-tongass-national-forest/2019/08/27/b4ca78d6 -c832-11e9-be05-f76ac4ec618c_story.html.

19. "Remarks by President Trump and President Macron of France in Joint Press Conference | Biarritz, France," The White House, issued on Aug. 26, 2019, https://www.whitehouse.gov/briefings-statements/remarks -president-trump-president-macron-france-joint-press-conference-biarritz -france/.

20. Paul Bedard, "Trump: Slashing Regulations Boosted Economy More Than Tax Cuts," Opinion: Washington Secrets, *Washington Examiner*, Feb. 13, 2020, https://www.washingtonexaminer.com/washington-secrets /trump-slashing-regulations-boosted-economy-more-than-tax-cuts.

21. Eric Morath and Jeffrey Sparshott, "Rank-and-File Workers Get Bigger Raises," Economy, *Wall Street Journal*, Dec. 27, 2019, https://www.wsj .com/articles/rank-and-file-workers-get-bigger-raises-11577442600.

22. Ibid.

23. Ibid.
24. "Remarks by President Trump in State of the Union Address," The White House, issued on Feb. 4, 2020, https://www.whitehouse.gov/briefings -statements/remarks-president-trump-state-union-address-3/.
25. Background interview with Maria Bartiromo and James Freeman.
26. President Donald Trump, telephone interview with Maria Bartiromo and James Freeman, July 16, 2020.
27. James Freeman, "A Trump Rescue for the Obama Presidential Center?," Opinion/Best of the Web, *Wall Street Journal*, Feb. 5, 2020, https:// www.wsj.com/articles/a-trump-rescue-for-the-obama-presidential-center -11580934455.
28. David R. Henderson, "The Troubling Logic of 'You Didn't Build That,'" Foundation for Economic Education, Nov. 12, 2018, https://fee.org /articles/the-troubling-logic-of-you-didnt-build-that/.

Chapter 4: Trump's Tax Revolution

1. Joe Nocera, "Is Trump Serious?," Opinion, *New York Times*, Sept. 29, 2015, https://www.nytimes.com/2015/09/29/opinion/joe-nocera-is-donald-trump -serious.html.
2. Ibid.
3. *Economic Report of the President, Together with the Annual Report of the Council of Economic Advisers*, Transmitted to the Congress Feb. 2015, 223, https://obamawhitehouse.archives.gov/sites/default/files/docs/cea_2015 _erp_complete.pdf.
4. Ibid., n3.
5. Kevin A. Hassett and Aparna Mathur, "The Cure for Wage Stagnation," Opinion/Commentary, *Wall Street Journal*, Aug. 14, 2016, https://www .wsj.com/articles/the-cure-for-wage-stagnation-1471210831.
6. Ibid.
7. Ibid.
8. Ibid.
9. Ibid.
10. *Mornings with Maria*, hosted by Maria Bartiromo, Fox Business Network, Jan. 24, 2017.
11. Kenneth J. McKenzie and Ergete Ferede, "Who Pays the Corporate Tax?: Insights from the Literature and Evidence for Canadian Provinces," University of Calgary, School of Public Policy, *SPP Research Papers* 10, no. 7 (April 2017), https://journalhosting.ucalgary.ca/in dex.php/sppp/article/view/42621/30502.

12. "Remarks by President Trump on Tax Reform | Springfield, MO," The White House, issued on Aug. 30, 2017, https://www.whitehouse.gov/briefings-statements/remarks-president-trump-tax-reform-springfield-mo/.

13. *Mornings with Maria*, hosted by Maria Bartiromo, Fox Business Network, Sept. 28, 2017.

14. *Corporate Tax Reform and Wages: Theory and Evidence*, The Council of Economic Advisers, Washington D.C., Oct. 2017, https://www.whitehouse.gov/sites/whitehouse.gov/files/documents/Tax%20Reform%20and%20Wages.pdf.

15. "Remarks by President Trump Before Cabinet Meeting," The White House, issued on Nov. 20, 2017, https://www.whitehouse.gov/briefings-statements/remarks-president-trump-cabinet-meeting-2/.

16. "American Tax Overhaul Has Worrying Implications for Ireland," Cantillon, *Irish Times*, Nov. 18, 2017, https://www.irishtimes.com/business/economy/american-tax-overhaul-has-worrying-implications-for-ireland-1.3296168.

17. Pascal Saint-Amans and Thomas Neubig, "The OECD/G20 BEPS Recommendations: Boosting U.S. Tax Reform," The Hill, June 8, 2016, https://thehill.com/blogs/congress-blog/economy-budget/282675-the-oecd-g20-beps-recommendations-boosting-us-tax-reform.

18. Mike Lillis, "Pelosi Denounces GOP Tax Reform as 'Armageddon,'" The Hill, Dec. 4, 2017, https://thehill.com/homenews/house/363238-pelosi-denounces-gop-tax-reform-as-armageddon.

19. Lawrence H. Summers, "Yes, the Senate GOP Tax Plan Would Cause 'Thousands' to Die," Economic Policy/Perspective, *Washington Post*, Dec. 3, 2017, https://www.washingtonpost.com/news/wonk/wp/2017/12/03/lawrence-summers-yes-the-senate-gop-tax-plan-would-cause-thousands-to-die/.

20. Lant Pritchett and Lawrence H. Summers, "Wealthier Is Healthier," *Journal of Human Resources* 31, no. 4 (Autumn 1996), 841.

21. ABC News Politics (@ABCPolitics), "Chants of 'kill the bill, don't kill us!,'" Twitter, Dec. 20, 2017, https://twitter.com/abcpolitics/status/943355658929344514.

22. "State of the Union: Republicans Pass Tax Bill; Interview with Vermont Senator Bernie Sanders; What Do Bush and Obama Think About Trump?; Democrats Warn President Trump Not to Fire Special Counsel," CNN Transcripts, aired Dec. 24, 2017, 09:00 ET.

23. Theo Francis, Peter Loftus, and Heather Haddon, "The Tax Law, Just One

Month Old, Is Roaring Through U.S. Companies," Business, *Wall Street Journal*, Jan. 26, 2018, https://www.wsj.com/articles/the-tax-law-just -one-month-old-is-roaring-through-u-s-companies-1516899466.

24. James Freeman, "Mr. 5%?," Opinion/Best of the Web, *Wall Street Journal*, Jan. 25, 2018, https://www.wsj.com/articles/mr-5-1516907102.

25. *Economic Report of the President, Together with the Annual Report of the Council of Economic Advisers*, Feb. 2020, 3, https://www.whitehouse.gov /wp-content/uploads/2020/02/2020-Economic-Report-of-the-President -WHCEA.pdf.

26. Ibid.

27. Ibid., 5.

28. Ibid., 13.

29. President Donald Trump, telephone interview with Maria Bartiromo and James Freeman.

30. Ibid.

Chapter 5: Boom Time and Beijing

1. Elliott Teaford, "Lakers 111, Phoenix 99: Bryant Gives Suns the Third Degree," *Los Angeles Daily News*, updated Aug. 28, 2017, https://www .dailynews.com/2012/02/17/lakers-111-phoenix-99-bryant-gives-suns -the-third-degree/.

2. J. A. Adande, "The Mamba Remembers," *TrueHoop* (blog), ESPN, Jan. 11, 2012, https://www.espn.com/blog/truehoop/post/_/id/35313/the -mamba-remembers.

3. Bob Young, "Malicious Mamba," *Arizona Republic*, Feb. 19, 2012.

4. "Lakers: Kobe Bryant Leads LA over Suns 111–99," Associated Press, in *Riverside (CA) Press-Enterprise*, Feb. 18, 2012, https://www.pe.com /2012/02/18/lakers-kobe-leads-la-over-suns-111-99/.

5. Noaki Schwartz and Christina Hoag, "Chinese Leader Xi, Biden Promote Trade in LA," Associated Press, in *San Diego Union-Telegram*, Feb. 17, 2012, https://www.sandiegouniontribune.com/sdut-chinese-leader-xi -biden-promote-trade-in-la-2012feb17-story.html.

6. Eva Dou, Jeremy Page, and Josh Chin, "China's Uighur Camps Swell as Beijing Widens the Dragnet," World/Asia, *Wall Street Journal*, Aug. 17, 2018, https://www.wsj.com/articles/chinas-uighur-camps-swell-as -beijing-widens-the-dragnet-1534534894.

7. Noaki Schwartz and Christina Hoag, "Chinese Leader Xi, Biden Promote Trade in LA."

8. Ibid.

9. Ibid.

10. Wallace Turner, "Reagan to Work for Nixon in '72," *New York Times*, Oct. 4, 1971, https://www.nytimes.com/1971/10/04/archives/reagan-to-work -for-nixon-in-72-backs-president-in-speech-to-gop-in.html.

11. "Nixon vs. Khrushchev—The Kitchen Debate (1959)," YouTube, posted Feb. 9, 2010, https://www.youtube.com/watch?v=-CvQOuNecy4.

12. David Stokes, "Buckley, Nixon, and Mao—1972," Richard Nixon Foundation, Feb. 29, 2008, https://www.nixonfoundation.org/2008/02 /buckley-nixon-and-mao-1972/.

13. Ibid.

14. William F. Buckley Jr., "Veni, Vidi, Victus," *National Review*, Feb. 28, 2018, https://www.nationalreview.com/2018/02/william-f-buckley-jr -nixon-trip-to-china/.

15. "China Policy," Milestones: 1977–1980, Office of the Historian, Depart- ment of State, United States of America, n.d., https://history.state.gov /milestones/1977-1980/china-policy.

16. Clyde H. Farnsworth, "U.S. Policy Increases Trade with China," *New York Times*, July 28, 1981, https://www.nytimes.com/1981/07/28/business/us -policy-increases-trade-with-china.html.

17. Bernard Gwertzman, "Reagan Decides to Relax Curbs on China Trade," *New York Times*, June 6, 1981, https://www.nytimes.com/1981/06/06 /world/reagan-decides-to-relax-curbs-on-china-trade.html?smid=em -share.

18. Milton and Rose Friedman, *Free to Choose: A Personal Statement* (Orlando, FL: Harcourt, 1980), 57.

19. Li Yuan, "Jack Ma, China's Richest Man, Belongs to the Communist Party. Of Course," Business, *New York Times*, Nov. 27, 2018, https://www.nytimes .com/2018/11/27/business/jack-ma-communist-party-alibaba.html.

20. Li Yuan, "Private Businesses Built Modern China. Now the Government Is Pushing Back," Business, *New York Times*, Oct. 3, 2018, https://www .nytimes.com/2018/10/03/business/china-economy-private-enterprise .html.

21. Milton and Rose Friedman, *Free to Choose: A Personal Statement*, 53.

22. Phillip L. Zweig, *Wriston: Walter Wriston, Citibank, and the Rise and Fall of American Financial Supremacy* (New York: Crown, 1996), 89.

23. Ibid., 627.

24. Julia Leung and Vigor Fung, "Entrepreneurs in China Are Quick to Seize Opportunity, Despite Official Delays, Hostility," *Wall Street Journal*, Mar. 11, 1985.

25. Mark D'Anastasio, "About Face: Soviets Now Hail China as a Source of Ideas for Reviving Socialism, but Free-Market Pragmatism of Deng May Not Fit Russian Economy Well—No Hong Kong Role Model," *Wall Street Journal*, Sept. 18, 1987.

26. Julia Leung and Vigor Fung, "Entrepreneurs in China Are Quick to Seize Opportunity, Despite Official Delays, Hostility."

27. Ibid.

28. Adi Ignatius, "Chinese Monopolists Hate to Pass 'Go' Without 200 Yuan; in Shanghai, Capitalist Game Is Big Hit with Socialists; Hotels on 'Parking Lot,'" *Wall Street Journal*, Oct. 4, 1988.

29. Ibid.

30. "GDP (Constant 2010 US$)—China," 1980–1989, World Bank, n.d., https://data.worldbank.org/indicator/NY.GDP.MKTP.KD?end=1989&locations=CN&start=1980&view=chart.

31. Mark D'Anastasio, "About Face: Soviets Now Hail China as a Source of Ideas for Reviving Socialism, but Free-Market Pragmatism of Deng May Not Fit Russian Economy Well."

32. "Remarks on East-West Relations at the Brandenburg Gate in West Berlin, June 12, 1987," Reagan Foundation, n.d., https://www.reaganfoundation.org/media/128814/brandenburg.pdf.

33. "The Collapse of the Soviet Union," Milestones: 1989–1992, Office of the Historian, Department of State, United States of America, n.d., https://history.state.gov/milestones/1989-1992/collapse-soviet-union.

34. NR Interview, "Reagan on Life," *National Review*, Dec. 23, 2003, https://www.nationalreview.com/2003/12/reagan-life-interview/.

35. Nicholas Kristof, "When China Massacred Its Own People," Opinion, *New York Times*, June 1, 2019. https://www.nytimes.com/2019/06/01/opinion/sunday/tiananmen-square-protest.html?searchResultPosition=4.

36. Te-Ping Chen and Chao Deng, "Tiananmen's Survivors and the Burden of Memory," *Wall Street Journal*, May 31, 2019, https://www.wsj.com/articles/tiananmens-survivors-and-the-burden-of-memory-11559295001.

37. Wang Dan, "What I Learned Leading the Tiananmen Protests," Opinion, *New York Times*, June 1, 2019, https://www.nytimes.com/2019/06/01/opinion/sunday/tiananmen-protests-china-wang-dan.html.

38. "Tiananmen Square Protest Death Toll 'Was 10,000,'" BBC News, Dec. 23, 2017, https://www.bbc.com/news/world-asia-china-42465516.

39. "Wu Renhua Still Struggles with Tiananmen Horrors," *Taipei Times*, May 29, 2019, https://www.taipeitimes.com/News/taiwan/archives/2019/05/29/2003715993.

40. Ibid.

41. "George H. W. Bush, Press Conference, June 5, 1989," USC US-China Institute, USC Annenberg, June 5, 1989, https://china.usc.edu/george-hw-bush-press-conference-june-5-1989.

42. Ibid.

43. Gerard Baker, "In 1989, the U.S. Decided to Let China Get Away With Murder," Life & Arts, *Wall Street Journal*, May 31, 2019, https://www.wsj.com/articles/in-1989-the-u-s-decided-to-let-beijing-get-away-with-murder-11559311545.

44. Chris Buckley, "30 Years After Tiananmen, a Chinese Military Insider Warns: Never Forget," *New York Times*, May 28, 2019, https://www.nytimes.com/2019/05/28/world/asia/china-tiananmen-square-massacre.html. Andrew Jacobs and Chris Buckley, "Tales of Army Discord Show Tiananmen Square in a New Light," *New York Times*, June 2, 2014, https://www.nytimes.com/2014/06/03/world/asia/tiananmen-square-25-years-later-details-emerge-of-armys-chaos.html. Minnie Chan, "How Tiananmen Crackdown Left a Deep Scar on China's Military Psyche," *South China Morning Post*, June 4, 2019, https://www.scmp.com/news/china/military/article/3012956/how-tiananmen-crackdown-left-deep-scar-chinas-military-psyche.

45. George H. W. Bush, Press Conference, June 5, 1989.

46. Adi Ignatius, "China's Economic Reform Program Stalls—Political Crackdown Threatens Free-Market Policy," *Wall Street Journal*, Sept. 26, 1989.

47. Lena H. Sun, "Communists on the Defensive in Beijing, Moscow; At Age 70, China's Ruling Party Confronts Old and New Troubles," *Washington Post*, June 30, 1991.

48. Lena H. Sun, "China's New Ideology: Make Money, Not Marxism," *Washington Post*, July 27, 1993, https://www.washingtonpost.com/archive/politics/1993/07/27/chinas-new-ideology-make-money-not-marxism/3d0390f5-7eea-43fb-89c9-948ee1ea6d00/.

49. Sheryl WuDunn, "Booming China Is Dream Market for West," *New York Times*, Feb. 15, 1993, https://www.nytimes.com/1993/02/15/world/booming-china-is-dream-market-for-west.html.

50. Ibid.

Chapter 6: Eyes Wide Open

1. U.S. Attorney's Office, Northern District of Illinois, "Suburban Chicago Woman Sentenced to Four Years in Prison for Stealing Motorola Trade Secrets Before Boarding Plane to China," Federal Bureau of Investigation, Chicago Division, Aug. 29, 2012, https://archives.fbi.gov/archives/chicago/press-releases/2012/suburban-chicago-woman-sentenced-to-four-years-in-prison-for-stealing-motorola-trade-secrets-before-boarding-plane-to-china.

2. Chuck Goudie, Christine Tressel, and Ross Weidner, "On Road to 5G, Allegations of Huawei Spy Craft Start in Chicago," ABC 7 Eyewitness News, June 24, 2019, https://abc7chicago.com/huawei-motorola-chinese-spycraft-chines-technology/5337601/.

3. *Mornings with Maria*, hosted by Maria Bartiromo, Fox Business Network, Dec. 11, 2018.

4. *Mornings with Maria*, hosted by Maria Bartiromo, Fox Business Network, Nov. 1, 2018.

5. Ibid.

6. "Attorney General William P. Barr Delivers Remarks on China Policy at the Gerald R. Ford Presidential Museum," Justice News, The United States Department of Justice, Grand Rapids, MI, July 16, 2020, https://www.justice.gov/opa/speech/attorney-general-william-p-barr-delivers-remarks-china-policy-gerald-r-ford-presidential.

7. President Donald Trump, interview with Maria Bartiromo and James Freeman, July 16, 2020.

8. Ibid.

9. Ibid.

10. "Briefing with Senior U.S. Government Officials on the Closure of the Chinese Consulate in Houston, Texas," Office of the Spokesperson via Teleconference, U.S. Department of State, July 24, 2020, https://www.state.gov/briefing-with-senior-u-s-government-officials-on-the-closure-of-the-chinese-consulate-in-houston-texas/.

11. Christopher Wray, Director, Federal Bureau of Investigation, "The Threat Posed by the Chinese Government and the Chinese Communist Party to the Economic and National Security of the United States," Hudson Institute, Video Event: China's Attempt to Influence U.S. Institutions, Washington, D.C., July 7, 2020, posted under "News: Speeches," FBI (website), https://www.fbi.gov/news/speeches/the-threat-posed-by-the-chinese-government

-and-the-chinese-communist-party-to-the-economic-and-national-secu
rity-of-the-united-states.

12. Ibid.

13. U.S. Department of Justice, Office of Public Affairs, Justice News, "Two Chinese Hackers Working with the Ministry of State Security Charged with Global Computer Intrusion Campaign Targeting Intellectual Property and Confidential Business Information, Including COVID-19 Research," press release no 20-675, July 21, 2020, https:// www.justice.gov/opa/pr/two-chinese-hackers-working-ministry-state -security-charged-global-computer-intrusion.

14. U.S. Department of Justice, Office of Public Affairs, "Chinese Citizen Convicted of Economic Espionage, Theft of Trade Secrets, and Conspiracy," press release no 20-598, June 26, 2020, https://www.jus tice.gov/opa/pr/chinese-citizen-convicted-economic-espionage-theft -trade-secrets-and-conspiracy.

15. U.S. Department of Justice, Office of Public Affairs, Justice News, "Harvard University Professor Charged with Tax Offenses," press release no 20-715, July 28, 2020, https://www.justice.gov/opa/pr/har vard-university-professor-charged-tax-offenses#.

16. U.S. Department of Justice, Office of Public Affairs, "Information About the Department of Justice's China Initiative and a Compilation of China-Related Prosecutions Since 2018," updated Aug. 4, 2020, https://www.justice.gov/opa/information-about-department-justice-s -china-initiative-and-compilation-china-related.

17. "Remarks by Henry M. Paulson, Jr., on the United States and China at a Crossroads," Paulson Institute, Nov. 7, 2018, https://www.paul soninstitute.org/press_release/remarks-by-henry-m-paulson-jr-on -the-united-states-and-china-at-a-crossroads/.

18. Christopher Wray, Director, Federal Bureau of Investigation, "Responding Effectively to the Chinese Economic Espionage Threat," Department of Justice China Initiative Conference, Center for Strategic and International Studies, Washington, D.C., Feb. 6, 2020, posted under "News: Speeches," FBI (website), https://www.fbi.gov/news/speeches /responding-effectively-to-the-chinese-economic-espionage-threat.

19. *Sunday Morning Futures*, hosted by Maria Bartiromo, Fox News Channel, May 3, 2020.

20. Christopher Wray, "Responding Effectively to the Chinese Economic Espionage Threat."

21. Maria Bartiromo telephone interview with John Demers, July 9, 2020.

22. Telephone interview with Maria Bartiromo, July 25, 2020.

23. Julia Limitone, "Pompeo Slams Huawei: US Won't Partner with Countries That Use Its Technology," Technology, Fox Business, Feb. 21, 2019, https://www.foxbusiness.com/technology/pompeo-slams-huawei-us-wont-partner-with-countries-that-use-its-technology.

24. *Mornings with Maria*, hosted by Maria Bartiromo, Fox Business Network, Dec. 12, 2019.

25. Chua Kong Ho, "Huawei Founder Ren Zhengfei on Why He Joined China's Communist Party and the People's Liberation Army," *South China Morning Post*, Jan. 16. 2019, https://www.scmp.com/tech/big-tech/article/2182332/huawei-founder-ren-zhengfei-why-he-joined-chinas-communist-party-and.

26. Christopher Wray, "Responding Effectively to the Chinese Economic Espionage Threat."

27. Gordon Corera, "Eric Schmidt: Huawei Has Engaged in Unacceptable Practices," BBC News, June 18, 2020, https://www.bbc.com/news/technology-53080113.

28. *Sunday Morning Futures*, hosted by Maria Bartiromo, Fox News Chanel, May 10, 2020.

29. *Sunday Morning Futures*, hosted by Maria Bartiromo, Fox News Channel, Feb. 23, 2020.

30. *Sunday Morning Futures*, hosted by Maria Bartiromo, Fox News Channel, June 21, 2020.

31. Ibid.

32. *Mornings with Maria*, hosted by Maria Bartiromo, Fox Business Network, May 31, 2020.

33. Jimmy Lai, telephone interview with Maria Bartiromo.

34. Ibid.

35. Ibid.

36. *Mornings with Maria*, hosted by Maria Bartiromo, Fox Business Network, May 28, 2019.

37. *Sunday Morning Futures*, hosted by Maria Bartiromo, Fox News Channel, July 19, 2020.

38. *Mornings with Maria*, hosted by Maria Bartiromo, Fox Business Network, Oct. 2, 2018.

39. *Sunday Morning Futures*, hosted by Maria Bartiromo, Fox News Channel, Dec. 16, 2018.

40. *Mornings with Maria*, hosted by Maria Bartiromo, Fox Business Network, Oct. 2, 2018.

41. *Sunday Morning Futures*, hosted by Maria Bartiromo, Fox News Channel, June 21, 2020.

42. Background interview with Maria Bartiromo and James Freeman.

43. *Sunday Morning Futures*, hosted by Maria Bartiromo, Fox News Channel, June 21, 2020.

44. Cate Cadell, "Hikvision, a Surveillance Powerhouse, Walks U.S.-China Tightrope," Reuters, Aug. 28, 2019, https://www.reuters.com/article/us -hikvision-china-insight/hikvision-a-surveillance-powerhouse-walks-u-s -china-tightrope-idUSKCN1VJ05C.

45. Background interview with Maria Bartiromo and James Freeman.

46. Thomas W. Lippman, "Bush Makes Clinton's China Policy an Issue," *Washington Post*, Aug. 20, 1999, https://www.washingtonpost.com/wp -srv/politics/campaigns/wh2000/stories/chiwan082099.htm.

47. Carl M. Cannon, "What We Did in China," *National Journal* 30, no. 29 (July 18, 1998), 1668–75.

48. "Transcript of Clinton Press Conference, July 2, in Hong Kong," U.S. Newswire, July 3, 1998.

49. Ibid.

50. *U.S. National Security and Military/Commercial Concerns with the People's Republic of China*, Vol. 1, Select Committee, United States House of Representatives, submitted by Mr. Cox of California, Chairman, top secret report date: Jan. 3, 1999; declassified report release date: May 25, 1999, ii–iv, https://www.govinfo.gov/content/pkg/GPO-CRPT-105hrpt851/pdf /GPO-CRPT-105hrpt851.pdf.

51. Jamie Dimon, interview with Maria Bartiromo and James Freeman, June 1, 2020.

52. Telephone interview with Maria Bartiromo and James Freeman, May 24, 2020.

53. Background interview with Maria Bartiromo and James Freeman.

54. President Donald Trump, telephone interview with Maria Bartiromo and James Freeman, July 16, 2020.

Chapter 7: The Media's Trump Boom

1. Jim Rutenberg, "Trump Is Testing the Norms of Objectivity in Journalism," *New York Times*, Aug. 7, 2016, https://www.nytimes.com /2016/08/08/business/balance-fairness-and-a-proudly-provocative-presi dential-candidate.html.

2. Ibid.

3. *Review of Four FISA Applications and Other Aspects of the FBI's Crossfire Hurricane Investigation* (Redacted for Public Release), Office of the Inspector General, U.S. Department of Justice, Oversight and Review Division (20-012), Dec. 2019 (revised), ix, https://www.justice.gov/storage/120919 -examination.pdf.

4. Ibid., 67.

5. Ibid., viii.

6. Ibid., ix.

7. Ibid., ix.

8. Ibid., x.

9. Ibid., 6.

10. Ibid., 234.

11. Ibid., 182.

12. Ibid., 177.

13. Ibid., 178.

14. James Freeman, "The Unbelievable James Comey," Opinion/Best of the Web, *Wall Street Journal*, Dec. 10, 2018, https://www.wsj.com/articles /the-unbelievable-james-comey-1544478713.

15. *Review of Four FISA Applications and Other Aspects of the FBI's Crossfire Hurricane Investigation*, 178.

16. Ibid., 179.

17. Ibid., 180.

18. Benjamin Mullin, "BuzzFeed Editor Defends Publishing Explosive Allegations Against Donald Trump," Poynter, Jan. 10, 2017, https:// www.poynter.org/ethics-trust/2017/buzzfeed-editor-defends-publish ing-explosive-allegations-against-donald-trump/.

19. David Bauder, "CNN at War with Trump over What Reporting Unleashed," Associated Press, Jan. 12, 2017, https://apnews.com/a012c6438 21e48c98ec3155493eb2e52/CNN-at-war-with-Trump-over-what-reporting -unleashed.

20. *Anderson Cooper 360°*, hosted by Anderson Cooper, Interview with Rep. Elijah Cummings, CNN, transcript, Jan. 10, 2017, http://transcripts.cnn .com/TRANSCRIPTS/1701/10/acd.01.html.

21. Ibid.

22. *Review of Four FISA Applications and Other Aspects of the FBI's Crossfire Hurricane Investigation*, x.

23. *Anderson Cooper 360°*, hosted by Anderson Cooper, Interview with Rep. Elijah Cummings, CNN, transcript, Jan. 10, 2017.

24. *The Rachel Maddow Show*, hosted by Rachel Maddow, MSNBC, transcript, Jan. 10, 2017, http://www.msnbc.com/transcripts/rachel-maddow-show/2017-01-10.

25. Ibid.

26. *Review of Four FISA Applications and Other Aspects of the FBI's Crossfire Hurricane Investigation*, 176–77n322.

27. Ibid., 181.

28. *Report of Investigation of Former Federal Bureau of Investigation Director James Comey's Disclosure of Sensitive Investigative Information and Handling of Certain Memoranda*, Office of the Inspector General, U.S. Department of Justice, Oversight and Review Division (19-02), Aug. 2019, 19–20, https://www.oversight.gov/sites/default/files/oig-reports/o1902.pdf.

29. Ibid., 3.

30. *Hardball with Chris Matthews*, hosted by Chris Matthews, MSNBC, transcript, Jan. 12, 2017, http://www.msnbc.com/transcripts/hardball/2017-01-12.

31. Ibid.

32. "IG Footnotes: Serious Problems with Dossier Sources Didn't Stop FBI's Page Surveillance," Chuck Grassley, United States Senator for Iowa, Apr. 15, 2020, https://www.grassley.senate.gov/news/news-releases/ig-footnotes-serious-problems-dossier-sources-didn-t-stop-fbi-s-page-surveillance.

33. David Ignatius, "Why Did Obama Dawdle on Russia's Hacking?," Opinions, *Washington Post*, Jan. 12, 2017, https://www.washingtonpost.com/opinions/why-did-obama-dawdle-on-russias-hacking/2017/01/12/75f878a0-d90c-11e6-9a36-1d296534b31e_story.html.

34. David Ignatius, "Why Did Obama Dawdle on Russia's Hacking?," Opinions, *Washington Post*, Jan. 12, 2017, https://www.washingtonpost.com/opinions/why-did-obama-dawdle-on-russias-hacking/2017/01/12/75f878a0-d90c-11e6-9a36-1d296534b31e_story.html.

35. Glenn Thrush and Michael M. Grynbaum, "Trump Ruled the Tabloid Media. Washington Is a Different Story," *New York Times*, Feb. 25, 2017, https://www.nytimes.com/2017/02/25/us/politics/trump-press-conflict.html.

36. Ibid.

37. Ibid.

38. Andrew Higgins, "Trump Embraces 'Enemy of the People,' a Phrase with a Fraught History," *New York Times*, Feb. 26, 2017, https://www.nytimes

.com/2017/02/26/world/europe/trump-enemy-of-the-people-stalin
.html?mod=article_inline.

39. Michael M. Grynbaum, "In Trump-CNN Battle, 2 Presidents Who Love a Spectacle," *New York Times*, Feb. 26, 2017, https://www.nytimes .com/2017/02/26/business/media/cnn-jeff-zucker-trump.html.

40. *Report of Investigation of Former Federal Bureau of Investigation Director James Comey's Disclosure of Sensitive Investigative Information and Handling of Certain Memoranda*, 20.

41. Timothy Egan, "Erasing Obama," Opinion, *New York Times*, Jan. 6, 2017, https://www.nytimes.com/2017/01/06/opinion/erasing-obama.html.

42. Maureen Dowd, "Game of Trump," Opinion, *New York Times*, July 15, 2017, https://www.nytimes.com/2017/07/15/opinion/sunday/game-of -trump.html.

43. Michelle Goldberg, "Odds Are, Russia Owns Trump," Opinion, *New York Times*, Nov. 27, 2017, https://www.nytimes.com/2017/11/27/opinion /trump-patriot-russia.html.

44. Yascha Mounk, "The Real Coup Plot Is Trump's," Opinion, *New York Times*, Dec. 20, 2017, https://www.nytimes.com/2017/12/20/opinion /trump-republican-coup.html.

45. Paul Krugman, "The New Climate of Treason," *The Conscience of a Liberal* (blog), *New York Times*, July 14, 2017, https://krugman.blogs.nytimes .com/2017/07/14/the-new-climate-of-treason/.

46. Paul Krugman, "Judas, Tax Cuts and the Great Betrayal," Opinion, *New York Times*, May 12, 2017, https://www.nytimes.com/2017/05/12/opin ion/judas-tax-cuts-and-the-great-betrayal.html.

47. *Mornings with Maria*, hosted by Maria Bartiromo, Fox Business Network, Apr. 12, 2017.

48. Paul Krugman, "Faust on the Potomac," Opinion, *New York Times*, Jan. 5, 2018, https://www.nytimes.com/2018/01/05/opinion/faust-on-the-poto mac.html.

49. Charles M. Blow, "Trump, Treasonous Traitor," Opinion, *New York Times*, July 15, 2018, https://www.nytimes.com/2018/07/15/opinion/trump -russia-investigation-putin.html.

50. Ibid.

51. Dominic Patten, "Fox News Tops Cable Ratings Again in Q2 Despite Well-Watched Dem Debates on MSNBC; Tucker Carlson up, Rachel Maddow Down," Deadline, July 2, 2019, https://deadline .com/2019/07/fox-news-ratings-top-cable-tucker-carlson-rachel-maddow -cnn-down-msnbc-second-quarter-1202641256/.

52. Jonathan Turley, "He Who Must Not Be Named: How Hunter Biden Became a Conversation-Stopper," Opinion, The Hill, Oct. 12, 2019, https://thehill.com/opinion/campaign/465520-he-who-must-not-be-named-how-hunter-biden-became-a-conversation-stopper?mod=article_inline.

53. Meet the Press (@MeetThePress), "WATCH: The president held a campaign rally last night and attacked Hunter Biden. We cannot in good conscience show it to you," Twitter, Oct. 11, 2019, https://twitter.com/MeetThePress/status/1182773349044408324?s=20.

54. John Gage, "Chuck Todd Refuses to Air 'Vicious' Trump Attacks on Hunter Biden," *Washington Examiner*, Oct. 12, 2019, https://www.washingtonexaminer.com/news/chuck-todd-refuses-to-air-vicious-trump-attacks-on-hunter-biden.

55. Ibid.

56. Jonathan Turley, "He Who Must Not Be Named: How Hunter Biden Became a Conversation-Stopper."

57. Cissy Zhou and Jun Mai, "Hunter Biden's China Investment Firm Is Small Fish in China's Private Equity Pond," *South China Morning Post*, Oct. 14, 2019, https://www.scmp.com/economy/china-economy/article/3032806/hunter-bidens-china-investment-firm-small-fish-chinas-private?mod=article_inline.

58. Donald J. Trump (@realDonaldTrump), "When are the Fake Journalists, who received unwarranted Pulitzer Prizes for Russia, Russia, Russia, and the Impeachment Scam, going to turn in their tarnished awards so they can be given to the real journalists who got it right. I'll give you the names, there are plenty of them!," Twitter, May 10, 2020, https://twitter.com/realDonaldTrump/status/1259450009734516736?s=20.

Chapter 8: The Cost of Covid

1. *Leading Causes of Death*, Centers for Disease Control and Prevention, National Center for Health Statistics, https://www.cdc.gov/nchs/fastats/leading-causes-of-death.htm.

2. "Key Metrics on Mortality," Ohio Department of Health, COVID-19 Dashboard, https://coronavirus.ohio.gov/wps/portal/gov/covid-19/dashboards/key-metrics/mortality.

3. "Fatalities," New York State Department of Health, https://covid19tracker.health.ny.gov/views/NYS-COVID19-Tracker/NYSDOHCOVID-19Tracker-Fatalities?%3Aembed=yes&%3Atoolbar=no&%3Atabs=n.

4. Joe Biden (@JoeBiden), "We are in the midst of a crisis with the corona-virus. We need to lead the way with science—not Donald Trump's record of hysteria, xenophobia, and fear-mongering. He is the worst possible person to lead our country through a global health emergency," Twitter, Feb. 1, 2020, https://twitter.com/JoeBiden/status/1223727977361338370?s=20.

5. Chao Deng and Josh Chin, "Chinese Doctor Who Issued Early Warn-ing on Virus Dies," World, *Wall Street Journal*, Feb. 7, 2020, https://www.wsj.com/articles/chinese-doctor-who-issued-early-warning-on-virus-dies-11581019816.

6. Guo Rui, "Li Wenliang: Chinese Academics Call for Justice for Corona-virus Whistle-Blower," *South China Morning Post*, Feb. 8, 2020, https://www.scmp.com/news/china/politics/article/3049634/li-wen liang-chinese-academics-call-justice-coronavirus-whistle.

7. Jonathan Cheng, "In China, Anger Simmers over Coronavirus Doctor's Death," *Wall Street Journal*, Feb. 7, 2020, https://www.wsj.com/articles/in-china-anger-simmers-over-coronavirus-doctors-death-11581061065.

8. James Freeman, "This Whistleblower Really Was a Hero," Opinion/Best of the Web, *Wall Street Journal*, Feb. 10, 2020, https://www.wsj.com/articles/this-whistleblower-really-was-a-hero-11581362030.

9. *Mornings with Maria*, hosted by Maria Bartiromo, Fox Business Network, Apr. 17, 2020.

10. Neil Ferguson et al., *Report 9: Impact of Non-Pharmaceutical Interventions (NPIs) to Reduce COVID-19 Mortality and Healthcare Demand*, Impe-rial College London, Mar. 16, 2020, https://www.imperial.ac.uk/media/imperial-college/medicine/sph/ide/gida-fellowships/Imperial-College-COVID19-NPI-modelling-16-03-2020.pdf.

11. "1918 Pandemic (H1N1 Virus)," Centers for Disease Control and Pre-vention, last reviewed Mar. 20, 2019, https://www.cdc.gov/flu/pandemic-resources/1918-pandemic-h1n1.html.

12. David Adam, "UK Has Enough Intensive Care Units for Corona-virus, Expert Predicts," *NewScientist*, Mar. 25, 2020, https://www.new scientist.com/article/2238578-uk-has-enough-intensive-care-units-for-coronavirus-expert-predicts/.

13. Chris Smyth, "NHS Now Likely to Cope with Coronavirus, Says Key Scientist," *Times* (London), Mar. 26, 2020, https://www.thetimes.co.uk/article/nhs-now-likely-to-cope-with-coronavirus-says-key-scientist-rn5m6nggk.

14. Eric Morath, Jon Hilsenrath, and Sarah Chaney, "Record Rise in

Unemployment Claims Halts Historic Run of Job Growth," *Wall Street Journal*, Mar. 26, 2020, https://www.wsj.com/articles/the-long-run-of-american-job-growth-has-ended-11585215000.

15. Marcus Walker, "A Global Conundrum: How to Pause the Economy and Avoid Ruin," *Wall Street Journal*, Mar. 30, 2020, https://www.wsj.com/articles/a-global-conundrum-how-to-pause-the-economy-and-avoid-ruin-11585567145.

16. Joe Concha, "Scarborough: Coronavirus Pandemic More Like World War II than 9/11," The Hill, Mar. 17, 2020, https://thehill.com/homenews/media/488001-scarborough-coronavirus-pandemic-more-like-world-war-ii-than-9-11.

17. "Research Starters: Worldwide Deaths in World War II," The National WWII Museum, New Orleans, https://www.nationalww2museum.org/students-teachers/student-resources/research-starters/research-starters-worldwide-deaths-world-war?mod=article_inline.

18. "Annual Population Estimates," United States Census Bureau, U.S. and World Population Clock, https://www.census.gov/popclock/.

19. John P. A. Ioannidis, "A Fiasco in the Making? As the Coronavirus Pandemic Takes Hold, We Are Making Decisions Without Reliable Data," Stat, Mar. 17, 2020, https://www.statnews.com/2020/03/17/a-fiasco-in-the-making-as-the-coronavirus-pandemic-takes-hold-we-are-making-decisions-without-reliable-data/.

20. Ibid.

21. Email from Casey Mulligan, July 25, 2020.

22. "Covid-19 News: A Cost-Benefit Analysis on School Closures," Goldman School of Public Policy, University of California Berkeley, June 23, 2020, https://gspp.berkeley.edu/news/covid-19/a-cost-benefit-analysis-on-school-closures.

23. "Scioto Analysis Releases Cost-Benefit Analysis on Covid School Closures," Scioto Analysis, June 22, 2020, https://www.sciotoanalysis.com/news/2020/6/19/scioto-analysis-releases-cost-benefit-analysis-on-covid-school-closures.

24. Ibid.

25. Mark McLaughlin, Marc Horne, and Rosemary Bennett, "No Known Case of Teacher Catching Coronavirus from Pupils, Says Scientist," *Times* (London), July 21, 2020, https://www.thetimes.co.uk/article/no-known-case-of-teacher-catching-coronavirus-from-pupils-says-scientist-3zk5g2x6z?fbclid=IwAR2gNTTf8SA_ycKPk8m0MWR-nEr7xzbSVJ8VgE4SFs9SlVNGZ7QPt0WwWCU.

26. Rebecca Martinson, "I Won't Return to the Classroom, and You Shouldn't Ask Me To," Opinion, *New York Times*, July 18, 2020, https://www.nytimes.com/2020/07/18/opinion/sunday/covid-schools-reopen-teacher-safety.html.

27. Charlotte Hays, "A School Teacher Makes an Emotional Plea to Play Hooky," Independent Women's Forum, July 21, 2020, https://www.iwf.org/2020/07/21/a-school-teacher-makes-an-emotional-plea-to-play-hooky/.

28. Mark McLaughlin, Marc Horne, and Rosemary Bennett, "No Known Case of Teacher Catching Coronavirus from Pupils, Says Scientist."

29. Ibid.

30. "Covid-19 Planning Considerations: Guidance for School Re-entry," American Academy of Pediatrics, last updated June 25, 2020, https://services.aap.org/en/pages/2019-novel-coronavirus-covid-19-infections/clinical-guidance/covid-19-planning-considerations-return-to-in-person-education-in-schools/.

31. Deepa Bharath, "Suicide, Help Hotline Calls Soar in Southern California over Coronavirus Anxieties," *Orange County Register*, April 19, 2020, updated Apr. 22, 2020, https://www.ocregister.com/2020/04/19/suicide-help-hotline-calls-soar-in-southern-california-over-coronavirus-anxieties/.

32. David Gunnell et al., "Suicide Risk and Prevention During the COVID-19 Epidemic," *Lancet Psychiatry* 7, no. 6 (June 2020), 468–71; published online Apr. 21, 2020, https://www.thelancet.com/journals/lanpsy/article/PIIS2215-0366(20)30171-1/fulltext.

33. James Freeman, "The Limits of Anthony Fauci's Expertise," Opinion/Best of the Web, *Wall Street Journal*, May 13, 2020, https://www.wsj.com/articles/the-limits-of-anthony-faucis-expertise-11589392347.

34. Josh Mitchell, "U.S. Unemployment Rate Fell to 13.3% in May," *Wall Street Journal*, June 6, 2020, https://www.wsj.com/articles/may-jobs-report-coronavirus-2020-11591310177.

35. James Freeman, "The Limits of Anthony Fauci's Expertise."

36. *Mornings with Maria*, hosted by Maria Bartiromo, Fox Business Network, May 6, 2020.

37. Jeff LeBenger and Mike Meyer, "Medical Lockdown Will Cause a Disease Surge," Opinion, *Wall Street Journal*, May 11, 2020, https://www.wsj.com/articles/medical-lockdown-will-cause-a-disease-surge-11589235129.

38. Harlan M. Krumholz, M.D., "Where Have All the Heart Attacks Gone?," *New York Times*, published Apr. 6, 2020, updated May 14, 2020, https://

www.nytimes.com/2020/04/06/well/live/coronavirus-doctors-hospitals
-emergency-care-heart-attack-stroke.html.

39. Email from Kristopher Sandlund, MD, Apr. 14, 2020.

40. Eric Morath, Harriet Torry, and Gwynn Guilford, "A Second Round of Coronavirus Layoffs Has Begun. Few Are Safe," Economy, *Wall Street Journal*, Apr. 14, 2020, https://www.wsj.com/articles/a-second-round -of-coronavirus-layoffs-has-begun-no-one-is-safe-11586872387.

41. Scott Grannis, "The Crisis Is Over, but at Terrible Cost," *Calafia Beach Pundit* (blog), Apr. 12, 2020, http://scottgrannis.blogspot.com/2020/04 /the-crisis-is-over-but-at-terrible-cost.html.Δiv

Chapter 9: Is Bidenomics Turning Out to Be Bernienomics?

1. "Live Results: Super Tuesday 2020," Election 2020, *Washington Post*, n.d., https://www.washingtonpost.com/elections/election-results/super-tues day/?itid=hp_hp-bignews4_web-delegate-tracker:homepage/.

2. Kevin Roose, "Biden Is Losing the Internet. Does That Matter?," The Shift, *New York Times*, Apr. 16, 2020, updated Apr. 23, 2020, https://www .nytimes.com/2020/04/16/technology/joe-biden-internet.html.

3. Sally Pipes, "Biden's Mask of Moderation Has Finally Slipped," *Forbes*, June 22, 2020, https://www.forbes.com/sites/sallypipes/2020/06/22/bidens -mask-of-moderation-has-finally-slipped/#7fb cv6b6ee7f51.

4. *Biden-Sanders Unity Task Force Recommendations: Combating the Climate Crisis and Pursuing Environmental Justice*, n.d., https://joebiden.com/wp -content/uploads/2020/07/UNITY-TASK-FORCE-RECOMMENDA TIONS.pdf.

5. Ibid., 11.

6. Constitution of the Bolivarian Republic of Venezuela (in English trans-lation from the original legal text), Human Rights Library, University of Minnesota, http://hrlibrary.umn.edu/research/venezuela-constitution .html.

7. *Biden-Sanders Unity Task Force Recommendations: Combating the Climate Crisis and Pursuing Environmental Justice*, 11.

8. Ibid., 16.

9. Ibid., 3.

10. Alex Leary and Timothy Puko, "Trump, Biden Square Off over Environ-mental Regulations," Politics, *Wall Street Journal*, July 16, 2020, https:// www.wsj.com/articles/trump-biden-square-off-over-environmental -regulations-11594917709.

11. Ibid.

12. *Biden-Sanders Unity Task Force Recommendations: Combating the Climate Crisis and Pursuing Environmental Justice*, 74.

13. Jaret Seiberg, "Top 10 Observations on Democratic Priorities for Financial Services," Cowen Washington Research Group, July 22, 2020.

14. Elizabeth Warren, "Companies Shouldn't Be Accountable Only to Shareholders," Opinion/Commentary, *Wall Street Journal*, Apr. 14, 2018, https://www.wsj.com/articles/companies-shouldnt-be-accountable-only-to-shareholders-1534287687.

15. Milton Friedman, "The Social Responsibility of Business Is to Increase Its Profits," *New York Times Magazine*, Sept. 13, 1970, reprinted in Scott P. Rae and Kenman L. Wong, *Beyond Integrity: A Judeo-Christian Approach to Business Ethics*, 2nd edition (Grand Rapids, MI: Zondervan, 2004), 131.

16. Ibid., 132.

17. Jonathan Easley, "Biden Strikes Populist Tone in Blistering Rebuke of Trump, Wall Street," The Hill, July 9, 2020, https://thehill.com/homenews/campaign/506634-biden-strikes-populist-tone-in-blistering-economic-rebuke-of-trump-wall.

18. Joe Biden (@JoeBiden), "We're going to beat Donald Trump. And when we do, we won't just rebuild this nation—we'll transform it," Twitter, July 5, 2020, https://twitter.com/joebiden/status/1279928045093228545.

19. Huaqun Li, Garrett Watson, and Taylor LaJoie, "Details and Analysis of Former Vice President Biden's Tax Proposals," Tax Foundation, Apr. 29, 2020, https://taxfoundation.org/joe-biden-tax-plan-2020/.

20. James Freeman, "Biden's Bigger Government," Opinion/Best of the Web, *Wall Street Journal*, July 9, 2020, https://www.wsj.com/articles/bidens-bigger-government-11594315921.

21. Ibid.

22. Michael Tesler, "Why Trump—Not Biden—Might Have an Enthusiasm Problem," FiveThirtyEight, July 15, 2020, https://fivethirtyeight.com/features/why-trump-not-biden-might-have-an-enthusiasm-problem/.

23. Change Research, CNBC "State of Play" Poll, National Likely Voters, July 10–12, 2020, https://9b1b5e59-cb8d-4d7b-8493-111f8aa90329.usrfiles.com/ugd/9b1b5e_cabe0094cdf847dc8a2f12309173b8dd.pdf.

24. Philip DeMuth, "The Biden Tax Hike Would Be Severe," Opinion/Commentary, *Wall Street Journal*, July 14, 2020, https://www.wsj.com/articles/the-biden-tax-hike-would-be-severe-11594767531.

25. Ibid.

26. Ibid.

Chapter 10: Trump's Unfinished Business

1. Erica York, "Tracking the Economic Impact of U.S. Tariffs and Retaliatory Actions," Tax Foundation, last updated Aug. 13, 2020, https://taxfounda tion.org/tariffs-trump-trade-war/#:~:text=According%20to%20the%20 Tax%20Foundation,179%2C800%20full%2Dtime%20equivalent %20jobs.

2. President Donald Trump, interview with James Freeman, Apr. 27, 2020.

3. Ibid.

4. President Donald Trump, telephone interview with Maria Bartiromo and James Freeman, July 16, 2020.

5. *Maria Bartiromo's Wall Street*, hosted by Maria Bartiromo, Fox Business Network, July 31, 2020.

6. James Freeman, "The Best Time Ever to Look for a Job," Opinion/Best of the Web, *Wall Street Journal*, Mar. 19, 2018, https://www.wsj.com /articles/the-best-time-ever-to-look-for-a-job-1521488877.

7. Lev Borodovsky, "The Daily Shot: The Number of Job Openings Matches the Number of Unemployed for the First Time," *Daily Shot* (blog), *Wall Street Journal*, Mar. 19, 2018, https://blogs.wsj.com/dailyshot/2018/03/19 /the-daily-shot-the-number-of-job-openings-matches-the-number-of-un employed-for-the-first-time/?mod=article_inline.

8. Victor Oliveira, *The Food Assistance Landscape: FY 2017 Annual Report* (report summary from the Economic Research Service), U.S. Department of Agriculture, Mar. 2018, https://www.ers.usda.gov/webdocs/publica tions/88074/eib-190_summary.pdf?v=0.

9. "Remarks by President Trump to the World Economic Forum," The White House, Jan. 26, 2018, https://www.whitehouse.gov/briefings-state ments/remarks-president-trump-world-economic-forum/.

10. "Job Openings and Labor Turnover Survey News Release," U.S. Bureau of Labor Statistics, Feb. 12, 2019, https://www.bls.gov/news.release/ar chives/jolts_02122019.htm.

11. Christopher Rugaber, "US Job Openings Jump to Record High of 7.3 Million," Associated Press, Feb. 12, 2019, https://apnews.com/bf2ff7ec 19c74f2a8451f4bf2876e7ee.

12. "Remarks by President Trump in State of the Union Address," The White House, issued on Feb. 6, 2019, https://www.whitehouse.gov /briefings-statements/remarks-president-trump-state-union-address-2/.

13. "Remarks by President Trump in Cabinet Meeting," The White House, issued on Feb. 12, 2019, https://www.whitehouse.gov/briefings -statements/remarks-president-trump-cabinet-meeting-13/.

14. Ibid.

15. Caitlin Dickerson and Miriam Jordan, "South Dakota Meat Plant Is Now Country's Biggest Coronavirus Hot Spot," *New York Times*, published Apr. 15, 2020, updated May 4, 2020, https://www.nytimes.com/2020 /04/15/us/coronavirus-south-dakota-meat-plant-refugees.html.

16. Michelle Hackman, "Trump Administration Plans to Raise Seasonal-Worker Cap," Politics, *Wall Street Journal*, updated Feb. 20, 2020, https:// www.wsj.com/articles/trump-administration-plans-to-raise-seasonal -worker-cap-11582248895.

17. Nick Miroff and Josh Dawsey, "Mulvaney Says U.S. Is 'Desperate' for More Legal Immigrants," Politics, *Washington Post*, Feb. 20, 2020, https:// www.washingtonpost.com/politics/mulvaney-says-us-is-desperate-for -more-legal-immigrants/2020/02/20/946292b2-5401-11ea-87b2-101dc 5477dd7_story.html.

18. "Final Rule on Public Charge Ground of Inadmissibility," U.S. Citizen-ship and Immigration Services, last reviewed and updated Feb. 24, 2020, https://www.uscis.gov/archive/final-rule-on-public-charge-ground -of-inadmissibility.

19. James Freeman, "Is China Finally Ready to Deal with Trump?," Opinion/ Best of the Web, *Wall Street Journal*, June 18, 2019, https://www.wsj.com /articles/is-china-finally-ready-to-deal-with-trump-11560895553.

20. Louise Radnofsky, "Trump Says Guatemala Is Set to Help Stem Migrant Flow," World, *Wall Street Journal*, June 18, 2019, https://www .wsj.com/articles/trump-says-guatemala-is-set-to-help-stem-migrant -flow-11560833062.

21. Joyce A. Martin, Brady E. Hamilton, Michelle J. K. Osterman, and Anne K. Driscoll, "Births: Final Data for 2018," *National Vital Statistics Reports* 68, no. 13 (Nov. 27, 2019), published by the National Center for Health Statistics, 3, https://www.cdc.gov/nchs/data/nvsr/nvsr68/nvsr68_13-508 .pdf.

22. Sheelah Kolhatkar, "At Uber, a New C.E.O. Shifts Gears," *New Yorker*, Mar. 30, 2018, https://www.newyorker.com/magazine/2018/04/09/at -uber-a-new-ceo-shifts-gears.

23. Ibid.

24. Stuart Anderson, "Immigrant Entrepreneurs Prove It Doesn't Matter Where You Were Born," *Forbes*, May 6, 2019, https://www.forbes.com

/sites/stuartanderson/2019/05/06/immigrant-entrepreneurs-prove-it
-doesnt-matter-where-you-were-born/#51ace44449b7.

25. President Donald Trump, telephone interview with Maria Bartiromo and James Freeman, July 16, 2020.

26. Ibid.

27. Ibid.

28. Ibid.

29. Ibid.

30. James Freeman, "Shelton Gets a Vote," Opinion/Best of the Web, *Wall Street Journal*, July 10, 2020, https://www.wsj.com/articles/shelton-gets -a-vote-11594418218.

31. President Donald Trump, telephone interview with Maria Bartiromo and James Freeman, July 16, 2020.